1,000,000 Books

are available to read at

www.ForgottenBooks.com

Read online
Download PDF
Purchase in print

ISBN 978-1-5282-0399-9
PIBN 10231716

This book is a reproduction of an important historical work. Forgotten Books uses state-of-the-art technology to digitally reconstruct the work, preserving the original format whilst repairing imperfections present in the aged copy. In rare cases, an imperfection in the original, such as a blemish or missing page, may be replicated in our edition. We do, however, repair the vast majority of imperfections successfully; any imperfections that remain are intentionally left to preserve the state of such historical works.

Forgotten Books is a registered trademark of FB &c Ltd.
Copyright © 2018 FB &c Ltd.
FB &c Ltd, Dalton House, 60 Windsor Avenue, London, SW19 2RR.
Company number 08720141. Registered in England and Wales.

For support please visit www.forgottenbooks.com

1 MONTH OF FREE READING

at
www.ForgottenBooks.com

By purchasing this book you are eligible for one month membership to ForgottenBooks.com, giving you unlimited access to our entire collection of over 1,000,000 titles via our web site and mobile apps.

To claim your free month visit:
www.forgottenbooks.com/free231716

* Offer is valid for 45 days from date of purchase. Terms and conditions apply.

English
Français
Deutsche
Italiano
Español
Português

www.forgottenbooks.com

Mythology Photography **Fiction**
Fishing Christianity **Art** Cooking
Essays Buddhism Freemasonry
Medicine **Biology** Music **Ancient Egypt** Evolution Carpentry Physics
Dance Geology **Mathematics** Fitness
Shakespeare **Folklore** Yoga Marketing
Confidence Immortality Biographies
Poetry **Psychology** Witchcraft
Electronics Chemistry History **Law**
Accounting **Philosophy** Anthropology
Alchemy Drama Quantum Mechanics
Atheism Sexual Health **Ancient History**
Entrepreneurship Languages Sport
Paleontology Needlework Islam
Metaphysics Investment Archaeology
Parenting Statistics Criminology
Motivational

EXTRACTS

—

FROM THE

DIARY OF A WORKHOUSES CHAPLAIN.

BY THE
REV. D. L. COUSINS, A.M.

"The short and simple Annals of the Poor."
GRAY.

LONDON:
J. HATCHARD AND SON, 187, PICCADILLY;
CHILCOTT, BRISTOL; LOVESEY, CHELTENHAM;
CHILD, WORCESTER: ELDER & CO.,
EDINBURGH.
184 .

LONDON:

PRINTED BY G. J. PALMER, SAVOY STREET, STRAND.

PREFACE.

MANY of my clerical brethren, to whom I forwarded a prospectus of this volume, expressed a fear that I was about to make an indiscriminate attack upon the chaplains of the various unions, for neglecting the duties of their office,—that I intended to wield the censor's pen and reproach them. The following pages will, I am sure, dissipate any such an idea, and prove that so far from uttering a single expression, which can be deemed in the slightest degree as approximating to the shadow of reproach, I have almost laid myself open to the opposite charge of giving too great commendation to the clerical body, as merited by their self-denying labours in behalf of the poor.

The subject of the state of religious instruction, provided for the union workhouses, has for some time engaged my attention, and but for a variety of causes, I should long ere this have brought it forward. Most gladly would I believe that the present publication is *after-timed*, from the fact that a better state of things is beginning to dawn; that even the very promoters of the new Poor Law are gradually opening their eyes to the one glaring defect in its provisions:—but with the strong convictions I have that whilst *some little* has been done, there remains much, very much yet undone—satisfied that one most important duty is neglected until the union chaplain is appointed *in every case*, not as a mere hireling at the smallest possible amount of salary, but with a real view to the benefit of those under his care, with such a stipend as shall secure his *undivided attention* to such an important sphere of labour, I commit the following pages to the press.

I have adopted the plan of extracting from my Diary, and giving the history of cases which have come under my observation, as being a more pleasing mode of directing attention to the subject in question, than that of mere outcry and declamation. The following tales will show in what light the poor in our workhouses regard the chaplain, and I record it as my deliberate opinion, that in no single union-house will a single individual speak of their spiritual adviser in other terms than those of the most sincere regard, and will constantly add, " We only wish we could see him oftener."

They only who have inquired into the subject, can know how much the services of the chaplain are valued, and I appeal confidently to my brethren who fill such situations in confirmation of this assertion. In few places are the people so grateful for spiritual instruction as in a workhouse, and I can point to many cases where on the sabbath-day, when the *solitary* service of the chaplain has been performed at the early hour of nine o'clock in the morning, (so that his workhouse duties may not clash with those which he has elsewhere to attend,) the inmates have not only rejoiced at, but looked forward with anxiety to the visits of christian ladies, who thought it no degradation to go and read the word of God to these children of misfortune and sorrow!

Some of my readers may think the following tales savour of exaggeration,—let me only add that the leading features of each tale are *those of sad reality;* the only charge to which I plead guilty, is that of having, in *some* instances, changed the language in which the events were originally related—in *all* I have studiously omitted certain circumstances whereby the originals might be recognised.

If the simple object I have in view be in the slightest degree helped on by the appearance of this volume, the many imperfections which it contains will, I trust, be lost sight of, and the *motive* which set the machine in motion, atone for any defects which may appear in its construction.

Eckington Vicarage.
May 1, 1847.

CONTENTS.

	PAGE
INTRODUCTION.—Spiritual Neglect of Workhouse Paupers	1
THE LAST OF THE FAMILY	25
THE PENITENT	63
THE ATHEIST'S END	98
THE WIDOW'S PORTION	117
THE MATRICIDE	151
THE JEWELLER	180
THE AUTHOR	225
THE OATH	269

INTRODUCTION.

SPIRITUAL NEGLECT OF WORKHOUSE PAUPERS.

Upwards of three years have elapsed since the Bishop of Exeter, in the legitimate exercise of his position in the upper House of Parliament, brought forward a motion on the state of "*spiritual instruction in the union workhouses.*" On first introducing the subject, he stated that "he did not intend to press that motion to a division," but that his intentions were to leave the question of "committee or no committee to inquire into the grievances of which he had to complain, to the responsibility of her Majesty's Government."

His arguments were unanswered, his statements met with no denial; indeed any attempt at the latter would have been futile, and yet in the face of those statements, borne out as they were by the arguments which he adduced, no legislative change has taken place to correct the evils of which he complained.

On the occasion to which I refer his lordship stated in a speech (from which I shall have occasion to quote hereafter) "that his attention had for ten years been most strongly directed towards the operation of the Poor Law Amendment Act, and that he had daily witnessed more and more of the evil effects of that measure."

Abler pens than mine have already canvassed the merits and demerits of this system, and I am most unwilling to provoke discussion on an enactment which, in spite of all the arguments I have heard in its favour, my own experience cannot allow me, in regard to several of its provisions, to consider a real social benefit. There is no class of persons through the length and breadth of the land, who have so good an opportunity of watching the operations, and coming to a right judgment on the beneficial effects or otherwise of the New Poor Law, as the parochial clergy. Their very occupation brings them into immediate contact with those who are to receive the relief it provides.

They are united by the strongest moral ties with the poor—their dwellings are in the midst of them, and in the daily round of professional duty, the parish priest must necessarily become intimately acquainted with the views and feelings of this very large portion of the community. Need I say that he constantly finds cause of complaint against the system? that laying out of the question the views which the poor themselves entertain with regard to it, he in his own judgment is too often compelled to pronounce the very same verdict on many of its harsh provisions. Take one instance, the case of '*out-door relief*.' How often might a timely assistance in this matter prevent many a family from becoming wholly chargeable on the parish? Work is slack, or the man has been laid up with an attack of sickness;—the little savings (which cannot amount to much, when his wages perhaps have not exceeded eight or nine shillings a week, with which he has to pay house-rent and maintain, it may be, a wife and four or five children) are soon exhausted.

He sees the hungry looks of his children, his credit is gone at the village shop; no other resource remains but an application to the workhouse for relief. And what reply does he receive?—"You must come into the house and bring your family; we cannot help you in any other way." The poor man well knows what he has to expect. As if the misfortunes of life were not enough, his fellow man, in answer to his appeal for assistance, replies, "There is a home provided for you; we will dispose of your few articles of furniture which you won't require here; your wife shall be taken care of in another part of the house, and your children shall go to the school. You will be able to see them occasionally, but of course that won't make much difference." . . . What is the sufferer to do? he must either watch his family sink under the pressure of want, or he must enter the asylum provided for him, when by the aid of a small sum, *weekly*, till the clouds of misfortune had passed over, he might have remained in his little cottage—his domestic treasures around him—the hope of better days shedding a light on the present gloom, and his poverty at all events made more tolerable by the presence of an affectionate wife and the faces of his dear children.

No wonder that the lower classes dread the very name of the Poor Law,—no wonder that they look upon the Union house as worse than a prison, and that in fact many rather than become the inmates of a workhouse, commit some petty felony that they may obtain, *to them*, a far lighter punishment—incarceration in a gaol ! *

But it is not my purpose to dwell on the many *social* evils which arise out of certain glaring

---

* A case in point now exists in my own parish. An aged couple, the man 78 years of age, the woman 73, who have brought up a large family without ever receiving the slightest assistance from the parish, are now through age and infirmity utterly unable to earn the smallest trifle. The cottage in which they live, (or rather *starve*,) with a small garden attached, is strictly entailed, and the eldest son (who earns only eight shillings a week and has a numerous family) refuses to cut off the entail. Again and again have this aged couple, who have literally *nothing to live upon* but the scanty produce of the garden, sought to obtain some trifling aid from the parish in which they were born and bred, and to which for many years they paid their quota of the poor's rate. Every such application, either from themselves or others, elicits one and the same reply, " Make over your interest in the cottage, furniture, &c. to the parish, and come into the union house." Can any person of feeling be surprised that the old couple who in the graphic language of the Scotch poet have for several years
" Clamb the hill thegither"
should be unwilling, at the eleventh hour, to be severed one from the other? Common humanity rejects such an idea ! but we fear, without wishing to express an uncharitable opinion, that such a grace is often lost sight of in the anxiety of the guardians to carry out the dictates of the authorities at Somerset House.

defects in the New Poor Law! My views as a clergyman—as one who has watched with some care the operation of this law in a spiritual light, are more than ever directed to the one grand defect which is so conspicuous in the whole system, the want of sufficient provision for what, in the ideas of every right-thinking person, is of far greater importance in *such* an establishment and amongst *such* characters, than mere temporal relief—*proper religious instruction and consolation to those who from a variety of contingent circumstances are brought to a workhouse.* I state it not as a mere unfounded assertion, but as what I believe to be a matter of statistical fact, that the balance between those who seek it as an asylum from misfortune, and those who are compelled to resort to it as a last refuge from their own vices, largely preponderates in favour of the former, and the sketches in the following pages will bear out this statement. Is then the union workhouse to be made a House of Correction?— if so, why not at least give it the same advantages which in a spiritual point of view are given to a house of the latter description? It would be difficult to find a gaol in any part of England which is not provided with a regular chaplain, whose remuneration is such that he is enabled

INTRODUCTION.

to devote the due portion of his time to the religious instruction of those over whom he is placed.

But what is the case in the majority of our union workhouses?—precisely what I have alluded to in the subsequent pages of this volume, that in nine cases out of ten the chaplain appointed is already an over-worked curate, the small amount of stipend rendering it out of the question for any disengaged clergyman to accept the appointment. In many of our gaols, both in town and country, the chaplain receives a salary averaging from £150 to £200 a year; in few of our unions does a like official receive more than £50 per annum; those which exceed this amount are infinitely fewer than those which fall below it.* Let us, however, on this point quote the statistical details given by the Bishop of Exeter in that memorable speech which he made in the House of Lords, Feb. 23, 1844. *—" There are in all," he observes, " 587 unions; to 414 there were chaplains; there were 102 which had no chaplains; and if Liverpool, London, Manchester, and one or two other places,

* Of course I allude to the statistical details which he made at the date referred to; some few alterations have since taken place, though not such as to affect the main question.

were excepted, it would be found that the average salary enjoyed by those chaplains *did not exceed* £37 *per annum!* In Liverpool the payment to the chaplain, was £250, in Manchester £200, and in London, where they have more than one chaplain, the gross payment to them all was £400. In the small county of Rutland, where they had but one union, the chaplain received £75, which was nearly double the amount paid by Durham, Northumberland, and Westmoreland! It was one and a half more than the sum paid by those three counties added to that paid by the North Riding of Yorkshire. These three counties paid but £50 a year, while the county of Huntingdon paid £150. In the North Riding of Yorkshire there were several chaplains, but in the union of Richmond, a very wealthy district in which many persons of opulence resided, they paid their chaplain the *magnificent sum of* £10 *per annum.*" . . . I have now before me the official notification which I received on my appointment as chaplain to a union, and for which I was the only candidate.

"Rev. Sir,

"I beg to inform you that you have this day been elected chaplain to the ——— union at a salary of £30 per annum. Your duties will be to read prayers and preach once on Sundays, to visit the sick, and catechize the children at —— during the week, and to give the usual lecture on Friday evenings." . . . .

These duties, let me observe, were to be performed in a union which averaged 190 inmates, (exclusive of the children,) by one who had already the care of 2000 souls in a parish with 30,000 inhabitants, and upon whom a proportionate part of the duties of so large a population naturally fell I know that I am open to the inquiry, "Why undertake such an addition to your labours, when you had already more than you could efficiently perform?" My reply is, simply because I knew that had I not undertaken the office, (the duties of which I had for some time before my appointment gratuitously performed,) those poor unfortunate ones in the workhouse would have been left, if not totally uncared for, at least dependent on the casual instruction of any who might have found "*a convenient season*" to impart the bread of life to those who were hourly perishing for lack of it.

The result has proved the truth of this; for when on leaving the parish I resigned an appointment which I had held for nearly four years, the inmates of that union were left without any service being performed *except by the master*, the utilitarian guardians (after failing in the experiment of sending some of the paupers to church) having in vain repeatedly advertised for a chaplain to undertake the above-named duties at the *extravagant salary of £20 a year!* *

Nor is this a solitary instance. I was lately informed by a brother-clergyman residing in the county of Northampton, that in one union the salary paid to the chaplain was £10 annually! a liberal stipend truly, and most expressive of the value at which the guardians of the poor estimate the labours of a clergyman to give the instruction so greatly required in such an establishment, and where so much spiritual consolation is needed!

None can know but those who have visited there, the sad scenes which call for commiseration; none can know so well as the minister of God who enters there on his errand of mercy, how rich the consolation which he can apply from

---

* A chaplain is now appointed, and he receives for the above-mentioned duties the annual stipend of £20! I know too that his sole reason for accepting the appointment was because the paupers should not be totally uncared for.

the spiritual treasury with which he is provided! For in that house he finds the buds which once gave promise of sweet flower insensible to the rays of hope which would beam upon it! There the cold hand of despair has seized with ruthless grasp upon its victim—there the world is excluded, life has lost its charm, and the angel of death is a welcome messenger, whose approach they long for as that which is to close their woes for ever! It is in the workhouse that the lessons of submission are to be learnt, but ofttimes they who should learn them have no teachers but their own rebellious hearts, and we speak advisedly when we say, that many have passed away to their great account in their solitary chamber of the union workhouse, without even the slightest consolations of a minister of God, who, although a frail and fallible creature as themselves, might at least, as every Christian knows, have been the means under God of soothing the pillow on which the dying head was laid.

But it is not only for the sick and dying that the offices of the chaplain are required; they who are in health are equally in need of religious instruction, and I regret to say that one often meets with characters in the workhouse who are very far gone in immorality, and ignorant of the simplest truths of the gospel.

The following evidence from one who had devoted a portion of his already fully occupied time for the benefit of the *Macclesfield* Union, presents a sad and melancholy picture. Writing to the Bishop of Exeter he says, (see Times, February 24th, 1844,) "I have the honour to lay before your lordship the following facts: 1. As to the union workhouse, the number of its inmates has sometimes reached 300, but at present it is slightly under 200, and I think I am correct in saying, that during the last seven months the number has varied from about 240 to 170. Of these the adults would certainly average more than 150, and the great majority would, if asked, either profess themselves members of our church, acknowledge that they had gone to no place of worship, or what is as common, " *to all sorts.*" He then adds,

"FOR THERE IS NO RELIGIOUS INSTRUCTION OR MINISTERIAL SUPERINTENDENCE WHATEVER PROVIDED BY THE GUARDIANS! The natural results are, that the very little religion which does, or at all events which till lately did exist, is entirely sectarian or savouring strongly of schism. The state of moral depravity and religious destitution is frightful, and the utter shamelessness and moral degradation which prevail among the young women in particular, are quite appalling. From the construction of the house, an old factory converted into a workhouse, anything like classification is impossible, and a moderately modest woman (unless indeed she should have the good fortune to be sufficiently ill to secure her a place in one of the sick wards, where it is practicable to afford stricter discipline) would, after a stay of some weeks, it is my firm conviction, go forth almost infallibly a hopeless prostitute!! The language which has sometimes met my ear has been most dreadful, and the governor, who is most anxious, I believe, to do his duty to God as well as to man, laments the state of things, but until the removal of the paupers to the house which is being built for them, he sees no prospect of amendment."

It is indeed to be hoped that in the new abode some new change has been effected, for what follows from the same pen is most affecting.

"In August last I found that excepting very rare visits of one clergyman, no one (save some Methodists on Sundays) went near the sick and dying, and at the time to which I allude, I found two or three persons actually dying *without any* care having been taken to warn, to instruct, or to comfort them. The paupers themselves have frequently complained of the way in which they have been neglected. An old woman one day said to me, 'Why, sir, no one has been near us since Mr. —— was obliged to give up, and here we are, a parcel of old blind creatures, hard at death's door, *and no one seems to think of us, or to care whether we go to heaven or hell!*' And oh, my Lord, she spoke the sad, the shameful truth! . . .

"The governor's constant complaint is, that the young men and women having nothing to do, and *there being no means of instructing them*, are . . . always in mischief. . . .

" A young woman who had been seduced in a very shocking and disgraceful manner, came to the house; of course she had a place assigned her among the common herd; fortunately she became very ill, and was for long confined to one of the sick wards. She seemed for a time exceedingly penitent, and I really believe that she sorrowed after a godly sort. She told me that she was very thankful that she had been brought into that ward, and that she felt how good the Lord had been in his dealings with her, for had she stayed in the room that she had previously occupied, she should have been driven distracted. She said '*I could have no notion how bad they were.*' And yet for the reformation of those persons not one step had been taken, excepting the efforts which I have been able to make, in aid of which I receive no kind of encouragement, nothing but the same permission given to the dissenters, not even a grant for books!"

Few, surely, can peruse such a statement as this without a feeling of the deepest sympathy for such a neglected class of one's fellow creatures. Happily for the character of England, such a statement cannot, we hope, be made of every union workhouse, but we surely speak within bounds when we say that *as a whole*, and *taken collectively*, the spiritual instruction provided for the destitute poor in the unions of England and Wales, is of a most defective character, and requires vital and efficient supervision. Not, perhaps, that we are entirely to charge this neglect upon the letter of the law itself, as upon the gross maladministration and perversion of what we in charity hope to be the spirit of it.

On this point, however, hear the Bishop of Exeter. "By the Poor Law Act the commissioners are bound to appoint—it is their duty to appoint—chaplains to union workhouses. They have themselves admitted that the appointment is essential, and they have told their assistant commissioner on no account to give way on this point. How stands the law with regard to other unhappy men? The prisoners in a gaol are entitled to chaplains, and if the unfortunate paupers were tenants of a prison instead of a poorhouse, they would be entitled to a chaplain with such remuneration that he could give up to them the whole of his time Suppose they were prisoners instead of paupers, or suppose that they had the misfortune of being lunatics, they would, in their lucid intervals, be entitled by the law to the spiritual consolations of a chaplain."

The question then seems to resolve itself to this; that they in whom the executive of poor law is vested—the commissioners appointed by the government—are incurring a *serious*, nay, *an awful responsibility*, by not insisting upon that which the law empowers them to do, the appointment of *proper* and efficient chaplains to each union in the land, and that official should not be a *mere hireling* at a salary which a gentleman would scarcely offer to his butler, but at such a stipend as will ensure the undivided duties of a laborious and devoted minister of God.*

---

* The following account of the Mary-le-bone workhouse bears upon the point. The average number of the inmates during the winter of 1846 and 1847 has been about 1600; there is a chapel within the walls holding about 1000 people,

INTRODUCTION. 17

One other quotation from the speech of the right reverend prelate who so ably pointed out the defects of the system under consideration, in that speech to which I have the greatest satisfaction in referring, and I will bring my observations on this question to a close.

"The commissioners have defined the duties of the chaplain (when appointed!) to be as follows. 'To read prayers and preach a sermon once to the paupers on Sunday, unless the guardians, with the consent of the Poor Law commissioners, should otherwise direct. To read prayers, not to preach, on Good Friday and Christmas day. To examine the children, and

in which are performed two full services on Sundays, and prayers are read every Wednesday. The stipend of the chaplain is £200 per annum, whose complete services, both in the chapel and through the wards, the guardians hold themselves entitled to. There is also a boys' school, a girls' school, and an infant school, each under separate instructors, and under the superintendence of the chaplain, who makes a weekly report to the board. And yet, as though such provision were insufficient, we find that a motion for admitting the missionaries of the London city mission into the refractory and casual wards was lately carried by a majority of 15 to 3. It is but right to add, that the reverend chaplain considered their admission unnecessary, and the evidence was most conclusive, that his exertions had not been wanting to reclaim the depraved inmates.

catechise such as are of the Church of England, at least once in every month." Well does his lordship ask, " Is that extent of spiritual instruction sufficient for the souls as well as the minds of young paupers? If the commissioners had consulted the rubric, they would have learnt that the instruction should be at least *weekly*. Then the chaplain was to 'visit the sick and administer religious consolation to those in the workhouse,' 'how often and when?' '*When applied to by the master or matron!*' These are the duties of the person who is employed as the spiritual instructor, mentor, and guide of the poor in a workhouse! All this is avowedly done to save expense." . . . He then enters into a statistical detail of what would be the cost of appointing a chaplain to each union at a salary of £100 per annum. "There are in England," he observes, " about 600 unions, therefore a salary of £100 a year for a chaplain at each workhouse would amount to between £50,000 and £60,000 a year. Now what is the annual amount of the property rated to the poor? at least £60,000,000. The rental of England and Wales was calculated, many years ago, at £32,000,000, and it has increased since. By a table published by the commissioners themselves, it appears that the land bears a proportion to other rateable property, as 52 to 38, so that the whole rateable property could not be less than £60,000,000 per annum. Taking it, therefore, as a question of economy, £1 in every £1000 of the property of the country would be sufficient for the purpose, and what is that in the pound? why *something less than one farthing!* so that this is the whole question of expense, and sordid guardians grudge the miserable pittance of a farthing in the pound, and for this they sacrifice the best interests, eternal and temporal, of the pauper!"

Let me, before I close, make a few observations on the instruction of the young in the union houses. In some cases a decided improvement has taken place in the plan and systematic arrangement of workhouse education, under the eye of an active chaplain; but great space for further amendment yet remains, and no really beneficial results can be expected until *every* school attached to a union be under the constant supervision of a zealous chaplain. "*Once a month's examination or catechising*" is perfectly absurd! Every one who has had the smallest experience in these matters knows that the class of persons who are generally appointed to these schools, are of such a description, that if left to themselves, their duties are most imperfectly performed; not perhaps so much from a want of principle as from an ill opinion of those who are under their charge. It requires no little tact to manage any school where the children of the lower orders are congregated together, but generally speaking, those who are consigned to the workhouse school are of the very worst description, brought into the world as the offspring of shame, doomed in their tenderest years to almost total neglect, and their naturally corrupt passions so long unchecked, that they obtain a double mastery over them, they require a double degree of intelligence and patience to bring back their wayward dispositions into the right channel. How unfitted for such a task many have been who have received the appointment, may be gathered from the following extract from a report presented to the Poor Law commissioners some few years since, by their then assistant commissioner, Mr. Tuffnell.

"By far the worst evil," he says, "to be apprehended from the present system, arises from the danger of sending forth into the world a set of beings, *vicious in habit* and *pauperized* in feeling, to be future burdens on the parochial rates, or candidates for the gaols and hulks. If there be any truth in the maxim 'As is the master, so is the school,' there must assuredly be, in many workhouses, little chance of the children ever becoming high-minded and respectable members of society. *There is no class of officers of whom such continual complaints are made, and for whose dismissal you have been called upon to issue so many orders!* I need not call to your recollection the numbers you have been obliged to discharge for drunkenness or other immoralities. I have reason to believe great cruelties have been practised at times on the children, which probably do not always come to light, as a schoolmaster has no difficulty in awing an unhappy orphan, who probably has not a friend in the world, into silence, and suppressing all complaints. In one case a child was beaten so severely, that had not the punishment been stopped by the fortunate entry of the governor into the apartment, death would probably have ensued. In another the schoolmaster was in the habit of tying up with a handkerchief the jaws of those boys whom he thought deserving of punishment, to prevent their screams being heard, and then beating them in the most savage manner! The persons who were guilty of these cruelties had been village schoolmasters, where they could not have practised such conduct, as a child so treated would have immediately complained to its parents and would have been taken away from the school, which would quickly have shown the master, from policy, if not from charity, the necessity of mildness in future. But where is a poor friendless orphan or foundling (for of these classes a great proportion of the workhouse children consist) to turn for assistance, when it knows no one in whom it can place confidence, or to whom it can utter complaints? Hence it seems incumbent on us, for humanity's sake, to be doubly cautious whom we select as schoolmasters for children thus situated, that is, *whom* we make rulers over these little worlds, lest we introduce a tyrannical despot, rather than a father! The following is extracted from a letter I received from the chaplain to a union workhouse. 'The evidence I produced against that man (the schoolmaster) was quite disgusting. I have now a schoolmaster and mistress of good principles. Their faithful discharge of duty has enabled me to exclude a man who, when schoolmaster, endeavoured at least to seduce several of the elder girls in the school.' This is a striking illustration of having chaplains, who are always regarded as the friends of the poor in the workhouses, who have no feelings of terror towards them. They come to the chaplain as to a minister of charity and mercy, as a friend of the wretch whom every friend forsakes." In Mr. Tremenheere's report on the schools at Norwood, it is said, " The very frequent presence of the chaplain, both on Sundays and other days of the week, has, as is to be expected, been mainly instrumental in establishing a tone of religious feeling and principle highly satisfactory."

With these quotations I close the remarks I have offered on the defective system of the provision made for the sick and dying, as well as for the young in the union workhouses of our land. I have already exceeded the limits which I had allotted myself for these observations, and yet feel that I have left unsaid much that I wished to comment upon.

Let us hope that in these enlightened days, when so much is done towards providing for the spirtual welfare of the country at large, when church accommodation is increasing, and schools are multiplied in every town and village, these children of sorrow and disappointment, who, whether from imprudence or otherwise, are compelled to enter the portals of the union, may not, in the expressive language of the editor of the

Times, " find that they are brought from their parish—congregated together in order that they may be isolated—to be marked out as it were, for separation from the church, and placed perhaps at the very door of the parish clergyman," without being able themselves to receive the spiritual consolation of which they so much stand in need.

Let them at least have some one to guide their erring steps, and if their own vices have brought them from being once respectable members of society to a state of pauperism and disgrace, do not withhold from them some faithful man of God who may cheer them with the message of mercy, and deliver the glad tidings to their despairing souls—"*There is joy in the presence of the angels of God over one sinner that repenteth.*"

THE LAST OF THE FAMILY.

With what strange variety of character does one meet in a workhouse! The world, we know, is made up of different classes, each one forming its own coterie, and associating in masses with those of like views and habits with themselves: but in the great multitude of which mankind is composed, their individual characteristics ofttimes escape particular attention. In any asylum, on the contrary, which serves as a "*refuge for the destitute,*" whether workhouse, hospital, or any similar institution, the sample generally consists of an extract from each distinct genus, and the leading features of character become more prominent from the contrast which is afforded in those of their immediate associates.

It has been in my experience as a " workhouse

chaplain," that I have so fully seen the force of the poet's dictum—

"The proper study of mankind is man;"

for never, I think, should I have obtained such an insight into human nature, or have so accurately detected the workings of man's heart, but for my experience in that office. Granted that a clergyman who is active in discharging a most important part of his ministerial duty, viz., "*Parochial visiting*," must necessarily (especially in densely-populated districts) meet with a vast variety of character, but in most cases they are those whose past life has been personally observed by him, and with whom he has had the opportunity of frequently coming into contact. Not so is it, generally speaking, with those who claim his professional services in a workhouse; there the inmates are such as are obliged to seek it, or rather are brought to it, as a *dernier resort* —poverty has haunted them with its attendant ills, disappointment has followed in their footsteps, and in every attempt they have made to succeed, has crushed the bright prospects which dawned upon them; or worse than this, vice has been the attendant of all their schemes, habits of idleness have been indulged in until they have become second nature, and then, when no other door opens upon them—when strength is gone and bodily vigour decayed—they claim their parish, and are thankful or otherwise, as the case may be, for the shelter and diet of a workhouse!

I can hardly say that either vice or improvidence opened the doors of the union to C—— M——. He had certainly tried his utmost to keep out of it, and when compelled at last by real necessity to make it his refuge, he never failed, whilst I was officially connected with the union, to vent his indignation against certain enactments of the New Poor Law, and that in no very measured terms: in fact, the language he adopted, could the walls of Somerset House have re-echoed it, might have caused a slight palpitation of the heart to the grave commissioners there assembled in conclave, and for aught we know, might have led to some valuable amendments in the system.

And yet, with all his complaints, and all the alterations he proposed, poor "*Charley*," (for such was the familiar cognomen by which he was known,) managed to pass his time pretty comfortably. He appeared to be one of that class of systematic grumblers whom we sometimes meet with in the world, who fancy that things cannot go right unless they have a hand in the direction of them, and who do not for a moment hesitate to "*speak evil of dignities*" if their plans of operation do not coincide exactly with their own.

It is not in all cases that we find such a really good-humoured censor as C—— M——. He always prided himself on taking, as he called it, "the common-sense view of the case," and yet, if you could by any fair argument induce him to think that your reasons, when pitted against his, displayed a *more* common sense view of the matter, he would immediately lay aside the cudgels, after securing, let me observe, a decent retreat for himself by one or two parting shots, and acknowledge that he " hadn't seen the question exactly in that light before, but now it appeared so plain he couldn't gainsay it." . . .

He prided himself not a little, moreover, on his political views. Charley was a bigoted Tory of the old school, such as we rarely meet with in these times. "*The Altar* and *the Throne*" was Charley's text, and however much he abused the ministers of the day, he always held the very letter of the archi-episcopal creed that "kings can do no wrong."

In speaking of the church I must, I fear in

truth, confess that the old man often overstepped the bounds of christian charity, for his hatred of dissent was most unqualified and unlimited; in his idea, any one who separated from the church placed himself almost beyond the pale of salvation, and had he been a fellow of any college in Oxford, I am persuaded he would have distinguished himself as a thorough-going Tractarian.

Much as I have reason to believe that I was a bit of a favourite with him, I know he could never forgive my extempore preaching; to him it savoured too much of dissent: he had so long been accustomed at the parish church to see "*the clergyman preach out of his book,*" that he looked upon that as the only proper and legitimate mode of public instruction. In fact, he one day went so far as to attack me with "I like your sermons, sir, very much, very much indeed, and I trust I've profited by them, but (I hope you wont be offended) I should like them better, and I think they'd do me just as much good, if you only preached them from your book!"

"And so I do, Charles, from the best of books!"

"Ah, sir, that's true, . . . but you know what I mean." . . .

Poor Charley was quite the master of the house,

and in spite of his constant outbreaks against the system to which he was doomed to submit—notwithstanding the many flaws which he detected and would have remedied after his own fashion if the power had been given him—I verily believe he did as much, if not more, than all the regulations of the commissioners, or the enforcements of the guardians, carried out by their subordinates, towards maintaining peace and good order in the W—— union workhouse.

Charley's opinion was enough amongst his fellows; did anything go wrong, he was forthwith appealed to; was there any cause for complaint, he was always appointed ambassador extraordinary, with full powers to treat, though it was seldom he undertook any mission which could not supply him with justice for credentials, so that, whether amongst the paupers in the yard, or amongst the guardians in the board-room, whatever case Charley took in hand, it was in nine cases out of ten considered as a just one.

I remember well, that on one occasion I found it necessary to lecture one of the paupers for some misconduct which I had observed during divine service; and after I had made some remarks, the old man, who was standing by, interrupted me with "Leave him to me, sir, I'll carry out what you've said; you won't be obliged to speak to J—— on that subject again."

Let me only add to what I have said above of C—— M——, that he was a fine hale old man, eighty one years of age, about five feet ten inches in height, with a figure which time had somewhat curved, a hoary head, which was to him "*a crown of glory,*" for it was found, "*in the way of righteousness,*" a most benign expression of countenance, to which the many troubles he had undergone almost added grace by the wrinkles they had caused—and the reader has a picture of the subject of this sketch.

He was, of all others, the last one would have expected to see in a workhouse; how he came to be there, with some of the chief incidents of his varied life, the reader will learn in the following pages.

In this case, as in one or two others, I shall not extract from my diary piecemeal, but present his story in a continuous form, though, as the reader will suppose, it was related to me at different periods.

My first particular introduction to C—— M—— was on as lovely a summer's evening as ever gladdened the face of nature. I had called at the house for the purpose of " privately bap-

... t;
... ...

... t;
... ...
then
and ;
 Ch...
fellow
appea...
he wa...
nary.
...ddo
...upj
who
...
ov...
en

most attentive a...... ... .
book before him. I ....
Bible, and was ....
relation of some .. ..
Poor old man! I ... .
before me as he ....
and recall the ....
telligent countenance ....
rays of the declining sun ....
escaping from beneath his ....
animated gleam of the eye to be ....
peculiarly striking even. The ... ...
formed a picture which, under the pencil of a
Rembrandt, would have been considered a masterpiece of design. This and another are the two
pictures of real life on which my "mind's eye"
has often lingered as in comparing the one for
the other, and I hardly know which of the two
to admire the most.

It was on a similar evening that I passed over a
common in my widely-extended parish to call on
one who had already passed the age of three-
>re years and ten, and was in a most declining
ndition. As I drew near his cottage, one of
1e many detached which dotted the unenclosed
1ste, I saw the old man's son, who was the
-eper of an adjoining manor, sitting at the door

tizing" a sick infant, and as I had some short time to spare, walked through the yard to see the paupers resting after their day's labour, and by entering into conversation with them, inculcate those lessons which, taught publicly from the pulpit, I have often found come home to the heart with twofold power when reiterated in the ordinary ministerial visitations. The former and the latter are, as every Christian knows, both equally inefficacious unless the Holy Spirit of God accompany the teaching; but knowing also that God is graciously pleased to employ human agency to make known his salvation, the duty is plain, that they to whom the commission is given should, after the really apostolical example, not only *publicly*, but also privately, and "*from house to house, cease not to teach and to preach Jesus Christ.*"

It was on the evening referred to that, passing into the yard, I found the men assembled in various little groups, each one attentively listening to its own chief, (if I may so term it,) who was reading to them, perhaps the remains of a worn-out newspaper, or some tract which had been distributed for the use of the paupers.

My friend, C—— M—— had by far the greatest number of listeners, and apparently the most attentive auditory; but instead of having a book before him, I found he had laid aside his Bible, and was indulging his hearers with the relation of some of the doings of his former days. Poor old man! I can imagine I see him now before me as he appeared on that very evening, and recall the effect produced I saw his intelligent countenance somewhat coloured by the rays of the declining sun, his silvered locks just escaping from beneath his glazed hat, and the animated gleam of the eye as he described any peculiarly striking event. The tout ensemble formed a picture which, under the pencil of a Rembrandt, would have been considered a masterpiece of design. This and another are the two pictures of real life on which my " mind's eye" has often lingered as fit companions the one for the other, and I hardly know which of the two to admire the most.

It was on a similar evening that I passed over a common in my widely-extended parish to call on one who had already passed the age of threescore years and ten, and was in a most declining condition. As I drew near his cottage, one of the many detached which dotted the unenclosed waste, I saw the old man's son, who was the keeper of an adjoining manor, sitting at the door of the hut with the opened Bible before him, evidently reading to the old man, whose easy chair had been drawn near the entrance that he might enjoy the fresh air of a summer's evening. I approached unperceived near enough to hear the words from the affecting parable of the prodigal son, "*I will arise and go to my father, and will say unto him, Father, I have sinned against Heaven, and before thee, and am no more worthy to be called thy son.*" . . . The scene in itself, with the beautiful language of penitent resolution dying away on the air, was a perfect picture, but, if incomplete, add to it the gun resting on the porch, and the three dogs, one a noble setter, lying close to the entrance, as it were mounting guard to prevent any interruption to the holy occupation, and I think the reader will agree with me that such a scene, though often pourtrayed in imagination, very rarely in every-day life meets the eye.

Such may be said of the appearance presented by C—— M—— and his attentive auditory. I would willingly have gazed on it undisturbed, but as I advanced farther into the yard, the old man, with his accustomed civility, rose up to acknowledge my presence, and as if influenced by the behaviour of their teacher, even had other motives been wanting, the circle around him immediately followed his example.

"Don't let me interrupt you, Charles; I dare say you are giving your companions some good advice."

"Why, as to that, sir, just as you came I was amusing them with describing some of the scenes through which I have passed,—they have been of a changing character, sir; . . . . but still, as I tell them, God didn't forsake me; 'twas his will, I suppose, that I shouldn't be prosperous long together, though several times I had every prospect of being so."

"Well, Charles, go on with your story now. I will be an attentive listener; for if you draw as good a moral from every incident as the one you have just given, I am satisfied you will benefit those who hear you."

"Thank you, sir, for your good opinion of me; but I only teach them the lessons God has taught me; they have many of them been unfortunate like myself, but murmuring won't lessen their troubles, as I often tell them. We are all too ready to cry out before we are really hurt, and I fear this is the case with a good many in this house; still I am constantly saying we are a great deal better off than many others."

" But you made some complaint to the board this morning, did you not, Charles ?"

" Oh! sir, that was a trifling one; they soon removed the grievance, for they know I never speak except when there is occasion for it. I never grumble, sir; but I like to see justice done. I learnt quite enough to cure me of discontent when I was in America,—if a man wants to be cured of that complaint, I recommend him to go there."

" I never knew you had been so far from home M——, I can't wonder at your adventures being so interesting to your hearers: I hope they attend to the lessons you give them ?"

" Pretty well, sir,—pretty well. They are a little restive at times; but when a man has seen better days, 'tis hard all at once . . . . We'll change the subject, if you please, sir;—'twon't do for me to be the one to set a bad example!"

The old man had excited my curiosity, and I confess I was anxious to hear his autobiography. Ere long my wish was gratified, and I can only wish, for the benefit of my readers, that I could relate what he communicated to me in the same graphic style that I heard it. This, however, I cannot do. The principal heads only appear in my diary, and they are perfect " *disjecta mem-*

bra." Memory supplies the "*feathering of the points,*" and consequently the full plumage cannot retain its original hues; 'twas that bright plumage when first presented which doubtless constituted the principal charm,—much must consequently be left to the imagination of the reader in perusing the memoir of "*the Last of the Family.*"

* * * * *

"You have, I dare say, sir, heard enough about me to know that I was born and bred in the village of D———, not far from this town. You know too, sir, the property which now finds an owner in Mr. C———: 'twas in the very house where he now resides, though strangely altered from what it then was, that I first drew breath nearly eighty-one years ago! 'tis a long time to look forward to; but, alas! 'tis as yesterday to look back upon; and long as is the time which has passed since I first left the home of my childhood, perhaps I know every inch of ground attached to it better than those who have since occupied it.

"I was but seventeen when it was sold. My father, who for twelve years had been a widower, had died the previous year without any preparation or settlement of his affairs, and, contrary to all expectation, instead of being a wealthy young squire, as I had been taught to anticipate I should be whenever he died, I found myself in possession of a very slender capital after the sale of all his property and the payment of his debts.

"The idea of living as little better than a beggar, where I had so lately revelled as a rich youngster, was more than I could put up with. The profession of the law, for which I had been destined, was soon laid aside, though perhaps had I diligently pursued it, I should not have met with so many hard rubs as it has been my lot in life to encounter; but the first step was wrong, and a right ending never yet came from a bad beginning.

"At the time, sir, of which I am now speaking, the unholy war which had so long been carried on between this country and her American colonies had just been brought to a close, and various individuals, availing themselves of the cessation of hostilities, embarked with their little fortunes for the new world, hoping to succeed better than they had a chance of doing in the mother country, which was at that time ground down with taxes by reason of the ruinous expenses incurred during the war.

It was not perhaps a feeling of this sort, so much as the motives to which I have referred, which led me to quit my native country. I had no ties to restrain me, and even had such existed, they must have been of a strong nature to make me forego my purpose.

"My passage was soon agreed on, and after a weary voyage, for they did not then go so fast across the Atlantic as they do now-a-days, I landed on the shores of America.

"I had determined to make Philadelphia my head quarters, and proceeded there soon after my arrival at New York. My plan was to engage in some commercial connexion, so that after having realized sufficient to live with credit in my native country, I might return and maintain my proper station in society.

"I soon found out, sir, that the Yankee temper and mine wouldn't exactly suit each other, and I had something to do to make a tolerably easy berth among my new friends. They were flushed with the success which had attended their struggle for independence, and dear as the victory cost them, whenever chance brought an Englishman in their way, they never failed to bore him almost to death with their wonderful doings.

"The surrender of Lord Cornwallis to Rochambeau and Washington at York Town was the eternal text, and you may be sure they always gave an eloquent discourse upon it; and though Lord Rodney afterwards had his revenge when he took the Count de Grasse *under his protection* to Jamaica—such in their estimation was a mere trifle compared with the delivery of Cornwallis's sword—whilst with some defect of memory they never alluded to the important part which the French took in that transaction. American valour did it all.

"Young and somewhat hot-headed as I then was, you won't be surprised to hear that I got into constant squabbles. I had been nursed too long in the school of loyalty to hear without resenting it a word against my country and good King George—such in my eyes was downright treason; and though this mode of thinking at first starting evidently interfered with my success, my perseverance in business in some measure compensated for it, and I soon found myself in the way of rapid advancement. I had enough to contend against at first, but my motto through life has been, '*Never despair*,' and on this I have ever acted.

"I may tell you, sir, that I managed to get

employment with a respectable merchant, and I really wonder when I think how closely I applied myself to the duties required of me—it could hardly be expected from one brought up as I had been—but I had an object in view, and that I suppose helped me on.

"Be this as it may, in ten years or so I not only contrived to double the little capital which emained to me after I got settled in a situation, but was in the annual receipt of as many dollars as enabled me without niggardness to lay by some of them every year.

"As my prospects brightened, I naturally wished to have some one to share my good fortune with me, and, like others of my age, I was not long in finding one whom I conceived would be an excellent match. She was the daughter of a man who, in my first struggles, had shown me more kindness than I had a right to expect at the hands of a stranger, and who, up to that time, had exhibited the same, if not warmer feelings towards me. His house, his table, and had I required it, I may add, his purse, was open to me; and it is but a small tribute to his memory to say that a more sincere or disinterested friend never fell to the lot of man. He was the senior partner of the firm which I served, and Maria was his only child. You may conceive, sir, the doting affection which he lavished upon her, and she was doubly dear to him from the sad event which made him a father and a widower in the same day. Well knowing, as I did, the favourable opinions he entertained of me, and flattering myself also that he could not have failed to notice the attachment which had sprung up between his daughter and myself, I yet trembled when I asked his consent to our union. That consent, however, was given when so little expected, though at the same time the accomplishment of our wishes was delayed for a year from the date of his consent. I was to undergo that period of probation, and if, at the expiration of that time, all was well, the day on which Maria attained her twenty-first year was to make her my wife, and myself a partner in the firm of ' B———s and Co.'

" Surely, sir, God seemed to smile upon me, so bright did the future appear; and yet (I know 'tis wrong to utter such a sentiment) often have I had occasion to wish the year of probation had never come to an end.

" It seemed long enough then, every day appeared a month, and the months never to come to a close; but the appointed time arrived at last, and the day which witnessed our union, and unfolded, as I fondly imagined, the roll of many happy years, proved to me the bitterest of my life: all my subsequent trials I have borne up under, because I never hazarded on any one venture the whole sum of my happiness; in this I did: I embarked my all, and when the bark which bore it foundered, I became utterly bankrupt in heart."

* * * * *

[The sad recollections caused the old man to pause; a tear rolled down his furrowed cheek, but hastily brushing it away, with many others that followed in its train, he resumed.]

"Long before our marriage, sir, I knew that Maria was naturally of a jealous disposition; but so far from its leading me to think that such would ever cause a moment's unhappiness between us, I rather hailed it as an omen that love for me was the mainspring of it, and that when once we became man and wife, every shadow of it would disappear. But, alas! I discovered at length that what was in her really a failing in the first instance was at last adopted as a foil to conceal her own designs.

"We had been married about two years, and God had blessed us with one lovely boy. I canno say that during that time there had been no little clouds hovering about the sunshine of our happiness so as occasionally to intercept its rays; far, far otherwise; a trivial expression, or still more a jocular commendation from me on any of our female acquaintance, was sufficient to fan the slumbering embers into a flame, and my endeavours to quench them had so often proved vain, that I at length learned to exercise patience until they burnt out of themselves. And yet, sir, in spite of these occasional outbreaks, how devotedly I loved her He only knew who can read the heart! Around my heart she was so entwined, that no wonder when a rude hand tore her away she carried with her a portion of that into which the fibres had fixed themselves.

"It was about four months after the birth of my second child, that on returning home unexpectedly from a journey which I had been obliged to make some distance from Washington, I found a young American, who was a junior clerk in our firm, seated at the tea-table with my wife. I did not make any observation at the moment, but after he had left, repeated what I had said, on former occasions, that I thought H—— was too frequent a guest at our house.

"I never liked the man, for I knew him to be a dissipated character, and it was only on Maria's account, who pleaded the connexion which had so long subsisted between him and her father, that I tolerated, rather than permitted his visits. At the same time she knew my wishes and apparently acted upon them, so that he never came without a special invitation. The tête-a-tête in which I found them engaged on my unlooked-for return certainly discomposed me; and I concluded my remarks on the impropriety of her receiving him in my absence, by adding my determination of giving strict orders that in future he never should darken my threshold.

"To my astonishment, Maria heard this determination with comparative calmness; true, she affected to rail at my jealousy, and used those weapons of sarcasm which women know so well how to handle when they can offer no plausible defence,—but her whole conduct led me to suppose that she saw the reasonableness and justice of my arguments. . . . Good easy man that I was, not to discover the deceit practised upon me.

"Too late was revealed how long the game had been played; that very meeting which I interrupted, was held to mature their plans, and that very night—she deserted her husband and her helpless babe to throw herself into the arms of her seducer.

* * * * *

"Heavily as fell the blow upon *me*, its effects were in one sense less disastrous than in the case of her father: it was more than he could bear up under, and before ten days had elapsed all that remained of the fondest of fathers and the warmest of friends was laid in the grave! ..

"I remained in America only long enough to arrange my affairs; and finding that every attempt at a discovery of the fugitives was vain, I set my face towards England with my two children, a widowed and broken-hearted man!

"My trials had commenced, and affliction seemed now to pursue me. We had been but a fortnight at sea, when my poor motherless infant closed its eyes in death, and its little corpse was cast into the deep dark Atlantic, whilst the vessel sped onwards in her gallant path as though eager to leave the spot which a woman's sin had marked with such a withering curse. Oh! sir, let it not appear harsh in me to say so, 'twas woman who brought the curse into the world, and though she also was the channel of the blessing, yet I can't help thinking, that as sin remains in the world, she is so perverted from the original end for which she was created, that she proves oftener a curse than a blessing."

"Well but, Charles," I interrupted, "I think you are judging somewhat unfairly in condemning the whole body because you happen to have met with a diseased member: how often is it that our sex reduces them to that degraded position in which we find them!"

"Oh! sir, I don't mean to make men faultless, because women are frail; but if there are degrees in vice, I think experience will prove that when woman *is* vicious she is far more so than man. You will say perhaps that, on the other hand, when they are true and virtuous, they are far more so than man. This may be the case; I can't gainsay it, because I have never proved the truth or falseness of the assertion, but nevertheless" . . .

"Well, Charles, we won't argue the point any farther: I dare say you speak as you feel on the subject; but remember we are all sinful, and should therefore learn to look with a merciflu eye on the sins of others."

"I hope I do, sir; my daily prayer has been that Maria has experienced at the hands of her

Father in heaven that forgiveness which her husband has given her! She did not live many years to indulge in her sin, and I have reason to believe that she bitterly repented of it before she died . . but to resume, sir. . . .

"Favourable winds made the voyage much shorter, and I was not sorry to catch a glimpse of the white cliffs of old England, although I had there no cheerful hearts to welcome my return! I was the last of my family, but I had a wish that the name should not utterly sink into oblivion without a struggle on my part.

"My plan was, as I had now the means to repurchase my paternal property, to settle there for the remainder of my days, and devote what of life remained to me to the education of my beloved child. He was all that I now retained as an object of love, and though too young to understand the extent of his mother's sin, he was taught to look upon her as dead, and to consider himself, as he really was, a *motherless* boy! Poor child! he had only a faint recollection of her. Hard indeed must have been her heart to have forsaken *him;* but worst of all to leave her babe, to whom at the time she fled she had so to speak but just given birth. Oh, unnatural monster! that so fair a face could conceal such a black heart! . . . but I will not again allude to this .. it unnerves me. . . . . .

"To my grievous disappointment, though perhaps hardly contrary to my expectations, the purchaser of my father's estate refused to part with it on any terms, even though I offered him double the sum which he had given for it.

My heart, however, yearned for a resting-place in my native village, and if I could not regain the house of my forefathers I was resolved to dwell as near the spot as possible. With this view I purchased some land in the immediate vicinity, a suitable house was soon reared and already began to assume a habitable appearance, when the American packet, for the arrival of which I had been anxiously looking to apprise me of the transfer of my American property into the English funds, brought me in its place the intelligence of the total failure of the concern in which all my earnings had been vested, and my liability to the creditors for nearly double the sum which I had expected to receive! How I recovered from the stunning effects of this fresh blow I hardly know; for a time I could not be brought to believe the reality, but a second packet soon brought stronger confirmation, if any had been needed, and I had again to embark to make my way in the world even without the capital which on a former occasion insured me against actual and immediate want. A second time was I obliged to quit the home of my youth, and it seemed that, like the Jews of old in regard to their temple, I was forbidden to attempt to rebuild on a spot where God had decreed that my home should not be.

"For some time I was at a loss what to undertake or in what business to engage. To return to America under all the circumstances of the case was the last thing I should have consented to, even had my inclinations at all led me that way; the remembrance of what I had suffered in that country would have proved an effectual barrier to such a step, and I preferred rather to move with my poor child to Liverpool, which was then rapidly rising in importance as a commercial town, and more likely to afford me an opening.

"After some delay, during which I was brought to the lowest ebb, I contrived to obtain a similar post to that in which I had first commenced my fortunes in America, and with almost pinching economy managed to obtain a tolerable subsistence for myself and my child.

"Sweet was the labour, however monotonous, whose wages not only enabled me to shield him from want, but by degrees to give him that training which would prove a treasure when wealth should fail; and often, when I have returned to my dinner after the principal fatigue of the day was over, did my little companion's cheerful prattle (giving me an account of what he had done and said at his school, where I daily sent him) make a lonely home appear a social circle; and peopled with unnumbered guests it would have been a solitude unless graced with the presence of my lovely boy!

"Already had he reached his eighth year, and gave promise of mental power which I fondly anticipated would one day place him in that rank of society in which his birth entitled him to move! But how strange it is, sir, that a man who entertains any proper views on the subject of religion, and I never forgot my duties in that respect,—how strange it is that a man should build on the future, when all beyond the present is shrouded in uncertainty! Surely I ought to have been wiser, for God had taught me by many severe lessons the folly of such a course! But so it is; we are always learning but never fully taught; and as you observed, sir, in your sermon last evening, 'God is obliged to speak in louder and more severe accents, because we will not listen and give heed when he addresses us in the tones of mercy and love—he is obliged to roar as in the whirlwind, because we turn a deaf ear to the still small voice.'

* * * * *

"Do not, sir, expect me to dwell at length and relate each detail connected with this portion of my history; let me only tell you that for three weeks I scarcely ever left the bedside of my suffering child after the first moment of his seizure: day and night found me in the same broken-hearted and desponding condition, heeding nothing but his recovery; and when that was pronounced hopeless—when I saw day by day, and almost hour by hour, the wasting form of my once lovely boy, till at length his gentle spirit passed away as though some angel had received it without disturbing his calm slumber, and he had parted with it without a struggle; then my long-tried powers gave way, then I felt the loneliness of my lot, and was indeed for awhile sorrowful as one that had no hope! Oh, sir, if I had had others around me, I could perhaps have borne the parting with this treasure, but he was then the one only tie which bound me to my kind; for him I patiently toiled, and to insure his welfare, I could have undergone anything and everything; . . . but God thought fit to remove him, he provided better for him than I could have done . . . and though I murmured at the time, I have since learnt to look upon the affliction as sent more in mercy than in judgment . . .

* * * * -

"Two months after my poor child was laid in the grave, I was miles away from his last earthly resting-place on my way to Jamaica. The house in which I was engaged was largely concerned in the West Indian trade, and the chief clerk, a man who had grown grey in the service of his masters, and to whom the management of everything was entrusted, observing the effect which my recent loss had produced, considerately proposed change of scene as a solace for my grief: and with this view I was despatched to the island of Jamaica for the purpose of superintending some mercantile transactions, which required the presence of some-one immediately connected with the firm.

Most gladly did I avail myself of the offer made me to undertake the mission. England had now no charms for me, the world was my home, and where I settled down was to me a matter of little moment, though I confess I looked forward to the hope of laying my bones in the tomb of my fathers.

"It was towards the end of the year 1806 when I left the shores of England; and although at that time, as you well know, sir, it was not a very safe passage across the Atlantic, owing to the warlike attitude in which England stood to other nations, we were fortunate enough to meet with no interruption, and after a fine run, reached Falmouth harbour. Scarcely had I been on the island a fortnight, and recovered the effects of the voyage, ere I fell a victim to the scourge of those western climates, the yellow fever, which, at the time of my arrival, was raging with more than common violence.

"Luckily I was in good hands, my constitution was good, and before this I had scarcely suffered a day's illness, but it was under God to a poor aged negress, that on the occasion I refer to I owed the preservation of my life. Through the tedious hours of sickness she nursed me with the affectionate care and attention of a mother to her only child, and I firmly believe that it was her skill more than that of the medical man which brought me round again.

"Happily it was in my power to make her a

return, which she valued far beyond the possession of any earthly wealth, by purchasing the freedom of her son a short time before her death, and he ever afterwards became one of my most attached followers.

"Ah, sir, it was whilst in that island, beautiful in every respect but for its accursed traffic in the flesh of our fellow creatures, that I saw in their full development the horrors of the slave trade. Many and many a tale could I relate of the sights I witnessed on the various plantations which business or pleasure induced me to visit. It was enough to draw tears from a heart of stone even to conceive, much more to behold, the sufferings of those poor simple creatures who, because nature had formed the colour of their skin different from that of other nations, were looked upon as a different species, not to be ranked amongst the noblest of God's works, but born to be as the beasts of burden to those who purchased or parted with them as an article of merchandize.

"It was at that time the common opinion that the intellect of the negroes was incapable of cultivation, that it was useless to attempt anything towards their civilization or moral advancement, because they were only one degree removed from the brute creation, and hence only to be treated as such! Thank God I have lived long enough to see such foolish opinions quite laid aside, and ——

. . . But, sir, you don't want to hear an account of slavery, as I said thank God the trade is put down, at least as far as our own country is concerned, though still, I must say, I never thought England abolished slavery in the way she ought to have done; but that's another business, things might have been managed differently—but never mind." . . .

"Come, Charles," I observed, "I should like to hear your views of the question; as an eye-witness your evidence is important."

"Ah well, sir, perhaps it might be; but it is a stale subject now, so we won't discuss it, at least not at present; I must go on with my story, or you will think I am never coming to the end of it. . . .

"Instead of remaining in Jamaica, as I had at first intended, about nine or ten months, I remained there nearly twice as many years. After recovering from the '*yellow Jack*,' as they called the fever which had attacked me, I proceeded in earnest to arrange the business for which I had been specially sent out, and whilst fully engaged in it, the offer was made me, by those whom I represented, to remain altogether on the spot, and receive a salary of £280 a year currency. I closed with the offer after very little hesitation. None were left behind in my own land who could mourn my separation from them. I had only myself to provide for, and my only wish was to secure a competency, so that when age and grey hairs came upon me, I should not be without a provision for my increasing wants. But there never was a truer saying than that *man appoints, God disappoints.* I laid up earthly riches, happy has it proved for me that I forgot not also to lay up a treasure in heaven, and when the former failed the latter was my support and consolation.

" During the nineteen years I remained in the island, I saved up no less a sum than £4000; and having done this, I thought I had realized sufficient to maintain me in comfort for the rest of my days, with something to spare to relieve the wants of those who were less fortunate and successful than I had been. My heart yearned towards England as my last resting place on earth, and having invested my savings in the English funds, I bade farewell to a land which had so long fostered me, and where providence had smiled on and prospered my exertions.

" I knew I was ' the last of the family,' and I

had now some hopes, that at least the 'family name' would not suffer reproach on account of its last possessor. . . .

"You will naturally suppose, sir, after the many changes and sad reverses which I had undergone, I had learned experience. Surely I ought to have done so, considering how dearly the lessons had been bought; but I suppose I must have been a very dull scholar, or you would not have heard me relate in a workhouse the history I have given you. Mine seemed to be a lot wherein it was appointed that I should never be so completely reduced as actually to want bread, and yet never continue rich enough to live in ease and retirement from active pursuits. For some time, however, after my return to England, I passed my days in comfort; the interest of the money I had invested produced me an income sufficient for my wants, at the same time that the capital was secure. Age was fast advancing, the boundary of three score years and ten was passed, and one might have thought I was too old to be caught by the specious bait which was held out to me, but caught I was: a proposal was made me to invest my capital in a sinking fund, and in consideration of my doing so, an annuity for life was promised me very far above what I was receiving from the funds! Whether it was that a foolish pride made me embrace the offer, in the anticipation that I might live in a station of society more suited to my birth, in the neighbourhood where I grew into manhood, or whether it was that God, by the way through which he led me, designed to teach me more strongly, the folly of such desires, and so wean me more from earth—in an evil hour—and yet I should not say so except in a worldly sense, I transferred the whole of my capital into the hands of swindlers, and after the first half year's dividend was paid my hard earnings vanished; the whole concern proved to be the speculation of an unprincipled gang, and, like many others who had been equally credulous, I was brought, in a short time, almost to the door of want.

"The idea of one arrived at my time of life commencing anew the work of earning a subsistence was too absurd to be entertained. I knew it could not be long before all my trials, as far at least as this life was concerned, would soon be terminated in the grave; and when the little which remained from the sad wreck was expended, seeing no other door open to me, I consented to enter within the walls of a workhouse! After all the scenes through which I have passed, all the bright hopes which I once formed—after all the expectations of happiness and comfort which for a time were realized,—it is a poor sequel, but it is not the wages of vice or extravagance, it is God's will, and from my heart I can say, 'His will be done!'" . . .

"Well, Charles, you don't appear discontented with your present condition, and though they say you are sometimes rather particular and give a little trouble, yet I always hear a good account of you."

"They would belie me, sir, if they laid any faults against me, for it is not the province of one who receives a bounty to find fault with the giver of it; such is not the case with me. I never complain of the provision which is made for the poor, but of the way in which that provision is administered. If a man who wants bread knows that by applying in a certain quarter he may obtain it, not as the sparingly bestowed alms of charity, but as a matter of right, he does not like, when he receives the bread, to have the wounds which misfortune has inflicted, made to bleed afresh, to be compelled to feel that he is punished because of God's providential visitations, equally with those who have squandered away their means of subsistence in waste and profligacy."

* * * * *

As I have embodied in another part of this work some of the observations of C—— M—— on this particular portion of the New Poor Law, I need hardly say, that to me his reasonings on the subject appeared, for the most part, very sound. Making every allowance for the garrulity of old age, and the disposition of one who had at one time "enough and to spare," to find cause of complaint, when at his time of life he looked upon himself as a *rated* pauper, I should have marvelled that he was so calm and contented as he was, had I not known that a higher power taught him the lessons of submission, and led him to look far beyond the care of the perishing body.

My connexion with the union of which I write has, for some time, been closed, though I often visit some of my old charges who still survive. When last there I heard of poor Charlie, but no longer as the inmate of a workhouse; through the medium of a friend who had known him in better days, he was transferred, almost before he could understand the change, to a comfortable

alms-house, where he is spending the winter
age, unvexed by the idea that the poor-house
the last refuge left him, and a pauper's fune
the last act of *respect* which will be offered to
"*Last of the Family.*"

THE PENITENT.

"Reverend Sir,

"You will please to pardon my troubling you at such a late hour, but as you wished to be informed if any change took place in Eliza S——, I have sent to say, that there does not appear to be much chance of her living through the night, and she has expressed a great wish to see you." . . .

Such were the contents of a note which I received at the close of a laborious day, and just as, after the usual evening sacrifice of social worship, I had dismissed the various members of my household for the night. My little *sanctum*, with its cheerful fire, close drawn curtains, and other comfortable arrangements, seemed to present an effectual barrier against the inclemency of the weather.

he pastor and his flock. I do not hesitate (even at the risk of being described as a partial witness) to record in these pages my deliberate conviction that there is no body of men who with such disinterested feelings and often under circumstances of great personal privation are so ready at any and all times to deny themselves and sacrifice ease and comfort in purposes to the flock committed to their charge, as the clergy of the Church of England; and although we grant that some instances may be brought forward from which an opposite fact may be elicited. I would rather say that such are the exceptions which prove the rule, and that such exceptions generally call forth more censure, because they are the more uncommon.

I say not these things in praise of the clerical body, or to claim for ourselves the least measure of human applause; we seek not our "reward of men," at the same time duty to our office and the Master whom we serve sometimes calls upon us in the spirit of the great apostle to "become fools in glorifying, because ye" (our enemies) "have compelled us." [2 Cor. xii. 11.] It requires us to adduce actually existing facts in evidence against mere assertion and clamour, lest by con

It was the very depth of winter, and the snow lay so thick upon the ground as completely to muffle the sound of the carriage wheels which now and then passed along, conveying some merry hearts either to or from the happy meeting of a Christmas party.

I had meditated on an hour or two of quiet study before retiring to rest, and had commenced the revision of my sermon for the ensuing first sabbath of the new year, when the summons above quoted overthrew my plans, and called me to exchange the dressing gown for the great coat, and to wend my way to the bedside of a dying saint!

The object of my visit was one of somewhat unusual interest to me, and perhaps on that account I felt the less disturbed at being obliged to quit a warm study to face such an inclement night; but even had it been otherwise, and the visit had been required to a comparative stranger of my flock, I trust those feelings of self-denial, characteristic of the majority of the clergy of the established Church, would not have been wanting in my case.

Much as they are maligned, much as they are spoken against by those who have never realized the affectionate sympathy which exists between the pastor and his flock, I do not hesitate (even at the risk of being discredited as a partial witness) to record in these pages my deliberate conviction that there is no body of men who, with such disinterested feelings, and often under circumstances of great personal privation, are so ready at any and all times to deny themselves, and sacrifice ease and comfort to minister to the flock committed to their charge, as the clergy of the Church of England; and although we grant that some instances may be brought forward from which an opposite fact may be elicited, I would rather say that such are the exceptions which prove the rule, and that such exceptions generally call forth more censure, because they are the more uncommon.

I say not these things in praise of the clerical body, or to claim for ourselves the least measure of human applause; we seek not our "reward of men," at the same time duty to our office and the Master whom we serve sometimes calls upon us in the spirit of the great apostle to "become fools in glorifying, because ye" (our enemies) "have compelled us." [2 Cor. xii. 11.] It requires us to adduce actually existing facts in evidence against mere assertion and clamour, lest by continued silence the latter should prevail to the injury of God's truth!

Take the various parishes throughout the length and breadth of the land, and with how few exceptions will you not find that the clergyman is the friend, the adviser, the *temporal* as well as the *spiritual* guide of his flock; whether in the dwelling of the rich, or in the humble cottage of the poor, he is the well-received guest, and whilst in many cases, it may be, that a portion of such respect may be laid to the score of the office he holds, the very existence in some solitary cases of the want of such a display of kindly feelings may generally be traced to some personal animosity aroused by the absence of those characteristics which are *always* looked for in the members of this body.

Why is it that the teachers of a dissenting communion have not such a hold on the affections of the people as the pastors of the Established Church? Many of them are men of prayer, men of unblemished walk and conversation, men who, humanly speaking, have much to command admiration and support;—and yet go into the villages of happy England—try to establish a dissenting chapel in a rural district where a faithful man of God, like Philip, "preaches Christ" unto the people, not only within the walls of their parish church, but from "house to house," and what will be the result? The "*tithe-grinding parson*," as he is contumeliously termed, is the one who has been tried and found to prove the real friend; and men who are generally considered ignorant in other matters, are sufficiently skilled to appreciate such a character.

I have now had some little experience, both actual and incidental, in the management of a rural population; and whilst I am willing to admit that great allowance must be made for what, for the sake of definition, we will call the *indigenous feelings of attachment to the parish church and the parish altar* at which our forefathers worshipped; this would be but a poor and worthless substitute for the services of one to minister at that altar in the person of the parish priest, and a vacancy would exist which, were every cottage in the parish to become a dissenting chapel, would never be filled up!

Some one, however, may point me to populous towns, and ask me whether the existence of dissent in them does not overthrow the position which I am endeavouring to establish? So far, however, from doing so, I am induced to claim it as a confirmatory argument in my favour, from the conviction which I have, that such dissent arises wholly and solely from the want of sufficient church accommodation, sufficient pastors to supply those churches, and to discharge what is perhaps the most efficient, as it certainly is the most necessary part of the clerical office—*the visiting the rich as well as the poor!* Only let us multiply churches—pastors will not be found wanting—and thus shall we not only most effectually quell dissent, but we may hope to witness not merely the *ideal*, but the *reality* of a Christian Church.

To return, however, to the subject of this sketch. I have said that the case of Eliza S—— was one which seemed to have a special claim on my attention.

She had been the object of many prayers, and the length and nature of her sufferings, together with her patience and sweet resignation, had made her case interesting not only to myself, who had long been the witness of what passed within, but to those who were enabled to judge according to outward appearance.

Many had surmised from various circumstances the history of her former life; it was, however, reserved for me to hear the accurate detail of her past follies and sins, as well as to witness her deep penitence!

Of the various intercourse I had with her, and the conversation which took place at my several visits, my diary contains the most circumstantial details.

Extending, however, as it does over a space of many months, during which period she was under my immediate visitation, it would exceed the limits I have assigned to this sketch were I to make a full transcript of all connected with her case. Deeply, moreover, as I myself may feel interested in its re-perusal, even now that she has long since gone to her rest, it would prove tedious to those who in this " daily chronicle" would find wanting one great charm, that of personally witnessing the progress of Divine grace.

I shall, therefore, only introduce such portions as immediately precede the closing scenes of a life which, early dedicated to the service of sin, was in its last stages doubly devoted to God in the only way that remained—that of heartfelt penitence and prayer.

It was about eight months previous to her death that Eliza S—— appeared to enter upon a new state of mental existence; until that time she had been rather an uninterested listener to the lessons of divine truth than an eager inquirer after them; and though I had observed on some occasions as a particularly striking or affecting portion of Scripture came under consideration in my course of instruction to those with her in the hospital ward, a long and deep drawn sigh indicated that some chord was vibrating within; yet her general demeanour would to a casual observer have confirmed the supposition that she had sunk into a state of apathetic indifference as regarded spiritual things!

Subsequent events, however, proved the contrary, and showed that the only weight which held her down, and produced what I may term the *concentration* of calm despair was a sense of unpardoned sin.

True, she spoke not of it, she complained not of it; for a time she confided not the fact of its existence to mortal ear; but the leaven was silently at work, and when, in God's good time, the whole lump was fully leavened, she was enabled to testify " how great things the Lord had done for her!"

It appeared strange, that frequently as I had communicated with her, I was never able to obtain much insight into her real state of mind;

and I had almost despaired of bringing her to a sense of her spiritual condition. For a whole year she had been unable to leave her bed; and her disorder was of such a nature, that though she did not, except at particular times, suffer acute bodily pain, there was no hope of her ultimate recovery.

It was my custom, at stated periods, to administer the sacrament of the Lord's supper to those sick and aged in the hospital who were unable to partake of it with the rest of the inmates. Eliza S—— had of course often witnessed the celebration of this sacred ordinance without being a partaker, and had never once hinted a wish, either to learn the nature of this feast, or the benefits to be derived, though she must often have *felt*, from being the only one in the ward who did not join in its reception.

On one occasion, however, whilst I was engaged in offering up that beautiful confessional prayer in the service which immediately precedes the absolution, somewhat to my astonishment, but still more to my delight, she distinctly repeated, after me, every petition, and at the close of it burst into a flood of tears!

The remainder of the service was interrupted by her repeated sobs, and from that hour the work of grace began to manifest itself. What subsequently followed shall be extracted from my diary, though long intervals must necessarily intervene between each extract.

* * * *

"August 18. How wonderful are the ways of God! how deeply mysterious the operations of his grace! After months of apparently spiritual desertion, hope has at length dawned upon the soul of Eliza S——. How refreshing to-day, after what I have so long witnessed, to find that light has burst in. . . . The bread cast upon the waters has returned after many days!"

"August 19. This day has indeed been one of encouragement, one which God sometimes grants to cheer us in our labours, and show us that fruit which, perhaps, often looking for too anxiously, we feel disappointment at not receiving · . .

"Eliza S—— has at last opened her mind to me, and I have discovered the cause of her long continued outward insensibility. On my visit to the house this morning, I had scarcely seated myself at her bed-side, when she exclaimed, 'Ah, sir, I have been anxiously expecting you—how glad I am to see you! I want to tell you of joys which I never felt before, and of comfort which I never knew till last night. I hope you are not angry at the interruption which I caused to the service yesterday, but . . . I never, till that hour, saw God in any other light than as an *offended Judge;* almost in a moment, a silent whisper told me he was something else, and now, . . . now, . . . blessed be his name, I see him as my reconciled Father, because he is the Father of my Saviour, Jesus Christ! Oh, sir, could you but know the weeks and months of anguish which have borne me down, and pressed on me *here* (pointing to her heart) like some deadly burthen, you would pity the poor wandering sinner who has so long been a stranger to the joys of her Father's home! Low indeed, sir, have I been brought into the valley of suffering, but never till now saw a ray of hope; . . . but it is past, and now, . . . oh merciful God, now all my past sorrows are more than amply repaid: . . . my sins *can* be pardoned, and God has given me the sweet assurance of it! . . . I was engaged when you entered, in reading the 103rd Psalm, . . surely I have cause to say, 'Bless the Lord oh my soul, and all that is within me bless his holy . . . *who forgiveth all thine iniquities.*' "

These last words she pronounced with peculiar emphasis, and I could not at first bring myself to believe, but that she who had made such an address, who had broken through, as in a moment, the barriers of taciturnity which had hitherto seemed impenetrable, was labouring under some strong delusion! Still there was a calmness in her mode of speech which opposed such an idea, and which bore with it the conviction that she was only giving utterance to the " words of soberness and truth."

"What then, Eliza, have been your ideas until now, when such a change seems to have taken place," was my first question; " you have hitherto appeared indifferent to all my instructions." . . .

"Ah, sir, I may have *seemed* so . . . perhaps I was . . . and yet it could not be; . . . but I always felt my sins had been so great as completely to cast off all hope, and until now I have lived in despair! but oh! . . . how good has God been to me, he has lifted up the light of his countenance, and now I can rejoice." . . .

This, the first allusion to her past life, made me somewhat anxious to hear from her own lips the burden which had pressed upon her so heavily; and I accordingly asked why she thought any sin too great for the atoning blood of Jesus to wash away. . . .

She looked round, and in a still lower tone of

voice than she had hitherto adopted, replied, "I have often, sir, felt a desire to relieve my mind of the sorrows which have so long overwhelmed me, and though my confession has long since been made to God, something urges me so far to humble myself as to make it to man: . . . to-morrow, sir, (she added in a whisper,) I am to be removed, by the surgeon's orders, to another ward, and if I am spared so long, may, in a few days, be enabled to tell you a tale which will, perhaps, grieve you, but which, nevertheless, must be told, if I would hope to fulfil, however imperfectly, the duty which I yet owe to God and man. . . .

"As you are about now to offer up your customary prayer, oh, entreat God to carry on the good work which he has begun, and to receive and pardon his sinful but repentant child!" . . .

* * * * *

October 3. Upwards of six weeks have elapsed, and I have not visited the workhouse until to day. . . . I pray God that the temporary absence from my duties, may, with the return of recruited strength, give me an increasing desire to promote the spiritual welfare of those amongst whom it is my lot to labour. . . .

I seemed to feel that God's blessing was upon

me during the interview which I had to-day, with Eliza S——.

My dear fellow labourer, H——, who had so kindly and faithfully supplied my absence, had given me reason to expect a gradual development of the work of grace in her heart, and I indeed found it answer his description; . . . a few extracts of her conversation will best explain this.

Adopting almost the same tone and the same mode of expression which she had done on the last occasion I visited her, her first greeting was . . . "They have not deceived me to day . . . they said you were come home, sir, and that I should soon see you . . . thank God you are returned . . . I hope better . . . for they said you have been very ill. . . . I do not think you will find I have gone back in your absence. . Mr. H—— has been very kind, but still, sir, I felt that you had been my instructor, and I could not listen to his teaching with the same advantage that I could to yours." . . .

What might be termed, in the language of the world, *a compliment*, but what, in this case, was no doubt the simple expression of a really existent feeling, did not deter me from conveying that reproof which, in every similar case, I should feel it my duty to administer.

The feeling which dictated the observation of, Eliza S. is one which though in a more matured form, pervades the great mass of professing Christians in the present day; and there is no folly more deserving of censure, none certainly which is carried to so undue an excess, as that of attaching oneself to *some particular teacher* merely because he happens to be the most talked of in the neighbourhood or parish—merely because he happens to be, what in common parlance is termed a *popular preacher!*

Let me not be misunderstood! Far be it from me to fall into the opposite extreme with some of our church, and to decry the preaching of the everlasting gospel, since scripture teaches us that it pleases God by the "foolishness of preaching to save them that believe," but I would at the same time affectionately entreat those who are the subject of this species of religious excitement to which I refer—to consider whether they are not in danger—nay, I would say in the greatest peril—of being led astray whilst they thus follow *men* rather than *doctrine*, whilst in the language of the apostle they have "*men's persons in admiration.*"

It may be, and doubtless is, most pleasing to the natural man to hear an eloquent discourse, from one who is highly gifted with this "power of speech," but when thus inclined to gratify our natural feelings, let us remember the spiritual object which we ought to have in view, and then, so far from joining in the cry, "I am of Paul, and I of Apollos,"—a cry equally if not more prevalent now than in the day in which the apostle reproved it,—instead of saying, (as I have heard many say,) "*I shall go to such a church to-day, because Mr. So-and-So is going to preach,*"—we shall rather seek the ministrations of him who is set over us in the Lord, and remember that though he may not be gifted with the same eloquence in delivering the message of salvation, the message, if he be a faithful man of God, does not on that account come with less real power, knowing that "*though there are diversities of gifts, there is but one and the same spirit.*" * . . .

---

* These observations may to the casual reader appear uncalled for, and the idea of rebuking a sufferer on a sick bed because she fancied one instructor more than another, may seem a harsh mode of proceeding; those, however, who from experience best know the line of conduct to be pursued in such cases, will understand the motives which influenced me in acting as I did. True that I had been, under God, the means of bringing this penitent one to a knowledge of the truth, and

"I feel I have been wrong, sir, in giving utterance to the expression of such feelings . . . but still I fear the lessons of Mr. H—— did not do me the good they ought to have done . . because I felt that you knew my case better . . . and yet he was very kind . . . I tried to profit . . . I hope I did. . . ."

It was but a weakness, and the simple rebuke was the means of showing me, by the result it produced, that she was growing in grace; she sought not to justify what she was sensible was an improper feeling, and whilst meekly acknowledging her error, proved that she was beginning to learn the hardest of all lessons, *the weakness of self.* . . .

Her conversation during this interview was in truth of a most gratifying nature, and it was now for the first time that I was enabled to gather an outline of her previous history. This outline was filled up at various subsequent visits, but as

she might on this account have naturally wished her further instruction to come from me; and yet such a feeling, however amiable and innocent in itself, ceases to be a right one, when it may lead us to value the channel through which the instruction flows equally with the instruction itself.

I will only add the wish, that the feelings which dictated her reply may be a model for those who in like case need a like reproof. . . . .

the result is what we are chiefly concerned with, I shall condense the original narrative, and only put the reader in possession of those facts which may be necessary to connect what eventually occurred. At the time I first knew her she was about thirty years of age, though bodily and mental suffering had, as in most similar cases, added ten or twelve years to her outward appearance.

Her first misfortune, and that to which she ascribed most of her subsequent sorrows, arose from the loss of both her parents within a short space of each other, and the consignment of herself and a younger sister at the age of nine years to the parish workhouse, where she received such instruction as the old system provided, and which, imperfect as it was, I am inclined to think was more adapted to those for whom it was intended than that which is now supplied under the newly-constituted order of things. The present system, when under the proper and immediate control of an active chaplain, may be made most efficient, but through the miserable parsimony which gives in some cases £20 a-year to an already over-worked curate to perform those duties which would employ *two* clergyman's undivided attention, left as the workhouse school too often is to the sole direction of a wretchedly paid schoolmaster, no wonder that so many brought up in such a way afterwards swell the gaol list, and cost the country more to banish them to some penal settlement, than it would have done to make them, by proper early training, good and useful members of society!

Three years passed away, and Eliza was transferred as an apprenticed servant to a farmer about ten miles distant from her native place, and there she remained for the next five years. Happily would it have proved for her had she never quitted it. Even then she looked back with delight on what she called her brightest days, when, with others in the same walk of life as herself, she was allowed to go once during the week on a stated evening to the vicarage, and receive the personal instruction of the good clergyman, who at such seasons was wont to assemble round him the younger ones of his flock, and simply teach them the lessons of heavenly wisdom. *

---

* This portion of the narrative of Eliza S—— has often recurred with peculiar force to my mind! Should these sketches fall into the hands of any of my reverend brethren, I would ask them to consider the subject here referred to . . the giving up one evening during the week to the instruction of the young persons in the parish. I allude more particularly to the agri-

Unfortunately for Eliza, a temptation too powerful to be resisted by one dazzled with the advantages held out, was presented in the offer of a situation in a neighbouring town; it was accepted, and she exchanged the quiet of a country service for the vice of a dissipated and "*fashionable watering place*," (as the language of the day terms it,) with a personal appearance of no ordinary pretensions, and scarce eighteen years of age!

Even in the midst of contagion she might have perhaps escaped unharmed, for vice in its grosser forms would have shocked rather than enticed her, but she had to contend with a subtle enemy, and his wiles eventually succeeded to her overthrow.

---

cultural districts. The clergyman seldom finds the young men and women at home in his ordinary pastoral visits, and if he should they are generally occupied in such labours as preclude the possibility of giving them the necessary instruction; without some other means, therefore, they are obliged to depend only on the public ministrations which they are not always able to attend.

I have for some time tried the plan of a weekly family lecture at the vicarage, and have been permitted to witness the fruit of such labours, whilst the attention and regular attendance of its members testify the value they set on such a course of instruction.

Her new mistress was distinguished for nothing so much as a practical unaffected piety; and Eliza, upon whom the lessons of religion had not been lost, felt happy in her new condition. Attachment to such a mistress almost insensibly sprang up, and attendant circumstances fostered its growth.

She had been long in a sickly condition, and Eliza well performed the duties assigned her; night after night did she watch by the bedside of the sufferer; no hand but hers could properly smooth the pillow, and, if she was not by, something was sure to be wanted which she only knew how to administer. . . .

Months thus passed on, and when at length her mistress was partially restored to health, she who had so faithfully attended her in the weary hours of sickness was not forgotten in the hour of recovery. All seemed to promise well, and no cloud threatened to darken the sunshine of Eliza's prosperity.

Placed where she had more comforts than usually fall to the lot of those in her condition of life, and apparently beyond the reach of danger, she perhaps little thought of the power of temptation; so that when the hour of trial came she sought not for grace to strive successfully against it—and fell!

Let her subsequent history be told as nearly in her own words as I can note them down; she attempted not to palliate or excuse her sin, but feeling the burden of it, took to herself the full measure of its guilt.

*　　　*　　　　*　　　*

"I need not detain you, sir, with the relation of the steps which preceded my commencement of a course of sin . . . the flatterer came and so successfully applied the poison that my ruin quickly ensued.

"For some time I endeavoured to conceal my shame, and by various contrivances succeeded in disarming suspicion as to the real cause of my altered looks, such being attributed to my constant confinement to the house rather than to the shadow of surmise as to the true reason. The very methods for concealment, however, hastened on the event which, in obliging me to leave my place on the plea of sickness for a short change, ushered into the world before its time a living monument of a mother's sin and shame.

"I was soon enabled to resume my accustomed duties, and though to outward appearance every thing seemed to go on as before, the pain of mind which I underwent was a severe punishment, so that when alone the thoughts of my sin almost led me to the verge of despair. How had the lessons so carefully instilled into my mind by the good clergyman long since gone to his rest, been lost sight of! How had I forsaken the good path in which he bade me walk; but how true is it that the ways of sin are the ways of sorrow, and God mercifully makes us feel them to be so!

"Perhaps I felt more severely in one sense the sin of which I had been guilty from the scenes which afterwards followed: the mistress, who was so deceived as to my real character, was, after a partial recovery, again brought to the weariness of a sick chamber, by a seizure which proved to be her last summons: and it was whilst watching her sink faster day by day into the tomb with the evidences of the sweetest peace and resignation, that I felt the difference between the deathbed of the sinner and the saint! Oh, sir, could you but have witnessed the rays of glory which appeared to light up her eye with heavenly brightness, could you but have listened to the sweet music of her voice as she spoke of Jesus, and told of the Saviour's love to poor sinners, and at the same time have known the deep anguish of my soul as I lent an ear, you would have understood how severe was the penalty I paid. . . .

"Even the very tears I shed as she spoke, and which were interpreted as evidences of my sorrow at her approaching end, were as burning coals upon my cheek; for unused to deception, though obliged from fear to practise it, my own conscience, not as yet hardened, uttered its silent reproaches.

"The blow fell at last, and I lost the only friend to whom had her state of health permitted it, I could and would have unburthened my sorrow . . . but . . . she died as she had lived full of faith in her Saviour. . . . Oh, that I had never lost sight of her pious instructions! . . . 'Tis a consolation that her last moments were not embittered by knowing how much she was deceived in one of whom she thought and would have hoped better things. Oh, that she could now look down from heaven and witness! . . .

"I am too weak to-day to tell you the various changes and sorrows which I have undergone until my poor child and myself were received into this house . . . . for his sake I toiled and laboured in the hope of keeping him out of the workhouse, and I might have succeeded had health and strength been given me, but over-exertion without proper food brought me to the brink of the grave in which I should long since have been laid but for the shelter here provided for me . . . still what great cause have I to thank God for thus sparing me, I can now look forward to something of joy beyond the grave. . . . Oh, yes! I can bless the hour when I was brought within these walls, where I have not only heard of, but really tasted the precious love of Jesus."

* * * * *

[It was on the occasion referred to at the commencement of this sketch, that I received a summons to attend what promised to be the death-bed of Eliza S———. She had some days previously been growing much weaker, and when I had left her in the morning was so persuaded that a change was on the eve of taking place, that I left such directions with the matron as induced her to send for me. Her disorder, however, was a treacherous one, at one time allowing the lamp of life to burn with almost its wonted brilliancy, at another moment allowing it to flicker to and fro so dimly, that one dreaded lest the slightest breath should extinguish it for ever.]

Dec. 26. On reaching the house, I found that the alarming symptoms in Eliza S—— had disappeared, and she had sunk into a calm sleep. After waiting some little time, and finding that she did not awake, I returned to my sanctum to resume the task which had been so interrupted.

Dec. 27. . . . " Thank you sir, for coming to see me last night. I feared the great change was about to take place, although God's work is not yet fully finished: he has some wise end in thus sparing me. I have put off from day to day speaking to you on a subject which lies heavy at my heart . . . 'tis about my poor child . . . . he will soon be an orphan, and his *mother's* guilt is stamped upon *him!*" . . .

Eliza S—— repeated the last observation with so much energy, that I replied, " Do not suffer any anxiety on his account to disturb you in your present weak state. He is well taken care of in this house, and if he goes on as he has hitherto done, will be put in the way of earning an honest livelihood." . . .

" I trust he will should all else fail, but whilst

THE PENITENT. 89

God spares me let me do all I can for him. You, sir, know all the circumstances connected with his birth, but I have never breathed to living soul the name of his father. He has seen his child but once, when he was two years old, and then he wished to remove him from me. . . . It was a mother's fondness which ruined the prospects of my poor boy, though it may not yet be too late to repair the evil. His father is rich, and I know that he is childless. God's chastisement has severely visited me, but it has fallen no less heavily upon him. . . . Can you, sir, do nothing? . . . It is the last favour I shall ask of you, . . , and one word from you would do all : . . . do not refuse me, . . . God will bless the endeavour, and a dying mother's prayers shall call down blessings upon you!" . . .

"Be calm, and all shall be done that can promote your object; but you must not prop yourself up with false hopes; the result is very uncertain!"

"It is, . . . but yet something whispers me that I shall be spared to see the accomplishment of my wishes, and that God will seal my pardon in allowing me to do so." . . .

*   *   *   *   *

How unpleasant was the task thus imposed on

me a task which might prove a most thankless one, to interfere in what might justly be regarded as an affair beyond the province of one who, in his relation to the workhouse, was merely as a paid official to perform certain specific duties. And still the path before me was one of christian benevolence, and the result proved in this, as it will in every similar instance, that in the exercise of christian duty, however thankless or ungracious first appearances may be, the end more than fully compensates for all.

I foresaw the difficulties which would arise in opening a communication with him whose address the sufferer had given me, and with whose character I was totally unacquainted. That he would deny the truth of her assertions I could not anticipate, so deeply was he inculpated by a letter which he had addressed to her, and which was in my possession; still a thousand imaginary obstacles presented themselves!

How soon, however, do the difficulties which man's fear raises up, sink into insignificance and nothingness before the overruling power of Him who connects the means with the end, and makes each link supply its proper and destined place in the mighty chain of events. The way was all smoothed before me, though I knew it not, and my feeble aid (humanly speaking) alone appeared wanting to work out the object which infinite wisdom designed to effect.

* * * * *

December 30. To-morrow I am to receive a visit from Mr. E——, who has replied to my application in a way far different from what I had anticipated. On visiting Eliza S—— this morning, she appeared in so weakly a state that I hesitated at first whether or not to communicate to her the good tidings which I had in store. Before I could speak, however, she had read in my countenance the wished-for intelligence; and after I had broken it to her as considerately as possible, and encouraged her to look for a happy result, she roused herself, and exclaimed, "Thank God—thank God for all his mercies! how good he is to permit such an unworthy sinner to have so much joy! Now I shall indeed see what alone I wished to live for, and if E—— will only own and provide for my poor child, all his past injuries to me shall be forgiven and forgotten." . . . . .

Few but those who are in the habit of watching the last moments of expiring nature would have detected the critical situation of the "Penitent."

Life (if I may be allowed the figure) appeared to be suspended on one frail cord, which was gradually becoming weaker and weaker from the degree of tension which had latterly been kept up; and I most plainly saw, that when the extra strain was applied in the excitement which must inevitably ensue, *that* one cord would be snapped asunder, and all would be over! Much caution and tenderness would consequently be needed in carrying out the now necessary operations.

With difficulty I quieted the disturbed breast of the sufferer, and allayed the anxiety which now arose from a fear that she should not be spared long enough to witness what she so longed for.

"I am now sinking fast, sir, . . . very, very fast, . . . I can feel the hand of death is upon me; . . . many, many times have I besought God, if it were his will, to shorten the period of my sufferings, . . . but now, my chief prayer is, that he would only spare me a little longer. . . . But I will not murmur, . . . oh no! . . . I dare not; I wish to bow in submission to Him, . . . *all is in His hands.*" . . . She paused for a few moments, and then turning her languid eye upon me, added, "Do you know, sir, . . . at times I feel much more to understand what is meant by "joy and peace in believing," ... when I think of God's wondrous love to sinners, and how much he must have desired their salvation in sending his dear Son to die for them; ... but, sir, these bright moments do not last without interruption; ... when I look within I find a great deal that is dark; ... my faith at times is weak, ... though I constantly call to mind those comforting words you once pointed out to me so strongly, "*He that spared not his own Son, ... but delivered him up for us all, how shall he not with him also freely give us all things.*' ... Oh pray, sir, *with* me, and *for* me, that God would strengthen my weak faith, that I may learn to lean more on Jesus."

How fervent were the petitions which that day ascended from the Penitent's chamber to the throne of grace, He alone to whom they were addressed can know. . . . . .

December 31. The last day of the passing year! a day always worthy of remembrance, but in this case doubly so to me, from the incidents which have occurred. It has been a day of much anxiety, and in some respects, one of satisfaction; my object having been gained without any of those attendant annoyances which I had anticipated.

Scarcely had I returned from a round of parochial visiting, when my servant announced a stranger, whose card, which she handed to me at once, revealed his name, and the object of his visit.

I was soon engaged in holding converse with my visitor. Above what is ordinarily termed the middle height, of commanding appearance, and somewhat gentlemanly deportment, there was a frankness and honesty in the expression of his countenance which seemed to invite confidence; and although, as might be expected from the cause of our interview, the flush of excitement was most visible, and indicated the strong feelings at work within, he evidently laboured to give me an impression of perfect calm and collectedness.

About 58 years of age, he might easily have passed for a much younger man, had not his hair, which had turned prematurely grey, caused the wrinkles of age to appear more conspicuous; a mild but expressive eye added a softness to features naturally pleasing, and the most skilful physiognomist would have judged him as the last man to be guilty of anything approaching to sensuality.

After mutual courtesies, he at once entered on the object of our meeting.

"You have addressed me, sir, on a painful subject, . . . is S—— still alive?" . . .

* * * * *

It is needless to detail all that passed, ... the last sad scene of all will best explain the result. E—— strongly expressed a desire of visiting the poor victim of whose ruin and consequent misery he had been the guilty cause; not so much from motives of curiosity, as from a wish to assure her that one burden should be removed, that the poor orphan should neither want home nor friends.

* * * *

It was a sad, it was a mournful scene,—never do I wish to witness such another! . . .

The last sun of the old year, whose rays seemed struggling for existence, and contending for the mastery with the chill atmosphere around, gained, as it were, a momentary triumph, and shed a parting ray on the couch of the "penitent," whilst a cold and cheerless gloom pervaded the solitary chamber as I entered.

There, the ruthless hand of the king of terrors rested on his prey; the dews of death were fast stealing over the sufferer's brow, and an occasional long-drawn sigh alone gave evidence that the lamp of life was not yet totally extinguished. The aged nurse who sat by the bed side motioned eagerly to me as I entered, to warn me that the last hour was fast drawing on.

I had desired Mr. E—— to await my summons before he ventured into the presence of the poor sufferer with whom he was so anxious to have an interview. With cautious step I approached the bed, but not unrecognised;—a smile, —it was the smile of childlike resignation, lit up for a moment the pallid cheek, and her outstretched hand was enfolded in mine.

"Is all well?" was the simple but touching inquiry; a slight pressure of my hand preceded my reply, which she interrupted.

"And he has really promised?" . . .

"He has promised to do everything, and now only ——" . . .

A movement at the door, which had not been fully closed, attracted her attention: the impatience of E—— had overcome his discretion, and led him to anticipate the appointed summons; . . . he had partially entered the chamber, unhappily not unobserved, . . . one piercing shriek awoke the solitude,—it was the shriek of death, the last pang of expiring nature, . . . ere its echo had died away all was over, . . . the "Penitent" had passed to her last account!

*　　*　　*　　*　　*

THE ATHEIST'S END.

Notwithstanding all that had been, at various times, said and written on the subject of Atheism, added to the fearful examples which had been adduced in support of the declared fact that men holding such tenets (in the fullest acceptation of the term) had existed, my own scepticism refused assent; for though I could believe that a man may, with the natural hardihood of a rebel against God, *profess* such a creed, and by his general conduct confirm to outward appearance the sincerity of his profession, I confess that my mind was still unconvinced as to the real existence of such a monster, until the subject of the following sketch came before me whilst chaplain to the W—— union.

In pity to others, I have omitted many circumstances which might lead to identification, and I trust no one will recognise the portrait, though suspicion may attach to the wretched being who is the sad original. . . .

* * * * *

E—— G—— had, for some months, been an inmate of the house, and, by the customary regulations, was obliged to attend the appointed services performed by the chaplain, he not having claimed exemption on the ground of being a dissenter.

I had frequently noticed him as one of my congregation, for his appearance was of too striking a character not to command attention. Much above the common stature, though bent down by age and infirmity, he presented a specimen of the decline of an able-bodied man. His countenance, which at first sight would have merely called forth a passing remark, on a closer view disclosed a dark and sullen expression, whilst a quick and rapid motion of the eye indicated the existence of inward feelings which no outward art could conceal. In his mode of address to his superiors he was ordinarily respectful, but his companions in suffering generally spoke of him as a *"surly and curious fellow."* "In fact, sir," said a pauper to me, one day, in answer to some inquiries which I had made respecting G——, "we can't make him out; he is always saying something strange about religion, and has often declared that he don't believe there's a word of truth in it!" . . .

My first serious conversation with G—— was on the subject of his inattention during the time of divine service; for I had on many occasions observed, that whilst the generality of those around me were at least orderly, and manifested some sense of awe for that God in whose immediate presence they were, G—— was as uniformly remarkable for the display of an opposite feeling, and on several occasions a smile marked the only attention which he paid to the ministrations of the gospel!

It was at one of my weekly services that I was preaching from Job xxxiv. 29, and had particular occasion, in the course of my lecture, to dwell on the omnipotence and omniscience of God, and it might have been from what I had previously heard of his character, my attention was more than usually directed to the subject of this sketch.

Such, however, was the result of my observation, that my first visit on the ensuing day was to the workhouse, where I desired an interview with G——, and on his entering the room, proceeded to give him a mild reproof for his unseemly and irreverent conduct in the chapel on previous occasions, and especially on the preceding even. His reply to my remonstrances completely staggered me; for in spite of what he had ventured to express to his companions, I little expected he would have ventured to declare his " abominable creed " so openly and unblushingly to me.

"Why, sir, I don't mean any disrespect to you, but I never attended what's called a place of worship till I entered this house; and now I am compelled to go to the chapel whether I will or not, and sit for an hour to hear what I don't believe!"

"What, G——!" I exclaimed, "do you thus boldly declare your disbelief in the truths of religion?"

"Why, sir, I know what the world calls religion, and men say there's a God whom we must worship; and it is all very well for those who think so to do what they do, but why shouldn't every man enjoy his own opinion? And as I think that their God exists only in fancy, and don't believe that there is any life after this, but that when a man dies there's an end of him, I can't see why I should be made to attend chapel!!"...

I will not venture to shock the feelings of the reader by detailing all that passed at this, to me, heart-rending interview. I have given the above merely as an introductory outline to what follows.

I found that G—— was really an *atheist at heart!* and had imbibed, from his earliest years, the horrid doctrines which he now so fearlessly maintained. He was familiar with all the writings of the most atheistical tendency, and the calamities of a long life (having now attained the age of 67 years) had fostered the conviction, that he was but the offspring of fate, brought into the world to bear his portion of its miseries, to undergo his share of its "labour and sorrow," and then to be annihilated in death!

All the glorious works of creation—all the attributes of God—all his bounteous provisions in nature and grace—were, to him, the mere results or effects of chance, and he claimed only to herd "*with the beasts that perish!*"

Before I proceed to the immediate extracts from my diary, which relate to the closing scenes of G——'s life, I will give the outline of his former career, as I was enabled to gather from himself at various periods. He was a native of G———, in which county his father was one of a respectable class of yeoman-farmers of the old school, who taught his children the lessons which he himself had learnt, to "fear God and honour the king," so that, whilst he gave them the opportunity of availing themselves of the advantages of a sound and plain education, he as strenuously opposed any of those innovations which tend only to make a man dissatisfied with that "state of life in which it has pleased God to call him."

Under the management of such a father, G—, though one of a numerous family, received an education which subsequently enabled him to earn a livelihood as an inferior officer at the Custom House, in London, a post which he held for some years.

It was whilst in this situation that he joined a class of young men who met under the title of the "*Freethinkers*," and who, from time to time, sent forth those pamphlets which, whilst they professed to free the mind from the influence of "*bigotry and priestcraft*," instilled a creed of rebellion as direct against God as it is offensive and disgraceful to a christian community.

By the vicious lessons here instilled, and all

restraints of religion being soon removed, as barrier after barrier of moral right was broken down, no marvel that the mind of G—— became thoroughly lost to all principles of rectitude, and having failed in his duty to God, he soon, as a natural consequence, failed in his duty to man.

He was detected, with others, in a system of deeply-planned fraud, which had been successfully carried on for some months, and after the usual formality of a trial, was sentenced to two years imprisonment, his previous good conduct having procured a mitigation of the full punishment.

Few, if any, have left a prison *better* men than they entered it ; few, if any, have failed to inhale the contaminating pollution of its atmosphere, or escape the contagion which that atmosphere engenders ; nor can we wonder if, under the present even improved state, they should do so. Much, it is true, has of late years been done in the way of moral amelioration of our prison discipline, but much, very much, yet remains to be done, ere the result of incarceration can be looked for with satisfaction, or our gaols become what they are at present, with an unhappy misnomer, termed " *Houses of Correction.*"

Under such a system it will excite no surprise

that a man of G——'s disposition should have emerged from his confinement fully prepared to add his quota to the mass of general corruption.

He had not failed to treasure up a stock of materials to be wrought out into a marketable commodity whenever the opportunity was afforded him; and accordingly but a short time elapsed after his liberation ere he was again actively engaged with his former associates in his former unholy vocation.

By the " wages of sin " which he thus obtained, he for years managed to keep from actual want; but the very means on which he was dependent for his daily bread naturally caused him to wallow deeper and deeper in the mire of infidelity; and he moved in the midst of his fellow men, glorying in the name which he bore, insensible to the withering curse which he breathed around, whilst he avowed himself *a confirmed atheist!*

Though the various changes of his eventful life are yet fresh in my memory, as well as noted in my diary, it is not my purpose to follow him through the different stages of his existence until I found him an inmate of the ——— workhouse. My present object is, to notice the closing scenes of his life, and though such notices must, from the sad nature of the subject, be necessarily brief, may their awful reality carry conviction to the breast of the worst infidel—to him who is a *practical atheist!*

April 16. "G—— is very ill, sir," said the master on my paying my usual visit this morning, "and yet I cannot persuade him to see you; but if you could contrive to see him. . . . He is in No. 7."

I did see him, but it was not, apparently, in the character of chaplain that I entered his ward, and during this my first visit little escaped my lips which could lead him to think that I intended (to use his own expression) to "*bore him about religion.*"

My plan, happily, succeeded! and so far from wishing me to leave him, he observed, when I was about to do so, "Perhaps you'll look in on me again, sir, when you come this side of the house; . . . I fear I sha'n't be able to get up for some time." . . .

Here was an opening! . . .

April 18. . . . Found G—— sitting up, and apparently changed for the better. With the temporary amendment he had adopted his wonted churlishness to those around, but appeared more subdued in his tone of address towards me than I had hitherto seen him on previous occasions. . .

April 21st. "G—— has received his last summons," were the first words which the medical officer addressed to me on my visit to the workhouse this morning. "Medicine can do little for him now, sir; he needs your assistance more than mine." . . .

"Is he in a dangerous state then?"

"He cannot last many days, and he begins to feel so himself. How *you* will be able to manage with him is another question; but he is, without exception, the most extraordinary patient I ever attended, and, but for certain symptoms, one whom I should pronounce perfectly deranged, so unusual is his language." . . .

However much the experience of Mr. F—— might have enabled him to detect the weakness of the physical man, and the progress of natural decay, he knew but little of the spiritual disease under which the man laboured within!

G—— was, of a truth, perfectly deranged, but it was with a madness which no human skill could minister to, no human art could ameliorate. His bodily sufferings, though great, were nothing in comparison to the anguish of his mind; for with all his attempts to disguise his feelings, the "still small voice," so long unheeded, now asserted her claim for attention, and in accents

" louder than the thunder's roar," scared away the props on which this wretched being had hitherto leant for support!

I have seen many instances of sudden and unexpected change in the tenants of a sick chamber, so sudden that even the lapse of a few hours has ofttimes seemed to have performed the work of years; but never, I think, had I witnessed, in the whole course of my existence, such a total transformation as three days had produced in the miserable G—— when I saw him this morning! His former surly look had settled down into an expression of perfect cowardice and alarm, which, in his now emaciated state, added to the harshness of features naturally unprepossessing, whilst his whole appearance would have given the most casual observer the idea of one unexpectedly detected in the commission of some notorious crime.

I did not let him imagine, for reasons which prudence dictated, that my visit was made purposely to him, but entering into conversation with one of the paupers at the door of G——'s ward, I waited his invitation to enter, and this was very soon given.

" Won't you please to come in and sit a few moments with me, sir?"

Ere long I was at his bed-side, and the door closed upon us. He looked from one side of the room to the other, apparently searching for some one in the chamber; and then fixing his eyes on me, he, in a most tremulous manner, faltered out, as though fearful of what he was about to say, " I am . . . very glad to see you, sir, . . . very glad, . . . not that I am going to talk about religion, nor do I want you to do so, . . . but yet, . . . have you seen the doctor, sir ?"

" I saw him as I entered the house, and he told me he had just left you."

" But what did he say, sir ? and (he added in an almost subdued whisper) does he think I am in very great danger ? . . . I didn't much like his manner when he was with me this morning!"

" He gives a very bad report of you, G——, and his belief is, that your case has assumed a dangerous appearance; but why are you so alarmed ? . . . you always professed not to be afraid of death."

" Nor . . . am I, sir, ex . . . actly a . . . fraid, . . . but still, . . . I'll tell you, sir, what it is. . . . One of the men, last night, got reading some horrid tract about punishment in hell after death; and though I don't believe a syllable of what he read, I don't mind saying so to you, in my weak state it made me very nervous and uncomfortable, so that I got no sleep all night. Couldn't you speak about it, sir, and prevent their disturbing me so?—I'm sure they do it on purpose."

Why should such a subject disturb you, G—? You have often said, whilst in health and strength, and even since sickness has come upon you, that you disbelieved everything connected with religion, and claimed liberty to enjoy your opinion, why then . . . ?"

"So I did, and I am not much inclined to . . . . . alter now . . . though I confess . ."

With a sidelong glance the poor trembling wretch gathered up his limbs in his bed, and as though haunted by some horrible vision of which he was unable to rid himself, he for several minutes lay shivering before me the concentrated image of despairing fear! An almost unearthly moan at times escaped him, whilst at intervals there appeared to be a struggle between madness and reason as to which should obtain the mastery.

The latter for the time prevailed; an hysterical laugh marked the termination of the conflict.

When in some measure recovered, he resumed the conversation, though in so languid a manner as proved the intensity of the inward agony which he had undergone.

"I wish, sir, you'd talk about something else . . . this subject disturbs me beyond what I can bear; and I'm almost ready at these times to think there is such a being as Satan, who is suffered to torment us . . . if so I am certain he has determined to torment me enough before I leave this world . . . . but don't, sir . . . pray don't let us say any more about it." . . .

This very speech afforded the strongest confirmation (if any were wanting) of the fact which I have noticed in the course of my ministrations, that where men have indulged in a long career of sin and impiety, the master whom they have so long served, and whose bidding they have been foremost to obey, is the foremost to torment them in the hour of peril. This retributive analogy also holding good in the opposite case, that where a man has lived a life of humble devotion to the service of God, when *distress* and *sorrow* are permitted to come upon him, the Master whom he has served is the first to manifest himself as a comforter and friend.

G—— had for many a long year served a hard task-master, and he now received the wages of his slavery in those pangs of conscience which racked his inmost soul during his waking hours, and which haunted his brain with infernal visions during the long and silent watches of the night! No blessed angel of peace hovered around his pillow to chase away disquieting thoughts and dreams, no staff of the Saviour was supplied him on which he might securely lean to uphold him as he was about to journey through the "valley of the shadow of death!"

His last request that religion might form no subject-matter for our discourse was, as the reader may suppose, unheeded to by me.

I now saw the path of duty so clearly marked out that I could not hesitate, and I too well foresaw that, with the sudden change which he had undergone, little time would be left him to converse on any subject whatever.

Still I had a task to perform which could be rendered efficacious in its object, not by man's might or by man's power, but by the Spirit of the living God alone!

[The reader may wish to learn the arguments which I employed to bring G—— to a sense of his real condition; this is, however, foreign to my purpose in the publication of these extracts: the result is what I am alone concerned to show, a result which I am unable even now to look back upon without emotions of the most overwhelming sadness!]

He suffered rather than attended to the observations which fell from my lips relative to the solemn truths of revelation, never once interrupting me, though at moments manifesting the impatience of one who, notwithstanding reason was against him, had predetermined not to assent to anything which might be urged to overthrow the doctrines which he held; and if man might have ventured to pronounce a judgment on that which can be known only by Him who searcheth the hearts, his was the case of one with whom the Holy Spirit had so long striven, and striven in vain, that at last it was altogether withdrawn! That gentle dove had gone to and fro, seeking a resting-place for the sole of her foot; but none was to be found amidst the turbulent ocean which raged within the bosom of G——, and she retraced her flight to the ark which she had left on her fruitless errand, leaving him to be engulphed amidst the angry waves whose fury he had aroused!

In spite of his seeming unconcern, I led him, by a variety of simple reasoning, to the point which I had in view; and during the whole of my discourse he maintained the same sullen silence; but when I spoke of the judgment to come, the sentence denounced against unbelief, and the eternity of torment, a chord seemed to vibrate through the heart of the miserable being which gave him a foretaste of the eternal woe to which he was fast hastening; and as we can conceive the greatest anguish to the lost would be the mention of those truths which were it then possible would make for their everlasting peace, so, in the case of G——, the subject of my conversation at length appeared to arouse the furies which raged within him, from the very consciousness that he had hitherto set them at nought, and now in their stead "*held a lie in his right hand!*"

"No more of that, sir,—I can't bear it! . . . If devils are to be my companions, and I am to perish in . . . the sooner I'm out of this the better, and I shall know the worst! . . . Oh! what a cursed fate is mine . . . to know 'tis coming . . . Yes, and has begun already, I feel it . . . damnation . . . No! no! 'tisn't for ever, 'tis false . . . You are only deceiving me

THE ATHEIST'S END. 115

... Oh! horrid ... horrid ... worse and worse ... I'm raging now ... the fire's consuming me ... the very devils are mocking me ... you are the worst devil of all ... leave me ... go instantly ... or if I reach you you'll become . . . ."

* * * * *

The torrent of blood which literally flowed from his mouth, choked his further utterance, and thus stopped the fearful ravings of which I have ventured to give but a faint outline.

The awful blasphemies, coupled with the self-imprecated curses, which fell from his lips, no pen can venture to record.

Assistance was soon procured, and the sufferer at length subdued;—the rupture of a blood-vessel was, however, his death-warrant; he never spoke again, and in somewhat less than two hours after I had left he expired in the most excruciating torments, and with groans that pierced the hearts of the most hardened of his companions.

So much had he become an object of terror, to those around, that the name of G—— was never afterwards mentioned by those who witnessed his last moments without a visible indication of mental horror!

* * * * *

If such were his falling asleep, what must have been the fearful awakening! . . . .

* * * * *

THE WIDOW'S PORTION.

I MARVEL not that any man who looks not up to the Great First Cause—who knows not that all things which happen are dictated and brought about by infinite wisdom, should sometimes fee at a loss to account for the strange vicissitudes which we meet with in the various portions of mankind. Here is one perhaps who, from childhood, has been accustomed to more than the ordinary comforts of life; has even been nursed, it may be, in the lap of affluence and luxury:— smoothly glides the little vessel onwards, and all around seems to promise perpetual peace and calm!—not a breath ruffles the wave— not a ripple is seen on the peaceful surface of the waters. . . . . But suddenly, as in a moment, the sun shines less brightly—the distant gathering in the horizon marks the coming storm, and almost, ere preparation can be made to meet it, it bursts with relentless fury upon its object, who escapes so bankrupt in hope as to wish that he himself had been overwhelmed in the tempest.

Here is another, on the contrary, who has been cradled in want and penury—who, as years advanced, knew nought but privation; trouble and suffering have constantly attended his steps, and nothing but clouds and darkness appear to hover around his path. When behold! the clouds unexpectedly give way—the darkness is exchanged for the bright sunshine.

Fortune rolls her choicest gifts into his lap, and leaves him for the time bewildered at the change!

This is not an ideal supposition, but plain simple truth of every day experience: and whilst he who connects not the *cause* and the *effect* is at a loss to account for these changes, he, on the other hand, who contemplates that omnipotence, whose fiat decrees what shall or shall not be, can in humble submission answer all inquiries, and hush to rest all doubts with the assurance, "*The Lord maketh poor and maketh rich, he bringeth low and lifteth up: He doeth according to his will in the army of heaven, and among the inhabitants of the earth: none can stay his hand, or say unto him, What doest thou?"*

These thoughts naturally arise in my mind as I am about to transcribe from my diary the memoranda which it contains concerning M——— H———. She had been a few months in the house before I was called upon to engage in those private and constant ministrations which the sick and dying so especially require. From the time of her admission she had been remarkable for her quiet and peaceable demeanour, and, to the credit of the master and matron who had the care of the establishment, she was made to feel less of the degradation to which she was obliged to submit than she would have felt had she been placed under a different surveillance.

I have already (in the preface to these pages) alluded to this point; but let me here repeat my conviction from all that I have witnessed, that the actual working of the poor-law system is left too entirely to the will and caprice of those who have the practical administration of it; the comfort of the inmates depends *too much* on the officials who reside in the house. If they are kindly disposed—if they can at all sympathize with the misery and suffering which they daily witness—they have it in their power to alleviate it in various little ways which those only can comprehend who are experienced in such matters.

Let me add my testimony that such was the case in the union with which I was officially connected, and I rejoice in being able to bear such testimony; but I do it, not so much in praise of those to whom I refer, as from the feeling which tells me that such cases are rare. In the majority of instances, more than half the suffering of the poor arises from the misconduct of those who bear rule, rather than from many of the actual provisions of the "New Poor Law."

What! is it not enough that misfortune, or, let me rather say, the afflicting visitations of Providence should overtake a man, without his burden being increased, his affliction added to, by the ignorance and brutality of those into whose keeping he chances to be delivered? Oh, it is enough to witness what I have to make one feel that man is more severe than his Creator, that the dispensations which God sends in love and mercy, man thinks insufficient, and therefore makes up what he conceives to be the right measure in cruelty and unkindness!

THE WIDOW'S PORTION. 121

Let me not be misunderstood, or be supposed to hold out an inducement to improvidence or vice; it is not so difficult a matter to draw the line of distinction between those whom misfortune has brought to a workhouse, and those whose vicious habits have compelled them to seek it as an asylum. My position is, and if it be a false one I am open to conviction, that the workhouse should not be, as it too generally is, converted into a house of correction, and that if we, as a Christian duty, nationally consent to provide for the poor and needy, we should do so without making those poor and needy feel that they are rather punished for their misfortunes than sympathized with for their distresses.

I have been led into this digression from the circumstances which attended the case of her who is the subject of these pages. She was allowed for a time (I believe by the permission of the master, though in opposition to the eighth order and regulation of the Poor Law Commissioners) to wear the sad memento of the loss she had experienced in the death of her husband; and which, if anything in this selfish and unfeeling world *can* excite sympathy, even the *most* selfish must gaze upon with something like emotions of tenderness. It is (unlike many others) the distinguishing mark of *perfect bereavement.*

A parent or a child, nay, even a wife, may be laid in the tomb, and there is nothing in the merely external " trappings of woe" farther than that which denotes the loss of a relative; but a *widow!* she carries her inward affliction in her outward garb! she has lost in a worldly sense *her all*, and therefore all her former adornments must now give place to the one peculiar dress— a token of her sorrow—a tribute of sad respect to the master, supporter, and protector she has lost.

I wonder not that the most beautiful images of Scripture are drawn from the ideas of marriage and widowhood: as no simile can so adequately convey the feeling of perfect union as the former, so nothing can describe so accurately the idea of perfect separation as the latter. When Christ is present with his Church, the bride and bridegroom rejoice together in peace and love; when he is removed the joy gives place to sorrow, and she mourns as a widow the absence of her Lord!

M—— H—— was with her four children, the eldest only nine years of age, admitted to the workhouse shortly after I had been licensed to the chaplaincy; and whilst she had to mourn over the sad reverses of her fortunes, though she rightly looked at them as the merciful dealings of an all-merciful Father, an additional pang was inflicted in the necessary separation from her children.

Hitherto heavy as her sorrows had been, they had shared them with her, and her care and attention for them had made her trials recur less to her mind. Now they were taken from her—they were consigned to the school, and it was some time before she could realize the melancholy satisfaction, though she did not often see them, of knowing that they were at least protected from the possibility of starvation.

As my diary relates only the last scenes, I will here put the reader in possession of the outline of her previous misfortunes; it is a plain unvarnished tale, but one over which sympathy may shed a tear.

Far removed from any such a termination to her earthly career were the dawn and noon-day of the early years of M——— H———. The daughter of a poor and hard-working clergyman, she had, as years of maturity advanced, been obliged to undertake, as, alas! too many are, the situation of a governess, soon after the loss of a mother. One after another she had followed to the grave a brother and three sisters, just as they were on the eve of launching forth their bark on the stormy ocean of life. To use her own language, " God removed from them that cup of sorrow which for his own wise purposes he has made me drink to the very dregs."

In her capacity as governess she might long have continued, but that her charge had shown symptoms of consumption, and was ordered to try a foreign climate in the vain hope of restoring to its full vigour a constitution which disease had already broken up.

This very change in her condition gave M—— H—— the opportunity of attending upon a dying father; and ofttimes have I heard her express her gratitude to God that he so ordered it; lonely and unfriended as such an event rendered her, it was some consolation to be with him in his last hours, and to minister to his dying wants.

Contrary to her expectations, she was not left without some means of subsistence; and after scrupulously discharging all the debts for which her parent was liable, she found herself mistress of a sum which, with economy, might for a time support her in tolerable comfort.

Her unprotected state, however, exposed her to many trials, and not wishing again to enter upon the duties in which she had formerly been engaged, from a feeling of its dependent condition, she at length consented to a union with one between herself and whom even in childish days an attachment had sprung up, and who was now, as regarded worldly prosperity, in a thriving position.

From what I could learn, he was in common parlance "*well to do in the world,*" and notwithstanding her superiority to him as regarded her position in life and in intellectual attainments — notwithstanding that she had been brought up in a different school, still that powerful principle which levels all, enabled her to accommodate herself to the sphere in which her lot was to be cast, and as she might have been an ornament to the highest grade of society, so she did not degenerate when called on to move in what our nation so justly prides herself upon, the *middling classes!*

Her tale is soon told,—alas! too soon; for between three and four years everything prospered around them.

The little town, of which her husband was the principal tradesman, had known few changes and his shop was the most frequented, not more out of regard to himself than that because his father had carried on the business before him, and had conciliated both town and neighbourhood by his obliging and active habits.

Happiness reigned in the circle at home; the husband knew the value of the partner he had obtained; the wife well fulfilled the vows she had made at the altar, when in the sight of God she pledged herself to "*love, honour, and obey.*"

Long might the tide of prosperity have continued to flow on, and accumulating wealth soon have raised them above the necessity of his continuing " the attendance at the counter," had not a desire to outstrip his competitors and become rich without toil seized the mind of our country tradesman. Had railroads then been in vogue, he certainly could not have escaped the contagious mania which has since so affected all classes of society, and caused the utter ruin of thousands: this kind of speculation was then in its infancy, but other modes of commercial gambling were equally rife, and equally, or at least nearly, as disastrous in their ultimate consequences.

A rage for building had sprung up in an ad-

joining town, and the husband of M——
H—— was induced, from the representations which were made, to join himself as a partner in the C—— W—— E—— Company, whose prospectus was put forth under the most auspicious appearances.

There was, to say the truth, every prospect of success; nay, more, as matters progressed, the speculation assumed the character of certain and actual gain. One after another houses rose into existence, were occupied almost before they were completed, and the shareholders were already calculating on the rich harvest they would reap from their good investment.

H—— in the mean time could not be said to have neglected his business, but the capital which ought to have been employed in keeping up or renewing his stock in trade being elsewhere engaged, he was obliged to adopt a system of credit which cannot fail of being, even under the most favourable circumstances, most injurious to the retail tradesman.

His outstanding bills, however, gave him little uneasiness; his fortunate speculation was about to prove a mine of wealth, and already, in the anticipation of his gains in that quarter, he was in treaty for the disposal of his "stock-in-trade, good-will, &c., &c.," as the advertisements have it.

Among his letters one morning was a circular convening a special meeting for the following day of the shareholders in the C——— W——— E——— Company, for the purpose " of laying before them a communication of the greatest importance just made to their solicitor, &c. ;" and with a light heart on the day appointed did H——— set out, little dreaming but that his El-Dorado was about to pour forth the long-expected and just at that time most needful supply. He quitted his home with a smiling face;— he was brought back to it more dead than alive. The announcement which had been made at the meeting, and of which not a suspicion had hitherto been breathed, came upon him like the thunderclap,—a paralytic seizure was the consequence, and in three days afterwards he was a corpse!

I may here state that the intelligence which produced such an awful effect on poor H——— was that by some oversight in the conveyance of the land on which the company had laid out such vast sums in the erection of houses, the title had not been sufficiently inquired into, and subsequently turned out to be faulty. I am not sufficient lawyer to describe the various quibbles which were raised on the occasion; the sum and substance appeared to be that the consent of a party who had some remote claim on the land in question had not been obtained to the sale of it to the C——— W——— E——— Company, and by the advice of one who was better versed than himself in the quirks of the law, he refused, when now called upon, to give his consent to the transfer and receive the proposed compensation. The result may easily be guessed; the land, with all upon it, reverted to the original vendors, and ruin could scarcely have been more complete than that which overtook the various shareholders;—men who had embarked largely in the concern, whose fortunes had been sufficient to support their station in life, and who had well and honourably hitherto maintained the appearance due to that station, now found themselves almost at one blow reduced to little more than penury. Many can remember the issue of that speculation, and (to speak literally) the flood of auctions which took place when the legal decision on the validity of the title was made known. . . . . But on this it is not my business to dwell; I am concerned only with the case of poor H———, on whom the intelligence given at the first special meeting on the subject produced such a fearful effect. From the time he was brought to his own home until the moment of his death his articulation was so feeble that not even his wife could understand him, and though at first the medical men gave some hopes of his ultimate recovery, that hope was speedily dispelled, and he was removed from the "evil to come." This evil was not slow in its progress; his creditors soon seized upon the little which remained to satisfy their demands, and the widow found herself, with her four infants, scarcely one step removed from beggary in the town where she had known not only the comforts, but even the luxuries of life.

Let me not, however, underrate the sympathy of her neighbours; a sufficient sum was raised to keep her, for the present, above actual want, and she was set up as the mistress of a small school, for the duties of which her previous education so eminently fitted her. In this calling, had health and strength been granted, she might have succeeded, as all around were anxious to assist her; *but her spirit was broken!* none could tell what passed within, the heart knew its own bitterness; and though the sweet consolations of religion were not wanting to give that inward joy with which a stranger intermeddleth not, she soon saw that success was out of the question.

I have said that her spirit was broken, and as mind so completely influences matter her bodily strength rapidly gave way. Unable, in consequence, to attend to the duties which devolved upon her, and which were, in truth, not so light as many may appear to imagine, she was obliged to give up her school, and after a short time was scarcely able to leave her bed except for a few hours in the course of the day. But one only resource was left her; and of this, however much in her heart she shrunk from it, for the sake of her children, she hesitated not to avail herself. Privation had already made its inroads on her once blooming family—want had already drawn its deep lines on their infant countenances, and without dwelling on the painful extremities to which she and they were reduced, ere long she was received as an inmate of the W—— union workhouse, and there survived only long enough to show, by her quiet demeanour, and the peaceful termination to her earthly trials, that whilst the *natural* strength was unable to bear up under the accumulation of providential dispensations, her *spiritual* perceptions enabled her to look forward to a sure resting-place in Him who is to his people, however the world may frown on them, a *" hiding place from the storm* and *a covert from the tempest."*

* * * * *

My general ministrations in the case of M—— H—— were soon changed for those of a more special character; for some little time after her admission into the house she appeared to rally under the more nourishing diet which the medical officer had given orders she should receive, but it was only as the brilliant rays of light which precede the setting sun; the last beam soon sank below the horizon of this world, and " *the days of her mourning were ended!*"

* * * * *

March 13. Had, to-day, a most edifying interview with poor M—— H——. She appears to like conversing on the state of her soul, and telling me of her inward feelings. She said she had been dwelling much on that passage in the Acts where St. Paul comforts the disciples, and exhorts them to continue in the faith, adding, at the same time, that it is through "much tribulation we must enter into the kingdom of God." " Do you think, sir, that the Apostle here referred to *temporal* or *spiritual* tribulations?"

" Why, in the original sense in which the

apostle used it, there can be little doubt but that he referred to the *temporal* persecutions to which the early disciples of Christ were exposed; nevertheless, in a secondary sense, I think it may safely be applied to those *spiritual* trials into which, more or less, God brings all his dear children. But why do you dwell so particularly on this?"

"Because I have for some time been brought up in the school of *temporal* tribulation, but yet I feel that my heart has not been so much humbled as I could wish it to be, on account of sin. Sometimes I doubt whether I can really be a child of God, not exactly from want of faith in his sweet promises, but because I do not experience those strong tokens of adoption which his word teaches me to expect."

"To what tokens do you particularly refer?"

"I mean *inward conflicts*. My outward tribulation has indeed worked patience, but my rebellious heart was for a time tempted to murmur. Yes! even against my own better convictions I was foolish enough to ask what I had done that God should so afflict me. . . . Temporal afflictions then cannot give a title to heaven, or mine would be secure, . . . though at times I have been inclined to think, that because I have suffered so much on earth, I shall have an abundance of joy hereafter in heaven." ...

"God grant you may do so! but remember, that outward afflictions, unless sanctified to us, do not answer the end for which they are sent, and that it is not *because* we suffer tribulation in this life that *therefore we are necessarily the children of God;* but it is when *that* tribulation weans us more and more from the things of time and enables us to look at eternity; when it shows us the vanity of the creature and the loving-kindness of the Creator, so that we look upon ourselves as only placed on earth for a time to do God's will as obedient children, and hereafter to receive that portion which the mercy of God has provided and the sacrifice of the Saviour has purchased for us, that such tribulation effects its legitimate object, and answers the real end and purpose for which it was sent."

"Ah, sir! your reply gives me much cause for self-inquiry: *has the end been answered in my case?* I have felt, it is true, the hardness of my lot, though I do not murmur at the condition in which I am placed! rather would I thank my God that I have found a refuge, but I fear that my duty to Him has been of a most imperfect kind. I have long been in that state for which God condemned the Laodiceans of old, *'I know thy works that thou art neither cold nor hot, I would thou wert cold or hot!'* I have never sufficiently mourned for sin though I know how powerfully it dwells in me. God only grant that I may have time and the aid of his Holy Spirit to effect this great and necessary work." . . .

"Let us unite our prayers to the throne of grace that such may be the blessed result, but at the same time remember that you must wait God's time, it may be his will that you may not yet obtain what you desire, therefore, in the language of Scripture, *' though the vision tarry, wait for it.'* "

"I will, I will! but what, if after all my sufferings here on earth, I should be a castaway at last! . . . Oh I dare not think so, . . . it cannot be! God has brought me so far, and even in the midst of the heaviest tribulations some ray of mercy has penetrated the thick gloom of sorrow. The ' bow was in the cloud, and it was God's blessed token that the waters of affliction should not finally overwhelm me.' . . . I do not refer to my temporal troubles, God knoweth they have been heavy enough, but though they have sorely weighed me down, yet have they made the lamp within burn more brightly, and as all human props have failed me, so have I learnt to lean more on the Rock of Ages."

A few words of prayer closed our conference.

March 15. How consoling is the promise, how encouraging to see its realization that the path of the "*just shineth more and more unto the perfect day.*"

Never has that text of Scripture, "*Whom the Lord loveth he chasteneth, and scourgeth every son whom he receiveth,*" received to my mind, a stronger practical commentary than in the case of M—— H——. In few instances have I seen such a perfect renvêrsement of earthly prosperity, such a complete withdrawal of earthly comforts; and although these changes, in a commercial community in particular, may be of daily occurrence, yet it is only as the sufferers are brought into communication with the ministers of God that the practical results are seen. Could the page of every-day life be fully exposed to the view, we should doubtless read many a history far more melancholy in its details than the case of the poor widow now before us; but perhaps we should find few, even in the pages of fiction, embellished with the meretricious ornaments and the fancied dreams of resignation which a powerful pen may

THE WIDOW'S PORTION. 137

depict, who, like her, have learned to kiss the rod that smites, and in the spirit of her great exemplar to say, "*Thy will be done.*"

One of her favourite hymns, which she not only repeated with her lips, but I believe really felt in her heart, was that in which occurs the beautiful stanza,—

> "Though dark my path and sad my lot,
> Let me be still and murmur not;
> Or breathe the prayer divinely taught,
>   Thy will be done!"

I found her reading it as I entered her room today. She pointed it out to me, and said, "It is the hymn my poor father was so fond of, and almost the first a dear mother taught me to lisp forth. In happier days I have often sung it to them, . . . but I shall never more sing on earth, . . . the last verse is most expressive of my desire,

> "'Then when on earth I breathe no more
> The prayer oft mixed with tears before;
> I'll sing upon a happier shore,
>   Thy will be done!'

"And that 'happier shore' is not far distant," she continued; "my little vessel draws nearer and nearer to the haven, and my eyes, so long accustomed to the wide waste of waters, catch a glimpse of the wished-for land! I hear the waves beating on the shore, but the murmur of them is sweet . . . O that my dear children were with me . . . but God has a work for them to do! . . .

"I am very weak this morning though better than yesterday; the sound sleep I was in when you came left me greatly refreshed, but I should have awoke if I had known you were so near me." . . .

"I did not wish you to be disturbed as I was told you had passed a restless night; but although without sleep, did you realize the presence of Him to whom the darkness and the light are both alike?"

"O yes! I found '*my Maker who giveth songs in the night*,' and even the hours seemed too short for me to number his past mercies to me! . . . but alas, I find it very hard to divest oneself of earthly thoughts, and fix the affections where they should be. I confess I could not at times help contrasting what I have been with what I now am . . . still, even in this temptation, God's mercy sustained me, for whilst I thought of my changed condition as regarded *temporal* things, He bade me look also at the change in *spiritual!*"

"Do you feel then that your prospects of eternal things are growing brighter than they were, and your sense of sin more clear, so that you understand more deeply its nature?"

"Not so bright nor so clear as both should be. Experience is, however, I humbly trust, gradually 'working hope;' but whilst I rest only on the '*sinner's friend,*' and put forth only the '*sinner's plea,*' the merits of my Saviour, I fear I have not a sufficiently strong sense of sin so as to loathe it on account of what it caused Him to undergo for me. . . . I can look at Jesus as a sin-bearing Saviour; yes, and blessed be his name, I can look at Him as *my* sin-bearing Saviour, but I do not think that I hate sin as I ought. I remember once reading, that 'in order to know what sin is we should look at its effects as manifested against the Saviour.'

"It is in this respect that I am so cold; O that my heart might warm more towards Him! I may truly say at present, in the words of the pious Adams, 'I see less malignity in sin, and can more easily forgive it, because I consider it not chiefly as sin against God but against myself.' ..

And yet how mercifully has God so long spared me that I may obtain what I so greatly need . . . wondrous forbearance has he exercised towards me! O when shall I be able to praise Him as I ought ?"

"Not until that day when '*you shall behold Him as He is !*' but in the mean time you can offer Him the sacrifice in which He most delights."

"I know it . . . but O how imperfect must that sacrifice be, offered as it is, with that clog which keeps us down to earth! We cannot loosen the ties, however much we may long to do so. Ever since I have been brought so low in sickness I have foreseen the end, and whilst I rest on the assurance that He who is the '*Father of the fatherless and the God of the widow,*' will protect my poor orphans, yet I cannot resign them without a struggle. . . . I was allowed to see them yesterday morning, all except my eldest boy; they tell me he has a cough and the medical man says he must not leave his bed for a day or two! . . . O why am I not at his side to nurse him ? . . . You will answer, sir, 'because it is God's will.' I feel this and I ought to be content, it is a portion of my cross, and the cross must be borne. . . . I should like, sir, to hear you read that beautiful chapter the 14th of St. John . . . it will now, as it has often done before, soothe and comfort me!"

* * * * *

March 16th. Poor M—— H——, I did not see her to-day, but what a weight of woe is again to fall upon her! my evening was passed at the bed-side of her dying child. The cough, as I well knew when she spoke of it yesterday, was of a most serious nature; in pity, however, I did not undeceive her in her belief that it would soon pass off. The medical officer had informed me of the violent symptoms of inflammation in the poor child, and added, that his course of suffering would be but short. This evening his prediction was fulfilled, and the little mourner closed his eyes for ever on a troublous world.

And now how shall I break the sad intelligence to the poor mother? The task has, perhaps, rightly been assigned to me, but need I say how I shrink from it? His death is in reality a dispensation of mercy, for he had only before him years of toil; but can a parent and a mother, at such a moment of bereavement, apply the healing balm which the case requires? It is his work alone who tempers the wind to the shorn lamb, and He assuredly will not " *break the bruised reed.*"

March 17th. With a heavy heart I bent my steps this morning towards the workhouse; for although I knew that I was in the path of duty, and that I should be rightly directed therein, the weakness of self prevailed, and made me wish that my task could be delegated to another.

M—— H—— was calm and tranquil when I entered, and began by thanking me for having visited her child on the preceding evening. . . . "They told me, sir, you were with him the last thing after your lecture, and this morning the nurse says he is '*easy and quiet.*' God grant that he may soon be able to see his poor mother . . . she will not be spared to him long." . . .

"But still you look forward to a happy reunion hereafter even though separated on earth, that is one of our greatest sources of consolation."

"Yes! yes! but he will have for a season to continue his sad pilgrimage alone, and yet I should not say *alone*, for his heavenly Father will be with him." . . .

"But it may please God to remove him whilst he still spares you; though so young, your child may yet 'outrun you and *come first to the sepulchre*,' and even should such be the case how much earthly sorrow will he be spared ! . . . would it not then be rather mercy than —— "

Before I could finish my observation poor M—— fixed upon me her dark eyes, now lit up with the glassy brightness of disease, and taking my hand exclaimed, " Are you preparing me for the worst . . . will not my dear child recover ? . . . O your looks tell me there is no hope . . . let me know all, indeed I can bear it . . . perhaps even now his spirit has fled . . oh, sir, in mercy let me know the worst!"

" But I have no really bad intelligence to communicate . . . my message is rather a cause of joy than otherwise. Would you not rejoice if you heard that your dear child was provided for far better than any earthly friends could provide for him ?"

" O, sir! I see it all . . . you need not tell me more ; my boy is indeed at 'ease and in quiet,' they told me truly, but not *all* the truth . . . they left it to you, sir, to announce to me the full extent of my loss! . . . O, Father of mercy, do thou support me under this fresh trial ! . . . My boy . . . my favourite child, never more will thine infant eyes look upon the sin and sorrow of this world ! . . . never more will thine infant limbs experience toil and suffering

... but thy mother should have closed those eyes ... thy mother should ..."

The fountain was at length unsealed, and tears relieved the almost bursting heart, a widow's tears for her first born! I looked on in silence, for it seemed like profanity to intrude a syllable at such a moment of almost sacred sorrow, and even had I wished to do so the powers of articulation would almost have failed! All I could do was to offer up a silent prayer that He who had torn and smitten would graciously be pleased to heal the wound which He had thought good to inflict.

Death-like, for a time, was the silence which pervaded the little chamber, when not, as it occasionally was, broken in upon by the widow's sobs. I could only imagine that all her former sorrows passed in review before her, and that the last seemed to place the crowning stone upon them.

Gradually she became calmer, and at length turning to me her still streaming eyes, she faintly whispered, "Had my poor child every comfort?"

"Be assured that he wanted for nothing which his condition required; the matron has been most kind to him and nursed him like her own child. You were told that I was with him last evening, and now perhaps it may be some consolation for you to know that his hand was in mine when he breathed his last! He fell asleep without a struggle, and is now, without doubt, resting upon the bosom of his Saviour. Would you then wish to have him back again?"

"No! no! not for all the treasures of earth!. ... but you can t understand, sir, nor enter fully into the feelings of a mother's heart. He was always a gentle child, always a delicate flower, and perhaps for that reason was more dear to me!... but ... he is gone! God has indeed broken another link of the chain which bound me to earth...."

* * * *

Fervent were our prayers at the throne of grace for that consolation which was so needed; and when I left the chamber I did so with the widow's blessing upon me!...

March 19. Yesterday being Sunday, I only saw M—— H—— for a few moments. To-day her poor child was buried, and when I first visited her this morning, she was, as may be supposed, in a state of great mental anguish. Although the violence of her grief had in some degree sobered down, though the waves rolled not so wildly through her bosom, the storm had not yet subsided, and its traces were plainly discernible in the wreck which remained. A strange alteration had taken place in her outward appearance, and one could plainly perceive that the last severe blow was hastening on an event, which even without such an additional impetus could not in all human probability have been very long delayed. The worm at the root had now made rapid advances, and the flower must soon fall. . . . " And to-day, sir, I am told my poor boy is to be laid in his cold grave . . . . Oh! 'tis very . . . very soon! . . . but a few days . . nay perhaps hours . . and they might have laid us in peace together! . . . And you, sir, will perform the last sad offices over him? . . . but will you think me wrong if I make one request? I have a clear presentiment that my earthly sorrows are fast drawing to a close, and when God does in his mercy think fit to take me to himself . . . I wish to be laid by the side of my poor boy." . . .

I hastily assured her that her request should not be unheeded,—at the same time adding that it mattered little where the *body* was placed so that the *spirit* gained its eternal resting-place. . .

"You are right, sir . . it matters little . . . yet 'tis a sort of consolation to think that our ashes will mingle with those whom we have loved on earth . . . I once hoped to have shared the same grave as my poor father and mother, who rest in the sweet churchyard of G——, but ... circumstances ... I ought not to talk of these things, they drive away other and better thoughts from my mind, and those which I wish to engage me now when eternity is so near ... and yet 'tis a sweet pleasure ... you knew my dear child, sir ... and to day .. almost as soon as you leave me you are going ... Hark .. I hear his knell ... Oh, could not this pang have been spared me! ... God of mercy, my heart is ready to burst ... Oh! leave me not to myself, lest I sink under the burden .... Thou hast indeed 'brought me low! .. let thy mercy in thine own good time raise me up!'" ...

A silence of some moments followed this last outbreak of sorrow,—the bell of the parish church, which was not far distant from the house, continued in mournful sound, and ever and anon the breeze wafted its boom so near that it vibrated through the chamber. The eyes of the poor widow were lifted up towards heaven, and the movement of her lips indicated that she was engaged in offering up to the throne of grace those petitions which He who sitteth thereon is ever ready to hear and answer. At length she again addressed me, though in accents so feeble, that I tried to dissuade her from making any further effort . . . my attempt was vain, and she faltered forth,

"I do not know whether I am much changed in outward appearance . . . but this last stroke has told me . . . of . . . speedy deliverance ! . . . 'twill be but a few short hours . . . and then . . . then I shall rejoin my lost child . . . yet not *lost* . . . then I shall rest my weary head on the same everlasting pillow. . . .

> 'I'll bid farewell . . . to every fear,
> And wipe my weeping eyes.' . . .

"Oh! the boundless love of my dear Redeemer to . . . a poor rebel such I am . . . to give me such a sweet assurance of pardon . . . yes, and peace . . . perfect peace . . . never more to be broken. . . .

"Let us once more unite together in prayer, sir, 'twill be perhaps . . . the last we shall offer up together . . . on earth . . . may we meet hereafter where prayer . . . will be swallowed up in praise." . . .

* * * *

Poor M—— H—— was right; it *was* the last prayer in which she was able to join . . .

THE WIDOW'S PORTION. 149

though at the time she made the remark, I was disposed to receive it rather as the dictation of weakness, than as the expression of sound and sober conviction. . . .

Hers, however, is not a solitary instance where I have observed that at the approach of death, the object has had such a clear perception of its nearness, as almost to specify the precise time at which the spirit is to leave its tenement of clay. Let me add, that in all similar cases which have come under my notice, the instances have been confined to those who have died "in the faith." What may be the secret origin of such "foreknowledge," it is not for man to presume to say,—but may not the bright glimpses of glory so completely turn away the eyes from earth, as to make the dying saint feel that Jordan is already more than half passed over ? . . . .

* * * * *

At about nine o'clock this evening, I was aroused by a message from the matron to the effect that poor H—— was almost at the last breath, and had expressed a wish that I should be sent for.

I arrived only in time to receive one glance of recognition as I approached the bedside, and e'er she could return the pressure of my hand her spirit had passed to its everlasting home!

* * * * *

The earth had not settled on the coffin of he child, e'er it was again disturbed, and in compliance with her dying wish, the widow was laid by the side of her first-born. . . .

THE MATRICIDE.

August 21. I had just closed my usual labours at the workhouse for the day, and was on the eve of leaving the establishment, when the matron requested me, if I had a few minutes to spare, to visit a man who had but a day or two since become an inmate of the house, and who had expressed a wish "to have some conversation with the chaplain."

I was soon conducted to the "*probation ward*," a portion of the building set apart for the reception of those whose disorder presented a fatal appearance when first admitted, in accordance with the regulation of the commissioners, "As soon as a pauper is admitted, he or she shall be placed in some probationary room, and shall there remain until examined by the medical officer of the workhouse."

Familiarized as I had long been to scenes of disease and suffering in their various forms, and by this very familiarity enabled in most instances to detect the stage of decay to which the patient had arrived, I saw that the time of J—— W———'s sojourn on earth would be prolonged to no very distant period. His frame gave evidence of a man originally of strong physical powers, which made the contrast the more striking between what he once must have been and his present enfeebled condition.

His countenance still retained, though in meagre outline, the traces of what in any class of life, and under any circumstances, would have been called handsome, whilst the expression of his features, now strangely altered by disease, and worn away with months of constant pain of body and mind, still manifested a characteristic distinctiveness which conveyed the impression that he was by birth of better condition, than the circumstances in which I found him would have warranted me in supposing. His subsequent history confirmed my surmises, and added a melancholy interest to the narrative of the unhappy pauper.

Soon after my admission to the ward, and a few kind admonitions from the matron, who, with her usual good feeling, seldom omitted an opportunity of encouraging those under her care to avail themselves of the offices of the chaplain, I was left alone with the object of my visit. A short conversation enabled me to become acquainted with the state of his mind, and the views which he entertained with respect to eternal things. His answer, however, to one question which I put will perhaps best explain what those views were, and how feeble was the hope he entertained of an interest in the atoning blood of his Saviour.

"Oh, sir! I am indeed a degraded outcast,—I have lived '*without God in the world*,'—I am now *without hope*, and when I am carried from this bed to the grave, as I feel I soon shall be, those who know my past life will only exclaim, 'No wonder that he came to such an end!'" . .

The poor fellow was evidently labouring under some deep mental excitement; the language, however, in which he expressed himself in his replies to my subsequent questions, and the indication he gave of his knowledge, not only of the text of the Bible, but of many of its leading and vital doctrines, called forth my surprise, and

I asked him how he became so conversant with the Scriptures, whilst in his present condition he apparently derived so little comfort from them.

"Mine, sir," was his reply, " is a long tale— a dark and fearful catalogue of sin upon sin . . . if God spares me long enough, you shall hear it; but—I am too weak to talk long now . . . do read me the thirteenth chapter of St. Matthew."

I of course complied with his request, and had proceeded as far as the fifth verse, when he interrupted me, and placing his now withered hand upon my arm, he exclaimed,

"That, sir, is precisely a description of myself, ... oft have I heard the word, and for a time I received it with joy . . . . . . but, alas! it did not take proper root, and now when I want the fruits . . . . will you offer up a prayer with me? it is never too late to seek for pardon. God may perhaps yet send a blessing; though I know it is long past the '*eleventh hour.*'"

Whatever may have been his former thoughts as to the salvation of his soul, whether despair had led him to cast aside hope, or conscience had brought his long career of sin in overwhelming review before him, so as hitherto to have closed up every avenue of comfort, he now seemed in earnest; and in complying with his request, I fervently besought the God of all grace to look with an eye of mercy on the wandering sheep who now sought admission into the fold of the good Shepherd.

During the offering up of my prayer, an occasional deep-drawn sigh alone marked the sufferer's participation in it; but (as I have frequently observed on similar occasions) most distinctly and reverently did he repeat after me every petition of the Lord's Prayer, with which I concluded.

Though now calmer and more resigned than he had yet been, I felt it would conduce to little practical benefit to lead him into a history of his past life, and was about to leave him with the promise of an early visit on the morrow, when he anticipated me.

" You would doubtless, sir, feel interested in hearing the circumstances which have brought me to the condition you now see me in—far different, I confess, from what but for my own waywardness it might have been . . . . but I am not equal to the task now . . . . another time . . . . another time . . . . thank you, sir, for your kind visit. . . . ."

He waved his hand as though wishing me to leave him.

August 22.—How little do we know what a day may bring forth! On my visit to the workhouse this morning I found W——b in so weak a state as scarcely to articulate,—

"Read me the eighth chapter of St. Luke, sir."

This was the parallel chapter to that which he had requested me to read on the previous day.

When I came to the thirteenth verse, he became greatly agitated, and as he whispered, "That will do, sir, ... I have now sufficient to meditate upon" . . . I closed the book . . .

August 25.—Two days have elapsed since my previous entry of anything connected with the case of J—— W——b, and twice since then have I seen him. Each visit was but short, his extreme weakness preventing him from holding any conversation. To-day, however, such is the strange variation of his disorder, he appeared better than I have yet seen him, and his spirits proportionately raised.

"I have been a great sufferer, sir, since our first meeting," was his address to me soon after my entrance; " but I trust the suffering has not been without benefit. . . . . I have much to say . . . . and it will ease me here (laying his hand on his heart) to unburden it to one who, I am sure, will sympathize with me. I wish I could undertake the task now, but . . . I know my time will be short . . . . if I am spared another day you shall know all; and yet the very idea of a recital of my guilt sinks me into perdition! . . . . do, sir, pray with me . . . ."

August 29th.—[I need not trouble the reader with the various extracts from my diary which record the circumstances of my last few visits to W——b, as they were mostly of the same character as those which I have already recorded. To-day I found him prepared to redeem the promise he had made me, to give a narrative of his life, and which I subjoin, retaining as nearly as possible the language in which he himself related it to me.]

"You may have wondered, sir, to hear me express myself in terms somewhat unsuited to the condition of a workhouse pauper, and you once expressed your surprise at my knowledge of the word of God; and looking at the miserable object before you, you may well find a difficulty in reconciling the idea of one well educated, and (on my father's side at least) nobly born, with such a perfect outcast as I now am! To both these advantages, if such they are, though in my case they have proved otherwise, I can justly lay claim; both, added to the influence of a naturally corrupt heart, have proved my ruin.

The first stage of my existence to which memory carries me back is as a child about four years old. I am now forty-one, and the visions of my infant years have, from the time and changes which have since intervened, naturally become somewhat indistinct. Still I can call to mind that I was then surrounded with every comfort and luxury which heart could desire, and was never suffered to move without a constant attendant on my steps. Even then, however, I displayed those passions which have since led me into such fearful excesses, and what perhaps in the *child* was looked upon as a trifling ebullition of temper, when uncontrolled in after life became a fearful curse *in the man*.

" I remember one whom I addressed as '*father*,' and who caressed me, but whom all around mentioned as '*my lord;*'—of my mother I will speak presently; but with her name and memory is involved the dark epoch of crime which I would give worlds, did I possess them, to blot out for ever from the page of my chequered existence. She, doubtless, has experienced at the throne of grace that forgiveness of her sins which with her dying lips she pronounced on her wayward child."

The sufferer's breast heaved convulsively at the mention of his mother, as though some wild vision passed in review before him. For a time he continued silent, and under the influence of the deepest agony, at length he resumed.

"As nearly, sir, as I can call to mind, about three years passed away in the enjoyment of those comforts which I have since learnt wealth and station can procure; and my days glided on, noted only by me as morning and evening called me to a mother's knee to lisp forth the prayer which she had taught me I was to offer up to 'the God who made me.' O long unpractised lessons! . . . . ofttimes, sir, have I attempted to resume the neglected duty in my subsequent course . . . . but . . . . I will proceed.

"At a short distance from the house in which my infant years thus glided away was a lake, on whose banks I have often wandered since the sad event which I have now to relate, and it was here that my father would frequently accompany my mother on a summer's evening, to pass an hour on the bosom of its calm waters...... Forgive me, sir, if I am somewhat minute in dwelling upon matters which are apparently unconnected with my present condition; they are in reality intimately interwoven with my after career, and I linger around them as the traveller who fears to quit the spring which he has found in the desert, lest haply he should fail to discover a second. My life, though I can give you but the outline of it, has but one such oasis—the spring-tide of boyhood—all beyond that is but dark and gloomy!

"I was one morning aroused by the bustle and loud voices of strangers, and, child as I was, soon discovered, from the disordered looks and anxious movements of those around me, that something very unusual must have occurred to disturb a household on all occasions so orderly and well arranged, that I was its most unruly member. I need not relate the various little circumstances which I could at such an age but faintly understand; suffice it to say, sir, that on the previous evening my noble father had, according to custom, ventured on the lake,—that in endeavouring to recover an oar which had slipped from his hand, he had overbalanced himself, and before they who had witnessed the accident could render assistance, he had sunk beneath the waters, nor was it until all hope of recovery was gone that the lifeless corpse was conveyed to its chamber!

"The pageantry of a rich man's funeral, such, moreover, as befitted the rank of my father, made perhaps greater impression on my infant mind than did the actual loss I had sustained, of which I could then form very little conception; but what the more sensibly affected me was my removal with my mother from the scenes of childhood to a humble cottage far remote from the spot of my former enjoyments. I have since learnt the sad cause of this removal in a truth from which I may date the curse that has embittered every hour of my existence.

"For some years we resided at the cottage at B——, and I was well nigh reconciled to the change; but my spirit was too fiery for the gentle control of a mother on whom affliction weighed so heavily, and in spite of my oft-renewed entreaties, not unaccompanied with the most violent threats, I at length became a pupil at a school in the immediate neighbourhood. Here, as I was not without some talents, my abilities soon obtained for me a position which nourished the dispositions I had manifested from my cradle. I was haughty and overbearing to all whom I considered my inferiors, (there were few who did not fall within my definition of inferiority,) and no wonder that I became an object of fear and hatred, always involved in some quarrel with my companions.

"I had but one in the whole school whom I could call my friend, and he, like myself, was a *bully!*—'*pares cum paribus*,'—you, sir, will remember the proverb. The establishment was conducted by a clergyman, who was no less distinguished for his simple piety than he was for his superior scholarship, and it was under his guidance, added to the instructions of a mother, that I acquired that *head-knowledge* of the Scriptures which has excited your attention. Would that Dr. G—— had alike had power to teach the heart! But *grace* must do its work; the 'stony heart must be made flesh,' ere the seed sown can bring forth fruit. Mine, indeed, has been barren ground, and though the seed did spring up and exist awhile, it soon died away, '*because it lacked moisture.*'

"I had been at the school about three years when one of my companions who, from his amiable disposition, was a general favourite, and

THE MATRICIDE.

who on that very account was an object of my deadliest hatred, so that I never let an opportunity escape of causing him some annoyance, goaded by my repeated insults, ventured to strike me, and for which he was loudly cheered by those who witnessed the act. The result was, as you may suppose, an appeal to physical strength; but you can hardly enter into my feelings when, in answer to my challenge, he replied, 'Prove your title to the name you bear and I'm ready, but not till then! I'm not going to fight with a —— !' . . .

"What subsequently passed I know not! the words have haunted me through life, they haunt me even now, on my death-bed, and no wonder, therefore, if, at the time they were first uttered, my senses left me! Guided by the influence of passions which I have never learnt to master, I soon reached my mother's cottage to demand of her the meaning of the language which had been used towards me, the import of which I sufficiently understood. She tried to calm me, but I was furious, rage almost checked my utterance, and rendered me still more ungovernable . . . till, like a madman I seized her to whom I owed my being with the grasp of a maniac.

* * * *

"Let me, sir, draw a veil over this scene of my life! Though she lingered long, my mother never recovered from the violence which I had offered her; and ere long I went forth on the wide world with a curse, infinitely heavier and more deeply branded than that of Cain, upon my brow, so that in the eyes of all who gazed at me I saw, or fancied I saw, that I was marked out as the *Matricide!*" . . .

The man's powers of articulation seemed utterly to have failed him when he arrived at this stage of his narrative! Large drops of perspiration stood upon his brow, and for some moments he appeared to be hovering on the confines of time and eternity. A few words of prayer answered the end in affording a temporary calm, but I saw that it would be, perhaps, fatal to allow him to resume his narrative in his exhausted condition, although he manifested a desire to do so. I accordingly left him for the day with the promise of seeing him before long.

August 30. Found W——b much changed in the lapse of a few hours. The scene of yesterday has left him in a most feeble state, and it may be has hastened on the event which is near at hand. He was sensibly alive to his enfeebled condition, and seemed to read in my looks that I observed the alteration.

"You see a difference in me, sir, since yesterday," was his remark; "it will soon be all over! I have just been reading the 51st Psalm, and it has given me comfort, because it so exactly expresses my state! Oh that God may accept the only sacrifice I can offer, 'a broken spirit and a contrite heart;' but dare I—can I hope that he will?"

After such words of consolation as I judged he stood most in need of, he interrupted me by saying, "I am now going, sir, to resume the history which my feelings prevented me from continuing yesterday; and though it is little better than an every-day tale of crime and its consequent misery, it will nevertheless enable you to judge how deep must be my guilt in the sight of God."

"I think, for your sake, W——b, I must not allow you to continue your story to-day; much as I should be interested you are evidently unequal to the task. The excitement of yesterday has been too much for you! Let your thoughts and meditations be rather fixed on Him whom you have so grievously sinned against. . . . If God should, in his mercy, spare you, I shall be able, another time, to hear the sequel of your wanderings." . . .

"No doubt you are right, sir; I will pray for pardon and peace . . . it is all I want!" . . .

September 2nd. J—— W——b has remained much in the same hopeless state, with no prospect of ultimate recovery, but still in full possession of his faculties. To-day he resumed his story as follows.

"Without wearying you, sir, with the account of my birth which I received from my poor mother, I learnt that the language which had so aroused my ungovernable passion had not been applied to me without some cause.

"The nobleman whom I had been taught to call father was indeed such, but my mother, who, from circumstances I need not detail, had consented to a private marriage with him, never discovered, until after his death, that his former wife was still living! Such a discovery, as you may easily conceive, gave a shock to a delicate mind which would of itself have shortened the course of my widowed-mother's life, even had not my brutal violence hastened on the event.

"After her death my situation was indeed critical; to return to a school which I had so abruptly left was of course out of the question, and scarcely had I seen the remains of one, the only tie which bound me to earth, deposited in the peaceful churchyard of B———, than, with the little property of which I found myself possessed, I sailed forth on the wide ocean of the world, wanting the only helm which might have enabled me to avoid its quicksands, *self-control!*

"True that I was not without some principles of religion; they had been instilled into my youthful mind with too much care not to find some lodgement, and under other circumstances it might have performed its legitimate office; but in my case religion had a doubly ungenial soil to contend against, and thus the blade no sooner appeared than it withered away.

"Like others, left as I was, their own master, I first directed my steps to the metropolis. In my sixteenth year, though tall and manly-looking for my age, and beyond my years in appearance, I was soon familiar with every description of vice which there meets one at every step in its various forms. It was not strange that a temper such as mine, looking only at the passion of the moment, should, amidst such temptations, have given full license to its natural tendency. A feeling of pride at first prevented me from mingling with all with whom I came in contact, and I drew, as I vainly imagined, a line of separation between the various shades of vice. I soon found, however, that such in reality is a *distinction* without a *difference*, as I sunk lower and lower into the vortex of sin.

"After some months' indulgence in such a course, you will not wonder, sir, that my fund of money was well nigh exhausted, and I began seriously to meditate on a departure from the scene of my iniquities, when a circumstance occurred which hastened that departure, and in a manner I had little anticipated. A robbery had been committed by some of my former companions, attended with the most violent outrage, and suspicions rested upon me as an accomplice, though in this case at least, however guilty in others, I was innocent; yet with my previous bad character I dared not face the accusation, and my only chance of escape was in immediate flight.

I succeeded, after much difficulty, in reaching a western port, where, as though providentially, I found a company seeking recruits to supply the vacancies in a regiment then in Ireland, on the eve of embarking for foreign service. Thankfully did I embrace the opportunity thus afforded me, and in a few weeks was tossing on the dark waters of the Atlantic, an exile from the land of my birth without the prospect of return.

"I had, perhaps, little to regret in leaving it, the only being who could have bound me to it had been sacrificed to my brutality, and though her lips, ere they were silent in death, had pronounced my forgiveness, the curse of a mother's blood accompanied me whithersoever I went.

"The discipline to which I was necessarily subject in my new condition as a soldier accorded ill with the uncontrolled fancies by which I had hitherto been led, and it was some time before I could bring myself to bear the yoke thus imposed upon me; but yet, sir, what with the new scenes which an Indian service opened upon me and the exciting life I then led, I contrived, if not to avoid any actual breach of duty, at all events to escape punishment on account of it; and in the exercise of those talents with which nature had endowed me and art subsequently cultivated, I succeeded in my new sphere of action to a degree which I had no right to anticipate.

"I must pass over the next ten years of my life, during which I experienced few changes beyond the ordinary routine of military life, and if I was not happy, as I could little expect to be whilst haunted with an accusing conscience, I was at least contented, and I trust thankful for what I was in the enjoyment of.

"You may wonder, sir, that my unruly passions so patiently submitted to the control they were subjected to; and though their occasional outbreaks often caused me much trouble, it is a wonder even to myself that they did not long before lead to the disastrous consequences which at length ensued.

"A trifling dispute had arisen between two privates in the company to which I belonged, and I was appointed, by mutual consent, to decide the point in contention. My decision involved me, certainly without any fault on my part, in a quarrel with the man against whom I had pronounced, and for some days he sought every opportunity with a view, apparently, of inducing me to commit some outrage which might bring me under the censure of my superiors. His object was at length gained, though in a way which he could little have anticipated. His insinuations on what he termed 'my want of spirit' in the presence of two of my comrades, brought on the collision which I had strenuously endeavoured to avoid, and unable any longer to bear his provocations, I lost all self-command, and in the struggle inflicted a wound which though not fatal, eventually disabled him for life. To escape the punishment inevitably awaiting me I availed myself of the assistance of a fellow-soldier and deserted, with, however, scarcely the shadow of a hope that I could ultimately quit the country with my life. For weeks did I lay concealed at no great distance from our quarters, as I naturally concluded I should thus best escape detection. We were stationed at Madras, and knowing the difficulty I should experience, amounting almost to an impossibility, in finding a passage from that port, I conceived the daring project of crossing the country some hundreds of miles, I believe, sir, nearly 700, in order to reach Bombay.

"To carry my plan into execution I assumed the native dress, and with the money which, as a servant to one of the officers of our company added to my pay, I had managed to save, I set out on my perilous undertaking, being aided in my escape by the kind offices of those who had witnessed the fray, and who knew the provocation I had received.

"It would, sir, fill a volume to give even an outline of my various and multiplied sufferings. My principal fears on first setting out arose from meeting with the numerous bands of *Looties*, or robbers, which infested the country; but whether the meanness of my appearance disarmed their cupidity, or my way-worn aspect excited their compassion, they proved more my friends than my foes, and to them was I often indebted for a meal and shelter.

"After five months of privation and suffering, such as perhaps scarcely ever yet fell to the lot of man, I succeeded in reaching the place of my destination, and by dint of much entreaty obtained permission to work my passage to England in a homeward-bound cotton ship. My reason for thus keeping up the semblance of poverty was, that (with a prudence, for which you will hardly give me credit,) I might husband my little property until my arrival in England, which, after an absence of nearly twelve years, I succeeded in reaching.

"My first business on my arrival was to seek out some remote spot where I might, under an assumed name, do something to earn a livelihood; and I know not by what singular fatality I settled down in the village of S———, about two miles distant from the abode of my infancy.

"Strange, indeed I have reason to say, are the ways of Providence, at least so they oftimes appear to short-sighted man, whose observations confined within the horizon of his own narrow circle, make him forget that he himself is but a speck amidst the myraids that surround him, and thus he fancies that but for him the world must stand still! Whilst I had been performing my part in the country to which my own imprudences had banished me, things had gone on their usual and regular course in the land of my birth; and yet I was surprised at the changes which had taken place, because I considered myself bound up in them.

"The possessor of what I considered my birthright, was the very man who in answer to my school boy's challenge, had dared to taunt me with illegitimacy, and was thus the cause of my subsequent misfortunes!

"The feelings of bitterness and disappointment, which arose on my making this discovery, you can perhaps have some idea of by placing yourself, sir, in imagination in my condition; but the baser passions which raged within me can be known only to Him '*who searcheth the hearts.*'

"Happily, prudence when least expected came to my aid, and the hardships which I had undergone, whilst they had so changed my outward man that I should have been unrecognized by my former acquaintances, had also, from the mental anxiety with which they had been attended, in some degree produced a change in the inner man, and thus saved me from an untimely end.

"His succession to the title and the property was nothing out of the usual course of such things; he, being the nearest of kin, had by the failure of other issue inherited the property, and thus obtained possession of what I can never cease to think as *morally*, though not perhaps *legally*, mine!

"As regarded my actual age, being then only in my thirtieth year, I was as one may say almost in the prime of life; although early dissipation, added to the causes before mentioned, made me appear a much older man than I in reality was.

"It was some time before I could make up my mind as to what I should engage in for my future support; but at length, after much discouragement, and many obstacles which I had little foreseen, I succeeded almost beyond my hopes in establishing myself as a schoolmaster in what I may truly call my native village; and small as the remuneration was which I derived from this occupation, it nevertheless enabled me to obtain a living without greatly trenching on the stock I had laid by, and which I carefully hoarded up against the day of sickness or adversity.

"For a time fortune seemed to smile upon me; my own conscience, however, was my perpetual scourge; and, added to the vision which sleeping or waking had haunted me for nearly fifteen years, I had now an additional torment in the fear of discovery and consequent punishment as a deserter. As, however, five years rolled on and brought with them an increase of prosperity, my little school being in a somewhat flourishing condition, I indulged the hope that, troublous as had hitherto been the voyage of life, I had glided into tranquil waters, and should at length be permitted to reach the haven in safety and peace.

"This hope was perhaps fostered by the circumstance of my having about four years after my settling at S——, been united to an amiable woman, of whom I can only say, that for the time we were permitted to remain together she was all that an affectionate wife could be, though my wayward temper and sudden bursts of passion, added to an increasing irritability of disposition which daily seemed to grow upon me, often called upon her to exercise that christian meekness which was her characteristic grace. She died about two years after our marriage, and though her loss fell heavily upon *me*, 'twas for *her* a merciful exchange, for her gentle disposition, ill-fitted to contend with calamity, must have sunk in the waves of adversity, which I have since had to encounter, and which shortly after her death opened in full tide upon me.

"I had seldom made my appearance in the village since the event which I have just related, when I was one day required to do so on urgent business. In my way to the quarter where my engagement was, I was attracted by a crowd of persons anxiously perusing a notice which has just been posted on the Market House; and prompted by curiosity I crossed over to learn its contents. Had any bystander observed my agitation, immediate detection must have been the consequence; *it was a list of deserters from the service!* and foremost on the list stood the name which I had formerly borne, H——H——, with a full description of my person, the date of my desertion, and under the head of "*remarks*," "supposed to be living somewhere in the county of W——," the very county where I then resided.

"My tale, sir, now is soon told. I saw it was useless to struggle on, *I was doomed*, and as my last chance, I immediately quitted the h which had so long sheltered me, with barely th means of subsistence for a few months; once more a houseless wanderer, to be hunted down at every stage where I ventured to think of obtaining a resting-place.

"For three long years have I thus wandered under every disguise that my ingenuity could adopt,—three weary years of the deepest and most heart-rending suffering, the casual dependant upon the half-withheld alms of those who spurned me as they gave, and oftimes exposed to the muttered curse of others whom I wearied with my importunities, when a morsel of bread would have been to me a greater blessing than heaps of untold gold!

"Truly I can say, sir, that I have suffered hunger and thirst, cold and nakedness in their most hideous forms; and if suffering on earth could expiate the crimes which on earth have been committed, surely the sin of the *Matricide*, heinous as it is must be, atoned for. . . .

"It is now some months since I reached this town, and whilst nature could support me I have crawled from door to door in search of food. This mode of subsistence could not of course last long after all that I had previously undergone, although, as you may see from the shattered wreck which now remains, I could once boast of a hardy and vigorous frame; and now the cares which have so deeply furrowed my brow, have given their aid to the work which is going on within. . . .

"I lingered awhile in utter destitution from the effects of disease, in a hovel not far from hence, until removed by the parish authorities to the chamber in which you now see me; and here am I . . . the offspring of rank . . . once the cherished object of the noblest of the land." . . .

The man's excitement as he uttered this last half soliloquy, half complaint, prevented him from proceeding farther, whilst the rolling of his eye showed me that for a moment reason had departed. With a sudden struggle he rose in his bed; but the exertion was too much for his exhausted strength, and his head sunk on his chest. Soon after I had replaced him in his original position he had calmed down, and as he feebly extended his hand faintly whispered,

"Forgive me, sir; I am thankful for what I have . . . far, far better than I have had for years . . . and infinitely more than I deserve . . . but I shall not want it long . . . O, that I could feel the assurance of pardon for what is past . . . but . . ."

* *

Sept. 4. The lamp of life still burns in J—— W——, but 'tis fast flickering away. This morning the poor sufferer was much easier . . . He lay with his bible opened before him, in which he had been reading the fifth chapter of the Romans. . . .

After my spiritual offices were ended, and I was about to leave him, he faintly said, "You will perhaps, sir, never hear my voice again . . . and I owe you much for your comforting visits. . . . Should you ever pass through the quiet little churchyard of B——, you will see a grave distinguished only by a single headstone bearing the name of H——C——, there sleeps the victim of the *Matricide!*"

* * *

THE JEWELLER.

Aug. 13.   *   *   *   *

What a daily round of painful duty is mine! what misery! what broken hearts is it my lot to come into contact with! No sooner is one sad scene ended than another presents itself upon the stage, and oftimes their continued occurrence comes with such force upon me, that I almost envy those strong temperaments which are little susceptible of impression from the miseries which they are called upon to witness!

They say that medical men by long practice become insensible to anything approaching to sympathy in bodily ailments; and in real truth such sympathy would unfit them for the duties of their profession;—but theirs is mere physical nerve, and whilst that from daily exercise becomes a second nature, I can testify from personal knowledge that they are not insensible to those holier emotions which moves them to "*weep with those that weep.*" And yet how many times have I wished that such physical fortitude might infuse itself into our moral constitution, that whilst at times we of the clerical profession are unavoidably the spectators of the most heart-rending sorrows, we might be able on such occasions so to control the feelings as not to be unfitted for other and more active duties. I have wished, in short, that the physical nerve might be transferred from matter to mind, so that the work in which we are engaged might be more efficiently performed, from the absence of those emotions which frequently render us unequal to the task.

And yet who can tell how much good our sympathy effects,—how it enables us to afford that peculiar consolation which the case may require!—what is deficient in one respect is more than compensated for in another;—and if there be times and seasons when our sympathy with the affliction is such as to prevent our adopting the active remedy which may appear needful, there is yet a pleasing result in the act that our very weakness becomes perfect strength in the hands of Him who overrules all for good.

But a casual observer may say, " Why complain of sympathy? 'tis one of the holiest feelings of our nature:"—we grant it, and God forbid we should say one word to weaken its ties, or loosen its bands! All we now speak of is *its excess;*—all we have at times wished for was its restraint within due limits, in those who are compelled by their position to apply the probing-knife, lest they handle it unsteadily to the injury of the patient under their care.

Too often have I felt this—too often has it been my lot to mourn over this excess of sensibility—(and I know such to have been the complaint of many of my brethren in the ministry)—so that we could not do what we would because of the wounds which we have been compelled to unclose. Little does the world know of the misery which it falls to the lot of those who " wait upon the altar," to behold; little do those who are blessed (may we not without being deemed uncharitable say *cursed?*) with all that this world affords; little do such know of the sad scenes which our office compels us to witness!

And they are not solitary instances; it is not

"*here a little and there a little,*" but link after link appears until the chain grows interminable, and we see the curse first pronounced upon man every hour receive its fulfilment!

* * * * *

How frequently at the close of a day's labour do I feel the inadequacy of my endeavours as regards certain individual cases to which my professional duty has called me!—a vague indefinite somewhat which tells me that I have not done all that I could: sure I am that the motive was not wanting; but misery in such hideous forms has quite unnerved me, has acted as a too-powerful check, and the needful reproof has been withheld from a too great sympathy in the woes and sorrows of one's fellow-men. What those sorrows have been, it were vain to hope that my pen could indite; my brethren in the ministry can well comprehend to what I allude; the Christian who knows his own heart can understand; the casual reader may imagine; but actual experience alone can fully unfold.

* * * * *

August 15.—"Forgive me, sir, for summoning you to my bed-side at so late an hour . . . I should not have thought of asking for you to-night . . . but they told me it was your lecture evening, and that you never refused to see any poor sufferer who wanted consolation. . . . ."

"Nor do I, my poor friend; but you appeared to have rallied when I saw you in the morning; do you feel weaker this evening?"

"Much . . . . very much feebler, sir, ... the hand of death has long been upon me . . . . but now it feels colder than ever. . . . . O that it had pleased God that I should once more look upon my beloved child! . . . she does not know where I am, nor do I wish her to; . . . . hitherto I have carefully concealed from her the extremity of want and distress to which I have been reduced, but . . . . she ought to know it at last . . . . it would be a bitter pang to her should I close my eyes amongst strangers, and she not by to soothe the dying pillow of her aged parent. . . . ."

"Then I suppose you wish your child to be sent for?"

"I do, sir, ... and yet what good can it do me now? it will soon be over!—something tells me it will not be long before the welcome messenger arrives to summon me to the land where sorrow will cease for ever! God knoweth mine has been a rough voyage here; but the sight of the haven almost makes me forget the perils of the ocean I have passed over. . . . ."

" Are you so satisfied, H——, with the prospect before you, as to be assured that the haven to which you are fast hastening will be to you the haven of peace?"

" I have scarcely a doubt on the subject *now!* there was a time when such a termination to my earthly course had little place in my thoughts, when surrounded by wealth, and in the midst of all that the men of this world esteem happiness, I looked not beyond the present; but blessed be God a change has passed over me . . . . I have awoke from my dream . . . . and after all I have gone through on earth, I cannot think that God will really cast me off!"

" But remember, H——, that earthly suffering is no proof of pardon with God; if that be all you have to rest upon, your foundation is far from being a safe one. . . ."

" No, sir, I do not rest *entirely* on that,—my hopes are better founded. . . . ."

* * * * *

Such is an outline of the conversation which I had this evening with J—— H——, a man whose appearance has excited the attention of all the authorities of the house, where he was admitted only two days since. In a state bordering on starvation, he applied for relief at its doors, and before that casual aid could be administered, had sunk down in a state of irrecoverable exhaustion in the presence of those to whom his application was made. Common humanity could not withstand an appeal more touching than the most affecting language, and by order of the guardians he was removed to the probation ward, until he might be in some measure sufficiently restored to proceed on his journey. Such a restoration, however, never took place. Continued privation had finished the work which a series of troubles had long since commenced, and the bed on which he was laid when he entered the workhouse of W—— was to him the bed of death. He was sixty-three years of age, as I afterwards learnt; but even the appearance of that age was added to by the ravages which want and sickness had made! Years do not always bring the semblance of age; for who that has passed through the vale of temporal suffering—who that has experienced the sad reverse from ease and plenty to disquietude and penury, or has witnessed this change in the case of another, but knows that one month's existence in such a condition will do the work of years! However great the mere physical powers may be, the mind receives from such an adjunct little assistance, but, on the contrary, affliction brings the most powerful physical matter under its entire subjection; the strongest man becomes a mere child when acted on by a *"mind diseased,"* and not even the fullest consolations of religion can in any way enable the mere animal frame to bear up under accumulated trial.

August 16.—I have just dispatched a summons to the daughter of J—— H——, written at his request.

He appeared much in the same state when I saw him this morning, though evidently fast approaching his end. His mind is apparently calm, and resigned to the change which awaits him. . . .

" . . . I hinted to you last night, sir, that I wished my child to be sent for . . . . it will be a sad meeting when she arrives, for how little does she suspect the condition in which her poor father now lies . . . . what trouble has my disappearance cost her ! . . . . O foolish, foolish man to quit . . . . but no matter, 'twill soon be all known . . . ."

" Will you write to her for me ?—do not tell

her where I am; but only say I am ill, very ill, and that if she does not hasten she will not receive my dying blessing. . . . . She gave me a home, but I could not bear the thought of eating my child's bread . . . . I—who, though unwillingly, deprived her of the patrimony to which she was entitled. . . . Her address is ———."

"Has she the means of coming to you without delay?"

"O yes, sir, she is placed far above want, though she has no cause to be grateful to me for it . . . . my child . . . , who ought now to take her place amongst the noblest of the land! . . . O if I had but strength to tell you all you would indeed mourn with me . . . . but God's will be done!"

* * * * *

August 18th.—This is the second day since I dispatched my letter, summoning the daughter of J—— H—— to the bedside of her dying father, and on my return home from a crowded meeting, I was informed by my servant that a lady was anxiously awaiting my return. I found her a person of agreeable manners and prepossessing appearance, about thirty-five years of age. She was dressed in deep mourning, and although great agitation was visible in the expression of her countenance, yet that expression wore an air of sweetness, which, when unruffled by inward distress, gave its possessor a peculiar charm.

"I believe I am addressing the Rev. Mr. C———, from whom I yesterday received this letter?"

"Your name is then ————."

"It is, sir; you have written to me of my father, ... can you bring me to him? . . . . How long have I been seeking him, and now perhaps it is too late. . . . ."

"Calm yourself, madam . . . . your father is alive, though I do not imagine he will be spared to you long; he was very weak when I saw him this morning."

"But where is he?—how came you to know my address? . . . . did he bid you to write to me? Oh! in mercy tell me — tell me all, sir! . . . ."

One after another did question succeed question, nor could agitation allow her to wait for my reply; with some difficulty I at length restrained it, and principally by showing her how necessary it was in the present state of her parent that she should control her feelings.

"I will try to be calm, sir; . . . but you cannot enter into my feelings: you do not know what it is to have a father, the fondest, the most devoted child ever knew, dying of a broken heart;—that is his disease—that is the secret worm which is preying upon him!—long has it been at work, and now its task is almost accomplished . . . . O lead me to him! . . . . lead me at once! . . . . where is he?—perhaps here in your house . . . . O sir, do not let me go distracted . . . . there has already been madness enough in one family!"

"He is not in this house; however he is in good hands, though not perhaps where you expect to see him: every attention, believe me, is paid to his wants;—at present he is————; but you had better come with me: I will go first and prepare him for your visit."

"But tell me where he is, sir! I can bear anything now . . . . I am quite calm . . . . indeed I am!"

Never did a countenance so contradict an assertion; and when in reply to her earnest entreaties, and with a view of getting over, as it were, the climax before she ventured to approach the sick man, I told her that her father was an inmate of the W———— Union House, a shudder visibly passed over her frame, as with an unnatural energy she exclaimed, "My God! .... is it come to this! my father the tenant of a workhouse! .... it cannot be! ... my father to die as a common pauper .... O this is bitter! .... this is the severest trial of all! ... "But" (she added after a pause) "he can be removed!—Yes, I have money ... more than enough for his wants;—I will have him removed at once!—O do not delay! .... lead me to him .... every moment may be fatal!"

Eager as she was, and almost vain as appeared the task of contending with her, I was bound to restrain, as far as I could, the exhibition of those feelings which would have been attended with the most fatal results to her dying parent.

Not without much difficulty did I at length partially succeed, and by the time we had reached the house, though still deeply affected, and almost ashamed to be seen entering its threshold, she had so far mastered the violence of her agitation, that after a short preparation of the sufferer for the interview, she was allowed to enter the sick man's chamber.

"My child!"—

"My father!"—

These were the only sounds which for a season broke the solemn stillness. The visit of the daughter was but the parting one ; for this evening, perhaps hastened on by the excitement of again beholding his child, death released her parent from his sufferings, and his last wish was gratified, that he might die in the arms of his child. She never left his side from the moment she was first admitted, and though pressed to take the food of which she so manifestly stood in need, every request of the kind was met with a thankful but firm refusal;—her only care was to attend to the last wants of her dying father— her hand supplied the moisture to his parched lips—the same filial hand arranged the sufferer's pillow, and if, as was the case, he was unable to *speak* his thanks, or express the consolation he felt that these offices were performed by the only being who could have soothed the last moments of his suffering humanity, — the look which glanced from his languid eye showed how much those sufferings were softened down by the presence of his only child.

Such a bond as exists between parent and child must be felt and experienced in order to be fully understood ; there is a chain whose every link has been forged in the fire of deep affection!—no selfishness can rust those links or weaken their power of tenacity,—no unthankfulness—no unkindness—not even disobedience or the coldest ingratitude of which human na- man nature is capable can loosen them ;—death alone can sever the ties, and even then, if here hallowed by the sweet influences of religion, the last enemy but prevails for a season in separating what shall again be firmly re-united and re-organized in a land where disunion and separation are alike unknown.

I have always lingered on the doctrine of mutual recognition in a future state, as one of the most consoling to the Christian in his most trying hours of bereavement. The feeling which prompted David to take comfort when he exclaimed, " I shall go to him, but he cannot return to me," is one which we conceive to be instilled into the believer's bosom by a God of infinite love. Otherwise death were indeed an enemy instead of a welcome friend, and we can hardly conceive of any severer pang short of perpetual exclusion from the presence of God and the Lamb, and the stings of conscience for opportunities lost and mercies despised, than the knowledge, which we shall doubtless possess, that we are *eternally* separated from those whose pure affection solaced us in the toilsome journey of life, and shed light on a path which, deprived of it, would have been dark and lonesome. On the other hand, what joy is there in the saddest hour, when the heart is bleeding for those who have " outrun us to the sepulchre," to rest upon the assurance that hereafter parent and child, husband and wife, brother and sister, friend and friend, shall share in uninterrupted intercourse, that communion which the grave has, though but for a little season, broken up.

* * * * *

August 19th.—I this morning had a short interview with the daughter of H——, who has taken up her abode in quiet lodgings, there to remain until after the last sad rites have been solemnized over the remains of her departed parent. On my briefly alluding to the circumstances which had brought him to the union, she observed,—

" Ah! sir, you little know the changes to which he and I have been obliged to submit. Could you know what we have undergone, and from what a position in society we have been cast down, you would not wonder that he whom you have so kindly interested yourself for, was unable any longer to bear up against the waves which opposed him.

"Thank God, he has done with all now! Care and sorrow will never more vex him, and the cold grave in which he is soon to rest will be a more welcome pillow than he has rested on for many, many years."

"Of what kind, then, have his sufferings been to have produced such an impression? Surely the mere loss of wealth could not ——"

"Not, sir, the loss of wealth so much as the sorrows which sprang out of it. Before I leave this place to resume those duties which this sad event has interrupted, I may perhaps be able to give you an outline of our afflictions; even if it do not interest you, it will at least prove to you that your sympathy is not lost. You have shown kindness to the stranger and his offspring, and in this cold world it is rare to find one who can prove himself a friend without some motive or some selfish end."

"That is a sweeping condemnation, and however in one sense it may be true of the men of the world, you must not forget that there is a class who are bound by a constraining tie to 'weep with those that weep,' and bear one another's burdens."

"There are doubtless such—I thank God there are,—but I have known few of this class!

Amongst those with whom my lot in life has been cast, I have witnessed none of those holier feelings of which you speak. I have seen the crowd of parasites who swarmed like locusts around whilst there was anything to be gained; all smiles, all professions of devoted friendship, whilst prosperity shed its golden beams on our path; but the moment the cloud supervened—the moment a doubt or a whisper was breathed that a change was on the eve of approach—that moment the cold look, or worse than this, the cutting sarcasm in the expression of a cold and mawkish pity was considered the only return which these wretches were called upon to make. Is it not enough, sir, to compel me to pass a sweeping condemnation, speaking as I do from such sad and bitter experience? He who is now at rest owned it and felt it, and lived long enough to curse the folly which brought him to become not only the witness, but the unwilling fosterer, of such detestable selfishness!"

*　　*　　*　　*　　*

"You shall judge for yourself," she resumed, after this outbreak had relieved itself in a flood of tears at the thought of what her father had undergone;—" you shall judge for yourself when acquainted with the circumstances which make me thus speak. I am now alone in the world, though not unprovided for; and had my dear parent been contented to share my means, he might yet be alive .... but ... no, I would not bring him back—the wreck was sorely shattered, but, thank God, it has at length reached the harbour."

"Your means, then, are sufficient to have kept your parent above want; how did he come to such a state of destitution?"

"Simply because no one knew where he was; but that forms the sad sequel to this narrative, and I cannot enter upon it now. Other things demand my thoughts, and I must rely on your kindness to assist the orphan stranger in the sad duty which she has to fulfil. I wish everything to be done which is needful to show a proper respect to the memory of one so dear to me; for though, by a strange combination of events, he has died in a workhouse, he must not at least be buried like a pauper! ... Oh! the idea is too painful to think of ... to me it seems as some horrid dream .... but, alas! it is a sad reality! Yes! he is dead .... he died in a workhouse!"

"Do you still persist in your intention of following the sad procession to the grave?"

"And why should I not?—why should I be deprived of the melancholy satisfaction of seeing him decently laid in his last resting-place?—O yes, let the tears of an affectionate child hallow the grave of an only parent, whose every anxiety in life was for those dependent upon him."

"My wish to dissuade you from it is simply lest the scene should be too overpowering for you under the painful circumstances with which his death has been attended. It is only from a kind motive that I have ventured to touch upon the subject; ere the moment arrives, I trust you may be more reconciled to the dispensation with which you have been visited."

"Thank you—thank you, sir, for your consideration! You know not how sweet to my ear are any accents approaching to sympathy,—sounds with which I have been so long unacquainted, and which I scarcely hoped ever to listen to again! May God reward you, I cannot."....

August 22nd.—To-day I performed the last affecting services of our church over the body of J—— H——. It was a sad and melancholy sight—to me still more so than it might have been to a casual observer. There was a calm and dignified sorrow about the chief mourner which for awhile enabled her to control her strong emotions; but it was when the clods were rattling on the coffin that the crisis had arrived, and with one piercing shriek she fell into the arms of one of the attendants, and was carried back to the chapel of the cemetery, where I found her scarcely recovered at the conclusion of the ceremony. Before she left the ground she again insisted on seeing the grave, and a conveyance having been procured, she was removed to her temporary home. There I saw her for a few moments in the course of the afternoon, and after some words of consolation, left her with the promise of a longer visit on the morrow.

August 23.— * * *

" I was just on the eve of calling at your residence, sir, for I have this morning received a letter which will oblige me to return home with as little delay as possible. I have not forgotten my promise to make you acquainted with the outline of our sad history. It will recall many and trying recollections; but I have now learnt to look on all that has passed as so many difficulties in the journey of life which are now surmounted, and which can never again, in the same form at least, obstruct my path. Trials of another kind may be, and doubtless are, in store for me, but their issue will be different, because the same combination of events can never again occur."

"But to judge from what I have now seen of you," was my reply, "your present position in life appears an easy one; and however great the change which you have experienced, does not

"Yes, sir; I thank God I am not only removed far above want, but am even enabled to lay by something against an evil day; how soon that day may come, He who foresees it alone knoweth,—our times are in his hand..... But I must not forget the main object of our meeting. Your sympathy has drawn me to open to you the secret fountains of my sorrow, and if you can spare a few moments this morning.... I shall not detain you long."

"My time is yours for the present, and I came with the full purpose of spending a spare hour with you. The relation of your troubles, if you feel equal to the task, may enable me to point you more effectually to Him who can make every affliction light, if we only exercise that patience which will enable us to see the end He has in view."

"I will enter upon the task at once, painful though it be; it will open many a grievous wound, but as you hear what I have to relate, you will judge whether my poor father had not enough to make him prematurely an old man, and bring him, if not to an early, at least to an earlier grave than with his strong constitution, and in the common course of nature might have been expected. . . .

* * * * *

"If you are at all acquainted with London, you will not fail to associate the name of my lost parent with the eminent jeweller, who some few years since lived at ———. My father was that person, and having commenced life as a humble journeyman in the house of R——— and B———, he was not long in reaping the fruits of his industry and integrity, so that he became, if not their equals, at least their rivals in influence and wealth. From being a workman in their house, he subsequently embarked in business for himself, and ever acting on the principle that whatever his calling the word of a British tradesman should be his bond, no wonder that all with whom he had any dealings were glad when the opportunity presented itself of again having intercourse with him.

"Do not think, sir, that I am speaking with the too fond partiality of a child for a parent; other evidences than mine have long since been afforded to his worth, and I but adopt the language of all who knew him, and who justly estimated his worth. They say that an ill name is easily gained, and never lost; but I think the contrary is also true, for the name which he gained, even when the storms of adversity beat in fullest force and finally overwhelmed him, never had the shadow of reproach or the blush of dishonour cast upon it.

"Wealth rapidly increased, and under the judicious direction of a master mind, was employed in schemes whose success increased that which was already more than sufficient to satisfy the wants of the most fastidious.

"My father was never what may be termed an ambitious man; but having risen from the working rank of society, he was so far proud of the position he had attained as to make those by birth placed above him feel his power. This he had many opportunities of doing. Oftimes has he told me that his office was beset by those whose extravagance had left them little more than their title of nobility, and who, knowing that he made it a rule never to take more than a fair and legal rate of interest, hoped to bring him to make a fresh advance for the supply of their urgent necessities by the offer of a higher premium.

"I have not yet spoken of one whose memory has been my solace in my heaviest trials, whose name is a synonyme for all that is good . . . my mother! . . . years have passed since she was called from a world in which, towards the close of her days especially, she knew nothing but bright prosperity. Her lot was but to behold life on its best side, and perhaps it was well that to one of her peculiar temperament the dark side of the picture was never visible. She was ill suited to struggle against the waves, and happy was it for her that her voyage was one of uninterrupted calm. Hers was a character which shone brighter in the quiet of the domestic circle: the full blaze of dazzling splendour with which we were afterwards surrounded, though it did not quench, nevertheless outshone the glimmer which proceeded from her unobtrusive spirit, and they only who were in its immediate vicinity could discover the purity of its flame.

"As I was their only child, you will not wonder

that all their affection—and O how intense was it!—was centred in and lavished upon me. Of themselves they were all in all to each other, and if I was not so much the connecting link between them, I was part and parcel of the chain on which their happiness depended.

"I was about seventeen years of age when a change took place in the plans and purposes of my father. Up to that time we had lived in a quiet residence adjoining his place of business, in one of the main streets at the west end. You may readily suppose that every thing around us was maintained in that state of comfort which my father's ample means could command, and certainly neither my mother nor myself desired any alteration; but our wishes always gave way to his, and however surprised we were at the announcement that we were to exchange our abode for a splendid dwelling in ———— Terrace, we knew that but one course was open to us, and that to submit.

"I cannot easily forget the manner in which the whole affair was settled: not a whisper had been breathed of his intentions, and in fact had any one hinted at the possibility of his removing from the place which he then occupied, we should have put it down as the supposition of one who knew but little of his character, and still less of his devotion to business.

"It was one morning, soon after our return from the sea-side, where I well remember that our stay had been that season longer than usual, after the breakfast was removed my father observed, addressing my mother,

"'I wish you and Fanny to come with me as soon as you can get ready, to look at a house for which I have to make some arrangements for a friend. You, Fanny, will see some good paintings there, and I know you are fond of such toys: the carriage is ordered at ten o'clock.'

"I mention this little circumstance, because it was the introduction to an important era in our family history, and one which more than any other materially influenced our future prospects.

"At the time appointed we were ready, and after a short drive stopped at a splendid mansion, whose appearance indicated a residence fit for the wealthiest of the land. If the exterior excited our admiration, much more did all that we saw within please and gratify the eye; the chaste but elegant furniture—the choice paintings—the air of comfort which pervaded the whole,—everything, in short, called forth our approbation. As we were leaving, my father (who had hitherto appeared only to listen to our praises) addressed the attendant,—

"'Let everything be ready by Monday next; the family will be here about four o'clock.'

* * * * *

"I pass over the surprise with which both my mother and myself received the intelligence that the mansion we had just quitted was in future to be our home. To my youthful mind it was rather a matter of joy than otherwise, though the pleasure was not unmingled with sorrow, because I saw that the proposed change was anything but gratifying to her whom I so affectionately loved. She clung to the spot where she had passed so many years of happiness since the day of her marriage, with a fondness only most natural, and nothing but the earnest entreaties of a devoted husband would have prevailed in making her quit that spot, or in any degree have reconciled her to the change.

"It seemed as if she had a prescience of what eventually happened; and it is but little expressive of her full feelings to say that she entered our new residence with a heavy heart. Its splendor had little value in her eyes compared with what she had left; and unlike most others in her situation, who would have indulged in a perfect ecstacy of delight, her cheerfulness appeared to have deserted her, and to linger at the fireside which she had quitted.

"My poor father was not slow to perceive and regret a result so different from what he had anticipated, and sought by means of society to reconcile her to her new position. Our house soon became the centre of attraction, and guests innumerable were glad to avail themselves of the profuse hospitality which was lavished on those so utterly unworthy of it. Titled personages, whose nobility was not of yesterday, condescended, as they no doubt termed it, to patronize the rich, jeweller—to honour his board with their presence, and consented to be fêted and feasted in return for their great condescension.

"Little does it become a child to speak of a parent's failings at any time; still less should the language of censure be employed when the subject of it lies in the cold grave. There all faults are, or at least should be, concealed; for the spirit has passed to render its account to One who 'judgeth righteous judgment,' and who weighs not our errors in the same uncharitable and selfish balances as our fellow-men.

"If then I speak of a weakness in the character of my parent, let me not be understood as adopting the language of condemnation or blame, but merely as making mention of it in order to connect the events which I am describing.

"Arising from a somewhat pardonable vanity, the weakness to which I allude was a fondness for having as his guests those whose only claim to distinction lay in the prefix to their aristocratic name, but whose brains were for the most part as deficient as their annual rent-roll. Their necessities were the means of their introduction to my father, and they were too glad of the opportunity afforded them of attending the fêtes which were given by the rich jeweller of ——— Terrace, whilst he was gratified at seeing the distinguished names of the peerage who were present at his table.

"Affairs had gone on for three or four years in this manner, when the health of a beloved mother, which had been for some time on the decline, could no longer bear up against the increasing power of disease. In vain was the foggy atmosphere of town exchanged for the more genial airs of the south of Devon; in vain was money poured forth with a lavish hand to ensure the first aid which human skill could supply; the constant attendance of the physician to watch her every look and mark her every pulse, though it succeeded in alleviating, failed in arresting the progress of her insidious malady, and ere long she was laid in the little churchyard of T—— where so many in like circumstances have found a resting-place from the sufferings of life.

"The effect produced by her death upon my father, was far more violent than might have been expected from one of his firm and decided character.

"He never entirely recovered the blow, and coming, as I have since understood, at a time when other causes were adding largely to his anxiety, its effects soon became visible in his altered appearance. For some months, however, no material interruption took place in our daily round of retirement; but even during that period, the hurried and anxious manner of my parent, together with an irritability of temper to which he had hitherto been a stranger, first led me to suspect that other causes besides grief for the loss sustained by the death of an affectionate wife were busy at work.

"One day, after our solitary dinner, I was about to retire from the dining-room, where he usually sat about half an hour before rejoining me for the evening. He had that day been more silent than ordinarily during dinner, and had evidently something weighing on his mind, for once or twice I saw a tear steal down his cheek, which he hastily brushed away as though fearful that his weakness should be observed.

"On my making, as I said, a movement to retire, he exclaimed,

"'Do not leave me to-day, Fanny; I have something of importance to say to you,—something in which your happiness is deeply involved, and in which, whatever my wishes may be, you yourself must alone decide.'

"'Your wishes, my dear father' was my reply, 'have ever been commands to me; and it must be something very unusual with which you desire my compliance now, to lead you to fear anything like a refusal.'

"'I do not imagine for one moment, my child, that you would refuse me any reasonable request . . . but in a case where your future welfare is so much involved, it is for you to decide, though that decision may of course be influenced by my advice and wishes.

"'To come to the point,—I have observed that lately the Marquis of B——, who in brighter and happier days,' . . . even now I can remember the emotion which agitated him as the recollection of an affectionate partner was brought fresh to his memory, for by a tacit agreement we seldom alluded to the one whose loss we both mourned . . . 'I have observed that his lordship, who used to be a frequent guest here, has latterly paid you a somewhat marked attention, and I am anxious to learn, my child, whether you feel that he is the man into whose keeping you can entrust your happiness, and whether you have ever thought of him in the light of a husband. I have a particular reason for asking, and therefore do not disguise from me your real feelings.'

"'Honestly, then, my dear father, the idea of marriage has never for a moment once entered my head. How could you suppose that I wished to leave you? Have I not everything which I can desire here, am I not happy with you? O yes! far, far happier than I should be with another!'

"'True, my child, a father's home is the happiest home, but you cannot always expect to share that blessing; the time must come, and it may be nearer than either anticipates, when I must leave you, for I find that trouble and anxiety are already doing their work upon me, and it would add much to my peace of mind to see you comfortably provided for. My chief reason, however, for speaking to you on this subject is that the Marquis of B—— has this morning proposed for you.'

"' Proposed for *me!*'

"' He has, Fanny; at least, which amounts to the same thing, he asked permission to be allowed to visit here in the character of my future son-in-law.'

"' And what was your reply?'

"' That I could give him no answer until I had ascertained your feelings; that all must depend upon your decision.'—

"' Which decision, my dear father, as you yourself just now observed, may be guided by your advice.'

"' Nay, my Fanny, not entirely; your own feelings must also have a considerable share in the matter. If you ask my opinion, I will candidly tell you that I think the Marquis of B—— is a young man of high principle and amiable disposition. He has, however, one vice, which was the means of his first introduction to me, but one of which I believe him to be now nearly cured by dearly-bought experience, *the vice of gambling!* Already have I advanced him large sums, of which I almost question the entire repayment, at least during my lifetime; but he has latterly not only ceased to borrow more, but has actually diminished my original claim upon him. In fact, I have no doubt of his perfect reformation; in every other respect I consider him a most suitable match for you, or I should have given a decided negative to his proposal this morning.'

* * * * *

"I am sure I have wearied you with these minute details: let me sum up all by saying that in a short time every thing apparently was settled, and I was, I confess it, not a little gratified by the prospect which awaited me. Even my poor father recovered somewhat of his former spirits, though at times a deep melancholy would steal over him, which all the comforts with which he was surrounded had not the power to dispel.

He had one morning been detained beyond the usual hour at which he quitted —— Terrace, to transact his business, and from which he never relaxed even in the days of his greatest prosperity, when a loud rap at the door announced a visitor, who was shown into my father's library. Sitting in an adjoining chamber, I could ere long distinguish something like angry voices. . . Suddenly the library bell was rung with unusual violence, and whilst advancing to the hall-door with hasty steps, my father's visitor in a loud tone exclaimed,—'Then sir, never again shall a son of mine disgrace himself by entering this house.' . . .

"My presentiments were soon realized, nor was I long left in doubt as to the interpretation of these words. With a flushed and disturbed countenance did my father enter the room where I was sitting, and could not for a few moments so far calm his excitement as to be able to address me. When, however, he succeeded in doing so, a few words sufficed to explain all. His visitor was the father of my intended husband, the Duke of ———, who had been vainly endeavouring to drive a bargain by the marriage of his son. Not only did he require a large portion of my expected fortune to be settled on the Marquis ———, but that my father, in addition, should liquidate the whole of his debts which, from gambling and other causes, amounted to no inconsiderable sum. In vain had my father, with the natural anxiety of a parent for an only child, represented the injustice and extravagance of such a demand—no arguments, no concessions could satisfy the grasping claims of this impoverished nobleman, and his decided refusal at last to comply with them had brought matters to an issue, and led to the announcement of which I had so unexpectedly been the hearer.

* * * * *

"I will not, sir, speak of my own feelings at that moment. A sense of proper pride and what was due to me made me rather congratulate myself on my escape from what proved to be a mere mercenary match, than grieve over the disappointment I experienced. Real troubles soon took the place of imaginary ones, and the splendour of wealth, which had so excited the envy of those who little dreamt of its many drawbacks, was soon to be exchanged for the obscurity of want, and the gloom of poverty and suffering.

"O, sir, none can tell but those who have experienced it, how the stroke of want becomes doubled in intensity when it falls upon those who have hitherto been, not only strangers to it, but who have viewed its approach as impossible. Its really gigantic form is magnified a thousand times by the light of contrast, until its hideous shape drives its beholders almost to the verge of madness. . . .

"Under the influence of a mania which has infected so many within the last few years, my poor father was induced to lend his name in support of a scheme which, like most of the kind, promised a '*vast return with little or no risk.*'

"I can hardly believe that in his sober senses he would have ventured to embark in anything approaching to such a hazardous experiment, but it was when his mind was distracted with grief for the loss of her who, with his child, divided his whole affections, and when, in consequence, his sound judgment was diverted from its natural equilibrium, that he fell into the trap so artfully baited for him. He saw his error when it could not be corrected, and although he would then have withdrawn at a sacrifice few but himself could have borne, that withdrawal was impossible, and he was therefore compelled to abide the result. For this, which he saw was almost inevitable, he began to make due preparations. Our residence was exchanged for one of a less expensive character, one more suited to our changed circumstances; but even in that, during the short season we were permitted to retain it, we experienced far more real comfort than in the splendid domain we had left with all the appliances of attendant pomp and display which marked the wealthy jeweller's abode. . . .

"Month after month did my father's purse supply the means by which to keep up the speculation, and which, notwithstanding outward appearances, he was led to believe would eventually return a rich harvest could it but contrive to outlive the fearful panic by which it was assailed. Subsequent events have proved that it would have done so, but alas! he who supplied the seed and watched the struggles with which, in its growth it had to contend, was not permitted to reap what he had sown; a broken heart, and all but a pauper's grave, are the only returns which have fallen to his lot!

"I speak only, sir, from what I have gathered from him; fearfully did he, and not without good reason, curse his own folly rather than the treachery of his fellow-men, for allowing himself to be led away by the phantom of gain when he had already more than enough to support him in affluence and credit. What gain could compensate for a tithe of the anxious days and sleepless nights he passed whilst waiting for a result which, "though long expected, never came;" a sinking constitution—a mind ever on the rack—the sickness of hope deferred—and the tide of ruin each day flowing nearer and nearer towards him,—these were the fruits which he gathered from the trees of his own planting, and which lined the path in which he had to walk for the remainder of his days.

"The end of his journey arrived sooner than he had anticipated. Everything he possessed capable of such a conversion, had, at no small sacrifice, been turned into ready money to meet the demands which were made almost daily upon him, and the large sum which one great sale had realized was deposited in the hands of his bankers.

"For some weeks I had perceived that a change for the better had taken place in my poor father's state of mind; a better and brighter prospect opened before him, and his wonted cheerfulness in some slight measure returned. It was, however, but the treacherous calm which preceded the coming storm, and though, to an unpractised eye, all appeared safe and promising, the small cloud had already risen in the distant horizon, and the note of the petrel came borne at intervals on the gale.

"On a certain day he was to pay, as he hoped, the last call to be made upon him, and when that day arrived he left his home for the purpose of doing so . . ."

* * * - -

"No marvel that on his return he had but strength to utter the sad announcement, 'My child . . . all is over . . . we are beggars!" . . .

* * * * *

"Never can I forget that awful moment! he sat with his eye fixed upon me, the perfect image of distraction! the cold unmeaning gaze of idiocy! Reason had fled, and the sad silence which followed the announcement of perfect ruin was only at last dispelled by the childish but heart-rending laugh of insanity! . . . Oh, sir, one must witness the reality in order to know the full intensity of the first symptoms of madness in those who are near and dear to us. The world talks of madness as a thing of course, we hear and read of those whom trouble has deprived of their senses; but it is when the stroke is thrust home, when we ourselves feel the sting, that then, and not till then, we can have any idea of the '*reality of insanity.*' To find yourself once the cherished object, not only no longer so, but the *object* of *aversion*—to watch the total overthrow of all natural feeling, and the insensibility of all social sympathy . . . it is enough to make madness a raging epidemic, and inoculate all with whom the sad objects it is brought into contact!

"In the case of my parent, that which was at first the raging swell of insanity, by degrees sank down into the calm of idiotic indifferentism.

The helm of reason was so far damaged that it could not be repaired, and whilst, as a natural consequence, the physical strength wasted away, the utter prostration of his mental powers rendered his ruin as complete as his bitterest enemy, if he ever had one, could have hoped for.

"It is over . . . it is gone! the sad dream has had its fearful awakening, and I would not again call its fantasies into existence! now numbered with the past, there let them remain, let no ruthless breath attempt to resuscitate the smouldering embers."

* * * * *

"I must close this melancholy history, sir; it is already longer than I intended it to be, but you have been so attentive and sympathising a listener. . . . The honest and upright tradesman—he who had been known as much for his integrity as his wealth—the famed Jeweller of ————, was gazetted a *bankrupt!* . . . He knew not the extent of his misfortune; in one sense, I may say happily, the intensity of this affliction was spared him, the wreck was soon complete, and then began the pinching privations in the humble and obscure lodging where we were glad to find shelter! But I will say little of these. . . .

"It would be unjust to assert that there were no offers of assistance when misfortune first assailed us, but they were of such a nature, and made in such a manner, that I could not but shrink from the acceptance of what, once received, would have laid me under obligations to those who would have lost no opportunity of reminding me of them, and I was more content when struggling to earn, by the aid of my pencil and needle, a scanty pittance for myself and the poor sufferer who now depended on me—aye, happier a thousand fold more than I should have been had every comfort been afforded me by the donations of a *pitying, self-commending* charity!

"The state of the poor bankrupt's mind precluded the possibility of any molestation being offered him even had his creditors been inclined so to act. For a time I kept our retreat a secret, and should have continued to do so had not an accident discovered it; and it was when our suffering was at the highest, and when in arrears for rent, I had already parted with all that could possibly be spared, that I proceeded to a shop to dispose of a drawing for which I hoped to realize sufficient to relieve present want.

I was doomed to disappointment, but a brighter change awaited us; the darkest night must have an end, and the day of comfort had already dawned on us, though I knew it not. I had been traced to our obscure home, and was the next morning visited by one of my poor father's chief creditors, who, in more prosperous times, had been one of his firmest friends. . . .

"I need not linger,—a few words will tell all. It appeared that every search had been made for us, only, however, to rescue an honourable though unfortunate man from total destruction. A sense of his worth was shown, not by mere cold expressions of pity, but in a more substantial form. A fund was raised amongst those who were the heaviest sufferers by his downfall, which, being invested, insured a provision, not only for him had he been spared, but more than sufficient for me now that he is gone. True that he was insensible to their benevolence, but their act was the more grateful, as he could neither recognise them when they visited him, nor understand how much he was their debtor; they were sufficiently repaid when they saw him in a state of comparative ease.

"For eighteen months did he thus share their liberality, but the malady which oppressed him made him alike unaware of what he had lost as of what remained. Month after month he languished on in hopeless idiocy without any prospect of ultimate recovery. Occasionally his mind still wandered through the vista of past happy days which he imagined were still present, and then he would speak so rationally of plans which he intended to carry into execution, that others, less interestedly observant than myself, imagined his reason would ultimately reassert her dethroned power, and successfully establish her claim. . . .

"It is a sad sequel to all which I have now to tell you. For some weeks past he had been in the habit of walking out accompanied either by myself or a female servant who, in my absence, attended upon him. The last time he did so was on ———, and as it would seem from the account given me, he complained of cold whilst seated on a bench in the walk which he ordinarily frequented at a short distance from our home. . . .

"At his desire the attendant returned for his cloak, and during the time for which she thus so imprudently left him, he disappeared. Afraid to return to me with the intelligence, or imagining that she should at length succeed in meeting with him, most important time was lost, and so effectually had the poor wanderer eluded our inquiries, that all trace of him was lost.

"In vain were messengers despatched on all sides; in vain were rewards offered; no tidings reached me on which I could rely until your letter arrived. . . . . You know the rest . . . . but you cannot know all that I have suffered."

* * * * *

THE AUTHOR.

May 17th. . . . .

"We therefore commit his body to the ground." . . . . " Earth to earth, ashes to ashes, dust to dust . . . ." Such were the beautiful and affecting terms of our incomparable Liturgy which I pronounced when the attendants had lowered into the grave the mortal remains of R———— W————, who but a few days before had closed his eyes on a scene which had been truly to him what inspiration has so expressively defined it, *" labour and sorrow."*

It was a *a pauper's funeral*, and they only who have been the eye-witnesses of one can tell how much descriptive reality is embodied in those words.

Any funeral, whether of rich or poor, can

hardly fail of exciting the most painful emotions; the train of mourners clad in garments whose colour seems so suited to the gloom which reigns within—the suppressed sobs of those who are committing to its parent earth the lifeless clay which so lately, in all the glow of life and health, was the beloved sharer of their joys and sorrows—perhaps a husband or a wife—a parent or a child who has now left the survivors to struggle on and pursue life's journey alone;— these, and a thousand attendant circumstances, invest such a scene with a melancholy and heart-depressing interest. Still the very respect paid to the dead by those who accompany the body to its long home removes in some measure the gloom of the occasion, and there is a gratification (sad though it be) to the survivors, in the knowledge that the last resting-place of the departed one has been hallowed by the tear of affection.

But a *pauper's grave!*—it is sad and solitary, and the very loneliness of death is made still more lonely from the absence of anything like sympathy.

How often is it that not even the decent exterior of a pall·covers the shell which encloses the cold ashes;—a few rough planks rudely joined together;—the black tinselled initials of the age and date;—the bearers in the grey frieze dress of the union—the badge of their misfortune, and who I have often thought, forgetful of the occasion—seem glad of the opportunity of again mingling with their fellow-creatures and breathing the air of freedom;—no sob, no sigh, no tear, not a breath or whisper of sorrow,—these are the significant marks of a *pauper's funeral!* Alone in life, worse than solitude attends him to the tomb, and the grave closes over him, and the green sod is replaced unmoistened with a single token of regret.

I could not but especially indulge in these reflections whilst wending my way back from the churchyard where I had been performing the last offices over the corpse of R—— W——.

I had seen but little of him before his death, for he had been an inmate of the house only three days when he breathed his last. Nothing there was known of him, save that (like many before him) he had been found in a lodging in one of the worst parts of the town, in a state of the most perfect destitution, wanting the common necessaries of life; and on a representation to the proper authorities, had been removed into the Union. He had nothing but the tattered clothes which he wore, and when I first saw him, (being by chance in the house when he was brought in,) a more miserable, emaciated, and care-worn object can hardly be conceived. He did not appear above forty years of age; nor was there anything very striking in what little expression remained in his sunken countenance. This, however, could hardly be expected from the state in which he then was. In the pockets of his coat (if, with the exception of its original shape, it deserved the appellation) was a bundle of papers, written in a small and at times not very legible hand, containing scraps of political ramblings both in prose and verse, and by far the greater part of them written in a spirit of the most bitter irony.

One unfinished scrap, seemingly of modern date, I cannot forbear quoting, not from any exact sympathy in the feelings displayed, as from their being expressive of the views he entertained with regard to the "New Poor Law." Could he, at the time he wrote them, have surmised the possibility of what eventually took place—that he himself would one day be a partaker of its "*tender mercies*," the bare idea would doubtless have added rage to his pen, and he would not have left uncompleted what he commenced in the following strain.

"Surely some imp from shades below
His d——ish power displayed;
When charging the messengers of hell
To weave for men some cursed spell,
They urged the ——, those plagues of earth,
To call the *Poor Law* into birth!
Arouse the piercing shrieks of woe."

* * * * *

Had his state permitted, I might perhaps have been able to learn from his own lips some incidents of his former life, and how with such talents, as some of the scraps showed him to possess, he had fallen so low in the scale of society. So utterly, however, was he prostrated both in body and mind, as to be quite beyond the possibility of paying even the slightest attention to his spiritual concerns, and from the time he was admitted into the house until the moment of his death, he scarcely uttered an articulate sound, or appeared to comprehend the meaning of a single inquiry which was addressed to him. Nothing, therefore, would probably ever have been known concerning him but for a circumstance which brought to light the following narrative.

The day succeeding his funeral I was called upon to visit a parishioner who was living in the same street where R—— W—— had been found in such a sinking condition. In passing the house from whence he was removed, and which was a sort of general receptacle for persons of that description, known by the name of "*tramps*," the woman who kept it, a perfect specimen, by the way, of her *genus*, and well suited to the occupation, was standing at the door, and of her I casually made the inquiry,—

"Do you know anything of the man who was found here in such a wretched state last week?"

"Why, sir, all I know is that he was here nearly ten days, and hadn't enough to pay for his lodging. I didn't like to turn him out, because he seemed so poorly, and as he paid me the first week in advance, and told me he should soon have some money, I let him go on."

"Did he tell you where he came from?"

"O yes, sir! he said he came last from C——, and that his name was R—— W——; he did nothing but write as long as he could, and it was only yesterday I found this under the mattrass in the room he had."

This said thing which she had found was a roll of paper neatly tied together, and on opening it I recognised at the first glance that it was in the same handwriting as the scraps before referred to. I told the woman what I supposed it to be, asking her at the same time if she wished to keep it.

"Why, sir, it is no good to me, but if it is worth anything, and will fetch any money, I ought to sell it to pay myself, for I can't afford to lose what he owed; it wasn't only his lodging, but I bought him lots of little things when he got so bad."

She was evidently trying to make the sum total of her demand cut a pretty respectable figure; I soon silenced her with a gratuity, and the manuscript was in my possession. She thought she had made a good bargain, and in heart perhaps gave me credit for being more rich than wise, in throwing away so much "gude siller" for a roll of what she considered waste paper. I however, in the anticipation of the perusal of my purchase, by no means grudged the price I had paid for the "*Ramblings of an Author.*"

The chimes of midnight had sounded from the clock of the old parish church, and my lamp, by its dim light, gave evident symptoms of a determination not to go on much longer, unless due attention were paid to its proper nourishment; still did I pore over the contents of this crabbed

MS., which in some places defied my utmost ingenuity to decipher. Yet did I persevere, so much was I interested with what I read.

In the version of it which follows, I have been obliged to omit some portions of an unconnected character, and here and there to add a few words to explain the meaning. On the whole, however, I have given a tolerably faithful transcript of the original.

" Where I was born, and who brought me into the world, are matters which cannot interest those who will peruse these pages. If those dear ones who have long since been numbered with the dead now look down from the regions of the blest on their neglected offspring, they can only, if such feelings are there permitted, curse the cold selfishness of their race, who whilst professing to honour and patroniz genius, take the first occasion to crush it, if no exercised for their self-aggrandizement and o their own terms! Long and weary have been the years since I first began to cultivate those talents which have proved to me a curse rathe than a blessing; for they have only converted the pillow which to the worn-out labourer is a downy resting-place, however coarse and homely, into one where, in my case, every feather was a thorn, and every thorn charged with the most excruciating anguish.

"O the days, the long, long days when the pen has almost dropped from my hand, and the night only brought visions of despair! and for what, for whom did I toil?—to pander to the appetites of self-styled patrons, wretches who lived upon my labours and grudged the scanty pittance which they thought was a recompense for my labour! Bah! the recollection of it is sickening—I dare not trust myself to write all I feel—let me only trace my course that others may profit by my experience!

"Thrown as I was at an early age on the wide world to trust to the tender mercies of my fellows, I entered on that path of honest independence which then appeared most suited to my capacities.

"Commerce was offered to me, and I might have joined the plodding herd around me, whose whole knowledge was summed up in the two words "*profit* and *loss*,"—whose ideas were limited to the perception of the *quality* and *quantity* of a bale of goods, and the percentage likely to be realized! but my feelings revolted from such a contact—the longings of my spirit were not to be satisfied by engagements in such grovelling pursuits. The bar, the church, medicine, were beyond my reach; for between me and the attainment of what was necessary to qualify me for either of them, the requisite outlay, and the want of means raised an insurmountable obstacle.

" And after all, where is the return for the expense and labour employed in the necessary qualification for these professions—to spend the four best years of one's life in the dry and formal study of an university—then called to the bar—and starve for years without earning the wherewith to liquidate the expense of one day's food!—or if ordained, to look forward only to a hard-earned subsistence as a curate, unless by fawning and flattery—by cringing and toadying some great man, you barter your independence for the sake of a provision for yourself and family.

" This is the return; the precarious, uncertain recompense for the sacrifice of time and principle. Let those who like the exchange follow their taste; mine led me another way, and as a writer, I fondly hoped to earn a moderate competence, whilst, at the same time, I maintained what to me has ever been dearer than life, *the spirit of independence*.

"Alas! want, pinching want, has at times checked its full development, and made me yield, *not the principle*, but soften down its harsher and more repulsive features.

"The pen, therefore, was my choice—the literary world, that in which I sought to move and to add my quota to the mass with which it was already stocked.

"But even in my first attempt I felt at a loss in what direction to turn my powers, so hackneyed had almost every subject become, from the labours of the many infected with the " *cacoëthes scribendi.*" My success, however, in that first attempt bade me hope, and already I saw visions of future fame and glory—already I had in fancy reached the summit of fame—the *monstrarier digito* was mine, and it was some time before I could quit the noble chateau of my fanciful creation, and feel the reality of the humble abode which I occupied.

"Dreams of genius! how often have thy pleasing visions spirited away for a time the sense of those miseries which it has been my lot to undergo;

how oft, when harassed by the slight and indifferrence, the scorn and cruelty of those whose subsistence almost depended on the creations of my brain, have ye led me to wander in the bright regions where ye dwell, and there forget that sorrow was ever to be felt, or wretchedness the portion of humanity! Alas! it was but a dream! O that such a dream had never had an awakening! would that I might have indulged in it through eternity!

* * * * *

"For a time I prospered, one production succeeded another, and although the remuneration I received was infinitely below what I felt was my due, yet was I "content with my wages," and submitted, though not without a struggle, to the petty exactions which were practised upon me by the publisher of my compositions. As long as these exactions had a certain limit I bore with them; but when avarice attempted to apply the screw beyond its due bounds, and to squeeze out as it were the very life's blood, endurance could go no farther, and spurning the mean wretch whose selfishness for once outwitted him, I sought to find one who might less greedily prey on the vitals of genius, and snap asunder the very heart-strings of humanity.

"What I experienced during that search I cannot find patience even at this distance of time to note down;—among the mercenary herd, I found but one solitary exception, one which was afforded only, as it seemed, to prove the rule that man lives only to grind down his fellows, and to damp every exertion which may benefit other than himself.

"For three years did that one of whom I write foster and encourage, by the most gentle treatment, those talents with which nature had endowed me. With him was no petty cavilling about the amount of remuneration; *value received* formed no part of his dealings, and if he *was* blessed, as he deservedly was, with an adequate share of this world's goods, no one could justly charge him with having added an atom to his wealth by the forced and unnatural pressure of an author's brain. He has ceased to adorn that trade of which he was at once the pride and the ornament; but the name of ——, whilst it graces the title of many a publication, lives far more indelibly impressed in the hearts of those whose good fortune it was to be either professionally or otherwise engaged with him.

"It was under the direction of him, to whom I have here paid a just though imperfect tribute, that my powers expanded, and if at times a cloud seemed to gather in the horizon, and a misanthropic spirit infused itself into my nature, so as to evidence itself in what flowed from my pen, his was the master spirit which allayed the storm and lulled the angry passions to rest. Those were my happiest days, a bright sunshine in the midst of a night of gloom . . . but alas! the clouds have intervened, and even those bright rays cannot dispel them . . . all again is darkness . . . all . . . all is deep impenetrable night! . . .

"And must I not say one word of thee, thou sainted one, whose spirit even now perchance hovers round me and sympathizes with my woes? O let me but hold converse with thee! let me recall the past, and bless the Author of all that thou hast not been spared to share the bitter afflictions which since thou wert removed from my side have befallen me! Thy gentle nature could ill have struggled with the cold blasts of this ungenial atmosphere! brought up in the lap of indulgence, cherished with a care and tenderness of which only such as thee are deserving, it is even a consolation to know that with me thou didst share only my day of prosperity,—it was but for ten short months—months of bliss, too perfect, too uninterrupted for the time to be prolonged. ... O that I could wipe away—from the moment I saw thee laid beside my beloved child in the cold, cold grave, all that has since come upon me, and blot it out from the page of my existence! ... but I dream ... surely it cannot be reality,—I never enjoyed such bliss! ... it is not, it cannot be the lot of man ... Surely my fancy has raised the structure only to crush me in its fall! ...

[The MS. is here illegible for some few lines; at least the words which I could here and there make out cannot be reduced to intelligible matter; what follows appears to resume the narrative which this apostrophe to his wife had interrupted.] ...

"From the day on which he who had led me on in the road to fame was called away, I may date my downward career, for though at times fortune appeared to smile upon me, yet was the smile like the fascination of the snake which paralyses the powers in order that its prey might be the less able to resist. It may be that the liberality of —— spoiled me for dealing with other men, whilst the recollection of what I had formerly gone through, made me view those with whom I was obliged professionally to come in contact, (from a sense of what was due to myself,) with that air of equality or rather superiority which many of them are unused to receive from those who are in a measure dependent upon them.

"It was my unhappy lot to fall in with one who knew too well how to play his part. With a fair smile and fairer promises, by almost forced aid at seasonable moments, and other deep-laid schemes which my blindness prevented me from detecting, he contrived to get me into his power, and for a season to make me wear his livery! It was in vain for me to resist, he had me in his toils long before I was aware of it, and bitterly did I repent when too late, of my folly and oversight. . . . He was indeed the wretch who deserved to be branded as chief of a

"Coward brood which mangle as they may,
By hellish instinct all that cross their way."

* * * * *

"I write strongly because I feel the sting so deeply. I had then been brought low by affliction, I had followed to the tomb the only being who had shed a bright light on my path in this dark and lonesome wilderness, and as if my cup of sorrow were not yet full, I lost the hand that guided me, the friend who directed me, and restrained my wayward fancies. When, therefore, obliged to seek other aid, I could ill brook the servility which was imposed upon me. Low in pocket, I was still high in principle . . . but the hawk's eye soon discovered my real condition, and hovering awhile, like that bird of prey, to pounce upon its quarry, when foiled in his first essay, he made up for his disappointment in the agonies he inflicted whilst witnessing the almost death throes of his victim.

"Life, however, remained though at apparently its last ebb! Though crushed and left doubtless for a future repast, the lacerated members revived, and in his eagerness to pounce upon another he forgot that his present prey might elude his grasp! . . .

"And I had my revenge—O how sweet was it! . . . Talk as you will *revenge is sweet!* 'Tis part of the curse of man—'tis the gratification of that satanic nature which is in us—'tis the fiend which haunts us . . . granted: 'tis wrong, 'tis sinful, it cannot exist in the breast of a Christian . . . we know all this, still *revenge is sweet*, and I had mine!

"I have lived to see the wretch who thus thought to trample on me, brought lower than ever he could have hoped to bring me; for in my case, however persecuted, let misfortunes come ever so thick, I still retained the powers which could inspire the pen, and thus enable me to ward off the pale spectre of actual want, though the luxuries and comforts of life might be denied me. He however, reaped the harvest of his avarice, and was brought to experience, in his own, what he had so often witnessed in the case of others, not only without a spark of sympathy, but even with feelings of exultation as bringing them more completely under his nod. The success of his dishonest dealings with those who from fear were compelled to submit, led him to attempt a like course with those who were under no such restraints ; a fraudulent bankruptcy was the result, and he who had so often been the means of consigning the poor writer to a gaol for some trifling debt, which had never been justly incurred at last now doomed to inhale its atmosphere as a swindler of no common character. Let me now dismiss the wretch, with all the sympathy which he deserves, expressed in the words of the author of my boyish days,—

"Rarò antecedentem scelestum
Deseruit pede Pœna claudo."

*   ⚊   *   ⚊   ⚊

It was whilst smarting under the treatment I

had received, and disgusted with the whole genus of those with whom I was compelled from the nature of my avocations to have dealings, that an introduction was by chance afforded me to a man who, high in station and really amiable at heart, might have become a sincere and valued friend, had one been able to put up with his pompous vanity, and forfeit all one's self-esteem.

"This foible led him to be guilty of meannesses which doubtless his natural disposition would have shrunk from; for to mention one point more immediately connected with myself, not only content with palming off as his own the productions of another's brain, he would assume even in private towards the very individual who supplied his demands an air of such intellectual superiority, that any one must have considered him the teacher rather than the taught, the originator of new, rather than the promulgator of another man's ideas!

"The means of my introduction to him was a pamphlet which I had published on the present state and future prospects of the Irish Church. In it I had happened to adopt views to which he was favourable, and as he then held the responsible post of ——, he doubtless thought that one whose sentiments so agreed with his own might be of service to him in the administration of his troublesome office.

"Be this as it may, he sought me out, and during the interview a discussion took place on the subject of the pamphlet. It may have been that I upheld that view of the question which I had taken, by some arguments which were new to him; he was evidently pleased, and thought them so conclusive, that he hesitated not to make them his own property, and triumphantly brought them forward that same evening in the house, where he was listened to with marked attention.

"Before our meeting terminated, the bargain had been struck between us, and I received the appointment as his lordship's secretary, with a residence in his house, and a salary which at least raised me above the necessity of visiting the dens of those from whom I had experienced such degrading and humiliating treatment. This in itself was a sufficient inducement for me to accept the offer, though in the opinion of many, I may have forfeited what I had hitherto so strenuously contended for, my *feeling of independence.*

"It is in human nature, however, to view things though a medium of our own creation when we would have them present an aspect conformable to our own wishes and desires, and this probably was the course which I now adopted, and I moreover satisfied myself with the assurance that I need not retain the post longer than suited my own convenience. The spirit which through life had been the ruling passion, was as strong within me as ever in my own opinion, and I saw only in the situation which I was about to undertake a channel through which my powers might be directed to my ulterior advancement; more especially as I should not be harassed by doubts of success, or fears of rejection from an overbearing publisher. The terms of our compact, however, I did not fully understand until I had actually entered upon my official duties; when thoroughly comprehended I began seriously to think that my independence would suffer a greater check than would be consonant to my feelings.

"But let me not anticipate.—After I had, as it were made a start in my new occupation, and rather congratulated myself than otherwise on the favourable prospect which had opened before me, I was one morning interrupted in my labours by the sudden entrance of his lordship with a pamphlet in his hand, which he hastily threw on my table, and in a most excited manner inquired, 'Have you read that, sir?'

"Glancing at its title, I replied that I had merely seen the announcement of it in an evening paper the night before, and was on the eve of procuring it.

"'This then will save you the trouble. I wish you to employ yourself this morning in an attentive and most minute examination of its contents, note its various points, and have a reply ready in less than twenty-four hours . . . observe me it must not be delayed longer than the time I fix . . . and . . . *the reply must sting* . . . Mark me, sir, I know the author of it, and the more bitterly you lash him, the deeper you cut, the better you will show yourself deserving of my confidence and favour! . . . I will not now detain you further than to say that the matter will be brought before the House on Thursday, you will therefore understand my reasons for this haste.'

"Notwithstanding that I looked for his lordship's exit after this announcement, he began pacing the room with a hurried step, as if he had something more to say which he could not get out, and which at the same time would not remain quiet within. He did not, however, succeed in producing the perfect sentence in my hearing, but after muttering something in which

I could merely detect the words '*renegade*,' '*turncoat*,' he exclaimed almost at the height of his voice,

"' Cut him to pieces, sir, ... don't leave him a leg to stand upon. . . . . Lash him into shreds, sir! You understand me. . . . Thursday indeed! He, above all others, to give notice of such a motion.'

" With these ebullitions of his indignation my noble patron left me to perform the task he had assigned me,—one certainly well suited to my inclinations, but one which I did not find so easy of accomplishment as I had at first imagined.

" The pamphlet which had so aroused his lordship's ire was admirably calculated to effect such an object; it was an attack on the policy of the existing government, more particularly in the administration of that department over which my patron Lord C—— presided; and when I pondered over the language in which his lordship was spoken of, I ceased to wonder at the excitement he displayed, or the desire he manifested to open the full vials of wrath on his unfortunate antagonist. To say that the author handled his subject well, is very indifferent commendation; the pamphlet was a masterpiece of its kind; and so strong were the arguments, that for a time I could really discover little whereon to found a reply; by dint, however, of perseverance and closer examination, I at last detected some fallacies, and these were to me a mine of wealth.

"I need not say that I made the most of every flaw I could discover, and employed every counter-argument I could call to my aid; when these failed, '*furor arma ministrat*,' invective of the severest kind, ridicule the most pungent the brain could conceive or the pen write; irony as bitter as human gall could make it,—all were pressed into my service, and by tolerable management contrived to make a very respectable ‛ Reply.'

The same night, about eleven o'clock, his lordship paid me another visit, in order to learn what progress I had made, little expecting, I imagine, to find me so far in advance; when I told him I was ready for the press.——

" ‛ Accept my best thanks, sir, for your expedition; if the matter only equals your activity, I need not doubt the result: perhaps you will favour me by reading the reply you have so speedily composed.'

" On any other occasion I should have wished

my Lord C—— quietly in his bed; but as I was in a measure so satisfied with my production, and was not unwilling to hear his opinion upon it, I did not grudge the extra labour imposed upon me. His interruptions as I read on were neither 'few nor far between;' but being more of a complimentary character, my self-gratulation made me pay but little heed to them. Now and then a sort of chuckle escaped him as any peculiarly cutting sarcasm occurred, and 'capital!' 'excellent!' 'most pointed, sir!' &c., were the expressions of delight with which he marked his approbation of my work.

"When I had concluded, he abruptly rose and said,—'I need not impose on you any longer, sir, . . . I will now seal it up and direct it to H——, so that he may have it the first thing in the morning; and I hope those for whom it is intended may digest it—ha, ha!'

"'But surely, my lord, you do not mean to make it appear as proceeding from your pen?'

"'Why, no—yes . . . . that is, not exactly . . . . do you think it advisable, eh?'

"'I should presume your lordship's own feelings will be the best guide in deciding such a question.'

"'Well . . . . perhaps you are right . . . .

it may be as well not to do so; still every one will guess the source from whence it originates.'

"They may or may not do so, thought I, but very few, I think, will give you credit for the authorship.

"As I made no audible reply to Lord C———'s last observation, he proceeded to indite a note to the publisher, whilst I sat coolly watching his countenance, in which I could discover only an expression of the most perfect satisfaction; and I really believe he looked upon the bantling which had cost me so much labour with the same paternal feeling as if it had been the offspring of his own brain. The wording of his note, which he read to me, showed the impression he meant to convey.

"'Lord C——— requests Mr. ——— will lose no time in bringing out the accompanying 'Reply, &c.,' as it is most essential that it *should appear immediately*. Mr. ——— need not answer *all* inquiries as to the quarter from whence it proceeds.

'——— House, Tuesday night.'

"'I think I need not add more,' said his lordship, after reading the above. 'You can look in at P——— in the course of the morning, and spur them on . . . . but now I will not intrude upon you, for I am sure you must need repose. . . . . Good night!'

"'There goes my lord very well satisfied,' was the commencement of my soliloquy as he left the room. 'His dreams will be pleasant to-night; . . . and I—I have to chew the cud of *independence*. Yes! *I am very independent!* no doubt I have done a very generous action! I have consented most liberally to let another engross the praise to which I am entitled, that I may receive in lieu thereof a certain annual consideration of £ s. d.'

"This is, forsooth, moral magnanimity! this is . . . . intellectual generosity!

"And now, when I look back at the events of those days, of which the circumstances above related form the outline, what are my feelings? those of self-congratulation? self-commendation?—far, very far otherwise! Even the dry crust on which I have often since been obliged to subsist, has been sweet from the reflection that it was not the wages of a mean and disgraceful contract.

"But it is past—it is gone—the remembrance only remains . . . . that is sufficiently bitter . . . . this is another of the pages of my existence which I could wish blotted out . . . . all my sufferings have become tolerable, because in them I have been more ' sinned against than sinning.'

[Again, the manuscript, though not exactly illegible, is continued in such an unconnected strain that I forbear transcribing it. The language is that of a man who seems to have got one idea into his head, brings that to bear upon every act of his life, and thus mars everything he undertakes. He fights, in fact, against a shadow of his own creation, and then proceeds to nurse himself in consequence of some imaginary wound which he has received in the encounter. This I fear is the case with too many; it is ever so with those who have not the fixed principles of gospel truth to guide them. As an ignorant and presumptuous sailor, who ventures without chart or compass to traverse an unknown sea, cannot marvel when his bark founders on some hidden shoal, so these of whom R—— W—— is a fair example, who think to pass through the troublous waters of life without the only compass which can point to the right track, need not be surprised, though they generally are so, when they make shipwreck of their best hopes.]

" At length the eventful Thursday arrived ; the

Reply was not yet out, but would be in the course of the afternoon, though not in time to have an extensive circulation until the following day.

"That night I went to the House to witness the result of the contest which was so charged with importance to my noble patron. His opponent, who brought forward the motion condemnatory of his policy, &c., (and who I had learnt was the author of the pamphlet which so troubled Lord C———,) rose with anything but an air of confidence, and the commencement of his speech betrayed a nervousness which must have been visible even to those who were most interested in his success, and consequently the less willing to observe or acknowledge it. He warmed, however, as he proceeded, and now and then an eloquent apostrophe drew down the cheers of his friends, and even forced a counter-cheer from some of his opponents! But in spite of all, there was evidently a sting which rankled within —a something which he could not shake off, and the whole of his speech produced little of its anticipated effect on a crowded and most attentive house; so that when he had finished, it did not take long for the echoes of the applause with which his partizans greeted him to die away, and my Lord C―― rose amidst breathless silence to discharge his battery upon his antagonist. Even now I see his noble and commanding figure, and the withering look of scorn which as he rose he cast at the opposition. Who that had then seen him could have thought that so narrow a soul dwelt within such a fair exterior?

"With scarcely any preface he plunged at once into his subject; but guess my utter astonishment when I heard him, with the most perfect coolness and self-possession, employ not only the very arguments, but almost word for word the very language of my reply!

"Much as I knew of the character of Lord C――, I at least was not prepared for this. It may appear nothing extraordinary that he should act as he did; but seeing his object so clearly, to identify himself with the authorship of the pamphlet I had written, so that no one could question its source—it was a meanness of which such as he alone would have been guilty, and still more. . . .

"And yet why should I have been annoyed? It was his property, he had bought it—he had paid for it—surely he had a right to do 'what he liked with his own.'

"His cause was triumphant; the motion against him was lost by an overwhelming majority. Lord C—— received the hearty congratulations of his colleagues for his masterly defence, and I—received my pay!

"Disgusted and wearied did I seek my bed that night! my golden dreams—my prospects of future advancement were crushed—crushed almost as soon as the flowers had begun to blossom; and instead of the path of honest independence opening before me, I found myself the slave—the drudge of a minister—a tool to be used as occasion required, and only to be employed in that particular service in which my owner thought fit to engage! Truly I had come to something at last! True it was that I was perhaps doing no more than what thousands with far greater capacities than myself would have endured anything to have the opportunity of doing; but what was this to me? could their willingness to submit make me more inclined to do so? was their tameness an argument why I should voluntarily assume the badge of slavery? Monstrous! ridiculous! No wonder that my dreams that night were mingled with the scenes of the day; no marvel that the applause of admiring senators rung in my ears as the cries of exulting fiends, and that the language of congratulation was changed into the hissing of the viper!

"I saw nothing of my patron during the following day,—he was no doubt too fully employed in acknowledging the fulsome adulation which was offered by his party on his unprecedented success; and I in my rounds heard nothing but the chant of his praises for the *extraordinary* ability he had displayed on the previous night. The pamphlet had, as already observed, appeared in the afternoon of the preceding day, and I saw its publication placarded in every bookseller's window that I passed; wherever I turned it met my eye, and heartily did I wish both it and its author at the bottom of the sea!

"I turned into a coffee-house I was in the habit of frequenting, after a ramble of some hours, and having partaken of a solitary dinner, was soon lost in the mazes of imagination. I had well nigh come to the conclusion of at once closing my connexion with Lord C————, and was balancing the reasons for and against such a proceeding, when a friend entered the room and took his seat. In no humour to hold communion with anything but my own thoughts, I sheltered myself with a copy of the '*Times,*' and shrunk almost like a guilty being into the farthest corner of the box. Not long was I permitted to remain in this listless state, and what recalled me to myself was like oil on the troubled waters. No traveller through the burning desert ever rejoiced more at finding the cool spring wherein to slake his raging thirst than did I at listening to the conversation which took place between two persons who were little aware of my proximity.

" My friend had been joined by a man whom I knew by sight, as an under clerk in one of the government offices, and he had hardly taken his seat when he began.

" ' Well, F———, what d'ye think of Lord C————'s display last night?—pity the ——— tells such a tale about him; he won't like it, I imagine.'

" ' What does it say; for I haven't seen it?'

" ' No?—then you'll have a treat! Waiter, is to-night's ——— in the room?'

" I with difficulty restrained myself from snatching the paper from the man's hand as he was carrying it to the last speaker; I however succeeded in doing so, fortunately, as such an act would have betrayed me, and I should have lost the exquisite delight with which I listened to the following paragraph, one which I cut from the paper, and have ever since kept by me."

[The paragraph was here pasted to the MS., and I therefore give it entire.]

" 'We can well conceive the feelings of self-gratification with which the noble ———— last night retired from the House. His success was brilliant; the more so, because most unexpected. All who witnessed the hearty congratulations, or listened to the fulsome compliments with which he was literally bespattered, need not be told what a burden was removed from the minds of the ministerial party by the result of last night's division on Mr. S——'s motion. We have, however, by a close comparison of his lordship's speech with a certain brochure, headed, '*Reply to an Attack on Irish Policy,*' &c., found so much resemblance between the two, that we are quite at a loss to discover which is the real *Simon Pure*—whether the pamphlet is a reprint of his lordship's speech, or the speech a re-issue of the pamphlet. They are both given to the public under his lordship's sanction; one is delivered from his lips in the House of Commons, the other proceeds in manuscript from

—————— House. We remember to have read somewhere, in days of yore, an apophthegm to this effect,

> ' Ne gloriari libeat alienis bonis.'

Perhaps his lordship's *private secretary* may be able to give him a free translation of this ——————.'

* * * * *

"Let me not attempt what the most eloquent pen would fail in accomplishing—a description of the feelings which agitated me as the reading of the above proceeded. I know of no language which can describe them; self-accusation, and self-commendation in turn prevailed, till at last, urged on by the two united, I hurried from the room without making myself known.

* * * * *

"It was late, very late, when I entered the rooms assigned to me in —————— House, but not *too late* to be told that Lord C—— had been waiting for me some time in his library, and was most anxious to see me the moment I returned. There was little difficulty in guessing the object for which he desired an interview, and if both wished to dissolve the existing connexion, no moment could have been more propitious. The double doors closed upon us as I took a seat, and his lordship began.

" 'You have read to-night's ——, I presume, Mr. W—— ?'

" 'I have not,' was my reply, 'though I can guess to what your lordship alludes.'

" 'Guess, sir ?—how can you do that if you have not seen the paper ?'

" I almost thought, from the expression of his countenance, that Lord C—— suspected me of being the writer of the paragraph in question; my answer, however, set him at rest on that score.

" 'Because, my lord, I heard it read aloud in a coffee-room but a few hours since.'

" 'And accompanied, I suppose, with the remarks and comments of coffee-room politicians! eloquent debaters, no doubt!'

" 'Pardon me, my lord, I heard no remarks which might have been made upon the article, for as I had remained unobserved during the reading of it, so I believe that I left the room unnoticed immediately after it was concluded.'

" ' Then what course am I to understand, Mr. W——, that you intend to pursue ?'

" ' I do not see that I am called upon to adopt

any particular line of conduct, your lordship having so completely fathered the pamphlet in your speech last night, its paternity can no longer be doubted,—at least as regards your lordship!'

"'But *it is* doubted, sir; the ——— dares to charge me with adopting what does not belong to me. You are no doubt prepared to meet the charge and disavow the authorship, so as to disprove the assertion which has been made.'

"'You surely cannot be in earnest, my lord, in making such a proposal; you are trying what material I am made of; you ask me ———'

"'I *am in earnest*, Mr. W———, never was I more so in my life; you must either consent to my terms, or you leave me to employ the only alternative which remains. Such an accusation as this cannot go uncontradicted, even allowing, for the sake of argument, that *you* did carry out the *ideas with* which *I furnished you!*'

"'Well,' thought I, 'this is cool; I shall next be persuaded that I really did not write the pamphlet at all!'—My mind was now made up.

"'Would not silence, my lord, be the wisest course?'

"'No, sir, undoubtedly not; a flat denial from you, sir, is the only course I can sanction. Are you prepared to give it?'

"'*I am not*, my lord!'

"Lord C—— with difficulty mastered his emotions; with as much coolness as he could command he merely stammered forth, 'I will think over this business; to-morrow morning you shall be informed of my future plans. Good night, sir.'

* * * * *

"I need not dwell at greater length on this part of my life. The following morning brought me a letter from Lord C——, enclosing a cheque, (double the amount of what he had previously promised me,) the former telling me that he no longer required my services; the latter, 'Pay to R—— W——, Esq., or bearer, &c. &c.' He should have been consistent; he should have added, '*value received.*' The note was consigned to the flames, and poor as I was, the cheque was returned to his lordship with one only alteration, —*a line drawn through his signature.*

"Behold me once more cast on the wide world, it was again open before me; there was, however, but one path which I could pursue in order to obtain a subsistence; yet such difficulties and ill-treatment I had experienced in before walking in it, that I in truth almost shrank from again encountering them. It was, however, my only resource, and bitter as the pill was I must swallow it!

"No sooner was it known that my connection with Lord C—— was at an end, than offers came thick upon me, and I might easily have engaged myself to fill a similar office; but one taste of its sweets had been sufficient to cloy my palate; my spirit had been too severely wounded to allow me again to submit; and as I had now learnt some of the secrets of political craft and chicanery, I imagined my powers might be well applied in that direction.

"My former patron did me essential service without perhaps in the least intending it; for his vanity led him to circulate a paragraph in all the morning papers, to the effect that, ' by way of giving the best and most unqualified contradiction to the insinuations of an evening contemporary, they were enabled to state, on the best authority, that all official connection between the noble —— and his late private secretary had ceased, &c. &c.'

"Though such a disclaimer might gull a few, I believe it opened the eyes of many more; certainly I rose in proportion, and being now beyond the power of those whom I employed to bring out my various publications,—writing for *myself* and not *for them*,—I succeeded beyond what my most sanguine expectations could ever have anticipated.

"But alas! I have ever been the sport of fortune; her character as a fickle goddess has never changed with respect to me,—always what the poet described her:—

> 'Hinc apicem rapax
> Fortuna, cum stridore acuto
> Sustulit, hic posuisse gaudet.'

"True, I flattered myself from first appearances that she was weary of persecuting me, and now intended to atone for past ill-usage by becoming more lavish of her favours; too soon, however, was I undeceived, and as usual was overwhelmed with bitter disappointment.

* * * * *

"For some time my publications found a ready sale; and teeming as the political world then was with matters of deep importance, I found no lack of subjects, in the divided state of party, whereon to apply my powers. And had it not been for those innate feelings which, though checked, were not yet sufficiently subdued, I might easily have obtained a situation which would have insured me a comfortable provision for life.

"But this was not fated to be my lot. The fires which raged within prevented anything like the approach of cool calculation; and what I have too late discovered to be *false notions of independence* forbad my accepting every offer which was made me, although many of them were of a most promising and advantageous nature.

"About this time I entered into an engagement with the editor of a popular journal, which gave me continuous and permanent employment. Here I was in my element—my pen ran riot—and constantly the excrescences of my articles were obliged to be submitted to the pruning book before they assumed a presentable garb Even this check-string, however, was at times insufficient; and in spite of all restraint, as if an eternal warfare had been waged between me and mankind in general, I so handled my pen that I at length became involved in a troublesome suit, in consequence of an attack which I had ventured to make on mistaken authority. The exposure which ensued, added to the constant harassment of mind and body, brought me so low, that my means were soon exhausted. To avoid a gaol I was obliged to quit London, though scarcely able to crawl from my bed. . . .

* * *

"And here am I—a poor friendless outcast—without one to whom I can apply—enfeebled in mind as well as body! . . .

"What have I to look for? I dare not discover myself! Even had not sickness paralysed my intellects, my pen must be silent, for I am marked out, and hunted down by the bloodhounds of the law! . . .

" . . . I feel the dews of death are upon me; —would God all were over! . . . It cannot be but that the curtain will soon drop—still perchance my part is not yet fully played. . . What if I have to linger on and perish from want? . . O hunger, thou tyrant! . . . . why dost thou haunt me? . . . . Ah! what vision flits before me? . . . 'Tis she! . . . 'tis the sainted image of my lost one. . . She does not beckon me . . No! . . . there's anger on her brow. . . . Why? . . . O my shattered brain! . . . Hunger . . . When? . . ."

* * * * *

Here closed this strange composition: the latter portion of it appeared to be of a fresher date than the rest, to judge from the colour of the ink, and the tremulous character of the handwriting. All of it had been written at different times, and my impression is that, finding all other means fail, he had composed it partly from fact, and still more from imagination, with a view to its publication with some other of his ramblings, as a means of procuring the common necessaries of life.

I have given it a place in these pages, though not coming strictly within the limits which I had proposed, but the moral which it conveys, as showing how the best talents may be perverted from their legitimate purpose, and be made a curse to their possessor, is my reason for doing so.

Here was a man with powers of no mean order —with intellectual endowments of more than common capacity—but the master spirit which could alone direct him for good was wanting.

Unbridled—self-opiniated—viewing every man as his inferior—he was too late brought to see his error, and by the false and absurd notions which he entertained, was a constant scourge to himself and others with whom he had any dealings. It is true that here and there in the narrative we trace the workings of a better spirit; they are, however, but as transient gleams in the firmament of darkness,—his headstrong passions soon drew the veil over them, and whilst all cannot but admire the proper exercise of what he caricatures as '*independence*,' in him it assumed the form of a vice.

He fancied all with whom he engaged were bent on crushing him—and on this account his conduct brought him at last to the condition in which, as the inmate of a workhouse, he comes under our notice.

He found indeed the truth of the words which he had perhaps casually read—" Our pleasant vices are made whips to scourge us :" or to adopt language, it may be, less familiar to him, " Pride goeth before destruction, and a haughty spirit before a fall."

THE OATH.

Dec. 16th.   *   *   *   *

"Don't, for God's sake, utter that curse again, W———; my blood runs cold every time I hear a fellow-creature invoke a malediction on another. But here comes our chaplain, and I am sure he will agree with what I say, although he cannot have the same reason to feel as I do on the subject."

A heavy sigh followed the conclusion of the old man's speech, which on inquiry I found had reference to an expression just uttered by one of his companions, who having been excited by some unfriendly act, had exclaimed, " Curse you for a meddling fool, I———mind your own business, and let me alone!"

It was to the first speaker that my visit this morning was specially made. Old F——— N———

has been about a month in the house, and is only waiting until the necessary steps can be taken to remove him to his own parish in the county of N———k. Of this removal, however, there appears but little chance, the distance being far too great for one of his declining years and enfeebled condition. Each time I see him the prospect of his ever being in a fit state for removal becomes less, and for the last few days the medical officer has ordered him not to venture into the open air.

His venerable appearance and benign expression of countenance strongly prepossessed me in his favour on our first interview; and so much reminded me of another subject of these sketches, C—— M———, that I imagined if ever I gained a knowledge of his past life, I should find it almost a counterpart of the adventurous career of " old Charles."

Almost on the verge of the grave, it is indeed comforting to find that he is not a stranger to the way of salvation; but in every conversation I have found him familiar with the truths of revelation."

I should say that F—— N—— was naturally of a happy and cheerful disposition, but, like many in similar situations, some burthen on the mind—some weight within appears to prevent the full exercise of hope, and chains down to earth the spirit which is longing to be at rest. I have endeavoured on many occasions to induce him to unburthen himself to me, in order to administer the proper spiritual remedy; but though receiving such attempts with kindness and gratitude, he has hitherto always avoided their object.

His observation, as I entered this morning, led me to imagine I had found a clue by which I might trace the origin of his deep mental suffering, and therefore in answer to his appeal to me, I replied—

"You are quite right, F——, to reprove such a sin as that which W—— has committed; few things can be more offensive in the sight of God than pronouncing a curse on the works of his hands;—but why did you say that it so deeply affects you more than it would me or any other who dislikes to hear God dishonoured?"

"O, sir, don't ask me!—'tis enough that I do so feel it! And I feel it the more because my time on earth is so short—not but what I have had much time for repentance, but the longest time is too short for such a work."

"Well, F——, I came to have some conversation with you to-day; are you freer from pain than you were yesterday?"

"I can hardly say that I am;—like the patriarch of old, 'there is now but a step between me and death,' and O, I cannot feel I am fully prepared for the great change:—sometimes the thought overwhelms me—a guilty creature standing in the presence of his Creator—a culprit before the Great Judge, with no hope of escape —is it not an awful thing, sir?"

"It is indeed, F——, a most solemn subject to employ our thoughts; but is it not also most comforting to know that we have a Friend ready to stand by our side at the bar of judgment, whose merits and intercession, if now insured, will procure us not only perfect pardon, but joy and happiness along with it?"

"I know it—I know it; blessed be God, his Holy Spirit has revealed this sweet truth to me; but something—I well know what it is—prevents" . . .

Another sigh, whose intensity choked the old man's utterance, caused a responsive vibration in the breast of each one present. As I watched him turn his languid eye round the little chamber whose cheerless aspect was, in a trifling degree, removed by the sight of the bright fire in the small grate, I motioned to those who were huddled round it, (for the weather was intensely cold,) and who with eager looks were listening to the observations of old F——, to go into the adjoining room. After they had complied, I resumed the conversation by asking the invalid what it was that prevented him from applying to himself the rich consolations which God had so mercifully provided for every penitent.

"Do not press me, sir, for an answer. . . . . My sin is known to God, and though I trust I am penitent, let me carry its secret to the grave." . . .

"Then you cannot expect me to offer you fitting comfort, nor apply the proper remedy, unless I know the particular nature of the disease, however greatly I may wish to do so: of what nature"——

"I am sure you wish to comfort me, sir, and perhaps you may think me obstinate in refusing to unburthen my sorrow to you;—but believe me, sir, I don't do so from any feeling of that sort. I cannot—dare not recall the horrible scene which a moment of anger . . . No! no!—may God pardon the sin!" . . .

"To God, then, my poor friend, confess the

sorrow which weighs down your soul—nor doubt for a moment but that, if you are really penitent, he will, in his own good time, ease your burthened conscience. It is for a wise purpose he allows you to feel the acute pangs of your transgression, of whatsoever nature it is—but remember that there is no sin, however deep the die of it, for which the blood of Jesus cannot atone!"

" 'Tis that blessed assurance, sir, which has alone kept me up through many trials,—but they will soon be over . . . O how sweet is the prospect of peace . . . sweet peace!" . . .

The reading of a portion of scripture followed by prayer, closed my morning's interview with F—— N.

* *

December 19th.

I am glad to find you so much better this morning, F——; you seem to have rallied from what you were when I last saw you."

" You are right, sir; I am better, far—far better than I have been for some days—and for this simple reason, I feel that my rest is nearer at hand, and I hope I am more prepared for it. . . . The last few days that God has spared me, though in much suffering, have made the prospect of home far brighter than it was."

"Mercy has then followed your steps . . . Give God the praise, and O seek the continuance of his Holy Spirit!—the nearer you approach the close of your journey, the more you will need his supporting arm.". . .

December 20th.

F—— M—— remains much in the same state as yesterday, but with brighter hopes and stronger confidence. Less of doubts and disquietude. . . .

December 21st.

I spent some time in N——'s room this morning, and his conversation was of a most cheering description. He seemed much impressed with a sense of the love of Jesus, and the abounding consolations of the Spirit. On the latter, as Comforter, he laid great stress, and after some remarks and inquiries, observed, "The nearer, sir, that I approach the last stage of life, the more does light break in upon me. Much I imagined I knew before, and I can now comprehend more and more of the wonders of redemption. O, what a subject to employ our thoughts! God's own beloved Son dying to pay the penalty of our sin, and then sending his Holy Spirit to assure us that all he did and suffered to effect our redemption has been accepted by our offended but now reconciled God! What a source of comfort is the Holy Spirit! The sufficiency of Christ's sacrifice would have been lost upon us, had we not been assured of it."

"I am most thankful, F——, that you are able to see these things in such a light. What unbounded mercy that God has spared you to come to such knowledge as this; had you been called away before it was vouchsafed to you, what comfort would you have lost!"

"Comfort, sir! I believe it! I can conceive of nothing which can be compared with it! Even the thought of past sin adds to it—because it increases the greatness of God's love; and were it not for the one plague-spot of my existence, I should not at this moment have a single care. . . . But His will be done! I am paying the penalty of my sin here—O God, teach me to submit!" . . . .

"What is that plague-spot, F——? It may be that you are needlessly disquieting yourself; sensible as you appear to be of the love of God towards you, feeling an interest in the atoning blood of the Saviour, and knowing, above all, somewhat of the consolations of the Holy Spirit, what can be the sin which presses on you so heavily as to intercept the full beams of light which ought to shine down into your soul?"

With an expression of the most affecting character, in which, if one can realize it, was conveyed a look of deep anguish, and at the same time one of sensible forgiveness, the aged sufferer replied,—

"That sin does not now so much affect me, because I am assured of forgiveness; but God makes me feel its burthen as the penalty of having committed it. . . . . For years I have been weighed down by it—but it is now only for a few hours longer that it will oppress me. . . . Each moment the load becomes lighter. . . . But O! it is still heavy . . . very, very heavy."

"You are satisfied, then, that life is drawing to its final close?"

"The moment is far nearer, sir, than you seem to imagine; apparently I am outwardly stronger, but something within gives far more convincing testimony. . . . Will you come, sir, to see me this evening, if it is not asking too much?"

"I shall not be able to come until a late hour, F——, as I have important duties elsewhere; but you may expect me about nine o'clock."

cepted by our offended but now reconciled God! What a source of comfort is the Holy Spirit! The sufficiency of Christ's sacrifice would have been lost upon us, had we not been assured of it."

"I am most thankful, F——, that you are able to see these things in such a light. What unbounded mercy that God has spared you to come to such knowledge as this; had you been called away before it was vouchsafed to you, what comfort would you have lost!"

"Comfort, sir! I believe it! I can conceive of nothing which can be compared with it! Even the thought of past sin adds to it—because it increases the greatness of God's love; and were it not for the one plague-spot of my existence, I should not at this moment have a single care.... But His will be done! I am paying the penalty of my sin here—O God, teach me to submit!"....

"What is that plague-spot, F——? It may be that you are needlessly disquieting yourself; sensible as you appear to be of the love of God towards you, feeling an interest in the atoning blood of the Saviour, and knowing, above all, somewhat of the consolations of the Holy Spirit, what can be the sin which presses on you so heavily as to intercept the full beams of light which ought to shine down into your soul?"

With an expression of the most affecting character, in which, if one can realize it, was conveyed a look of deep anguish, and at the same time one of sensible forgiveness, the aged sufferer replied,—

"That sin does not now so much affect me, because I am assured of forgiveness; but God makes me feel its burthen as the penalty of having committed it. . . . . For years I have been weighed down by it—but it is now only for a few hours longer that it will oppress me. . . . Each moment the load becomes lighter. . . . But O! it is still heavy . . . very, very heavy."

"You are satisfied, then, that life is drawing to its final close?"

"The moment is far nearer, sir, than you seem to imagine; apparently I am outwardly stronger, but something within gives far more convincing testimony. . . . Will you come, sir, to see me this evening, if it is not asking too much?"

"I shall not be able to come until a late hour, F——, as I have important duties elsewhere; but you may expect me about nine o'clock."

"Thank you .... thank you. ... God's blessing, and the blessing of a dying old man, rest upon you. ... And now, sir, one more chapter from the book of life—the only real book of comfort. O, how I love thy testimonies .... in keeping of them there is great reward!" ...

* * * * *

Never, perhaps, did the outward aspect of the season so little affect me as it did this evening. An intense—an exciting, though chastened anxiety, to witness the closing scenes of poor F—— N——'s life, imparted a zeal which I honestly confess set everything else at defiance. The snow, which had made its appearance unusually early this season, fell fast and thick about me, and the keen east wind, which blew full against me, compelled me to draw my comforter closer around my neck: but snow and wind were alike powerless as (after dismissing the evening class of Sunday-school teachers which my brother curate and myself were accustomed to assemble at our mutual residence once during the week, for the purpose of Scripture reading, and general discussion on the best mode of juvenile teaching) I wended my well-known path to the Union Workhouse, on my interesting, though painful and solemn errand.

It was and is a bitter night—such a night that the very sight of anything approaching to a fire would melt the coldest heart into lively charity towards our fellow-creatures. One wretched, and I may add, almost *solitary* being—(for few, unless necessitated to do so, would have trod the streets in such weather)—one poor wretched being, with an infant at her breast, vainly, as one may easily conceive, endeavouring to extract from the almost frozen fountain its necessary food, implored from me, in the most piteous accents, a trifle wherewith to procure a temporary shelter from the piercing cold, and food for herself and her famishing child.

" Come with me, and you shall have both, for to-night at least, in the union."

" O, sir, for pity's sake don't take me there. I have a home to go to, though at some distance from this town. . . . In mercy give me a small trifle for to-night's want, and to-morrow I shall be provided for!" . . .

" She is not the only one," thought I, whilst bestowing on her the trifle she asked for, " who would rather brave the inclemency of the most inclement season, than seek for shelter within the walls of a workhouse!"

The "*union bell*," which so many have pulled with a trembling hand, scarcely allowed its echoes to die away, mingled with the second peal by which the porter announced my arrival, ere I was met by the matron, (kind and warm-hearted creature that she is, and a pattern for every one placed in a similar situation,) who, with an expression of real pleasure at seeing me, answered my greeting with—

" O, sir, I am so glad you are come—though really I had almost given you up, knowing that this was your class night. . . . Master tells me poor N—— has been several times asking if he thought you would come." . . . .

" How is N—— to-night?"

" He's fast going, sir, and has altered *wonderfully* since you saw him this morning; . . . but he seems so happy . . . it is quite a treat to stand by his bed-side, he is so patient and so resigned:—I wish all in the house could see what it is to die as he does!"

I had soon an opportunity of judging for myself; and often as I have had the melancholy satisfaction of watching the departure of a dying penitent, the present case certainly did not fall below what I have witnessed in similar cases. There was something unspeakably calm in the expression of the old man's eye as he saw and recognised me on entering his little chamber. He really

"*Look'd* unutterable things,"—

for his articulation had entirely failed; a low indistinct murmur from the throat was all that could be distinguished as approaching to the sound of the human voice, and nature was plainly sinking to its last ebb.

There is something inexpressibly solemn in the chamber of death—but even that very solemnity, intense though it be, is softened down when one is permitted to view these evidences of childlike submission and confidence which light up the bed of death, and which, when matter and spirit are about to separate, can alone reconcile those who witness it to the mighty change which is about to ensue.

Familiarity with any sight, however solemn it may be, naturally deadens the feelings to its intensity, and they who are accustomed to stand by the death-bed, become from habit gradually, according to the peculiarity of constitution, less affected by it. But there are cases of dissolution—there are death-beds which few can stand by without being powerfully excited; and well can we understand the feelings which moved in the breast of the nurse who attended Voltaire in his dying moments, and which, when applied to to give her services to another in the hours of sickness, led her to inquire if the object of her future care was a Christian, adding, as a reason for the inquiry, " I have witnessed the death of one unbeliever, and for all the wealth which earth can bestow, I would not stand by to witness another!"

Far, very far different, however, was the scene to be witnessed this evening, and it would indeed have been a matter of deepest regret to me had anything interfered to prevent my attendance. The aged tree had weathered the storms of life long beyond the appointed time, and although the blasts to which it had been exposed had left their traces behind, sufficient of the noble trunk remained to show what a goodly tree it had once been. It was now on the verge of total decay—the sap was fast leaving its branches, and ere long it would sink from over maturity into the receptacle provided for it.

I know of few sights more grateful to a

minister of Jesus than that of watching an aged penitent dropping, like a shock of corn, in due season into his last earthly resting-place. His past life may not have been one of obedience to the will of his heavenly Father, and many and repeated acts of rebellion may almost have provoked God to withdraw his favour from him: but by some merciful dispensations the rebel's sin has been brought to his remembrance, and he has learned to mourn with that " godly sorrow which worketh repentance not to be repented of.' Still God for awhile makes him feel the bitterness of iniquity, and for a long season withholds that perfect assurance of pardon which is necessary to ensure joy and peace in believing. Thus we frequently see that the death-bed of many who we have every reason to believe are departing in the faith, does not present a scene of such perfect triumph as we might with our own feeble views expect to witness. God's ways are not as our ways, and when we can behold deep and heartfelt penitence for past sin, even though such penitence may not be accompanied by most infallible signs of the secret witness of adoption, dispelling every sense of fear—nay, though often attended, as I have seen, with much of doubt and uncertainty, we have nevertheless great reason to rejoice, and rest upon the assurance which lights up even the gloomiest hour, that they who sow in tears *shall* reap in joy; and though such now go on their way, even to the last stage of their journey, " weeping, they shall doubtless come again with joy, and bring their sheaves with them."

Penitence and pardon are so intimately interwoven with each other, that we can hardly conceive of their separation, when the former is of that heartfelt and sincere character which an omniscient God requires; and although we well know that no repentance can save us except it be united with faith in Him who has atoned for our guilt, yet as the one is not vouchsafed without the other, so the former is the first grand step towards the attainment of the latter. Penitence without faith is mere hypocrisy and self-deception: that real saving faith can exist without godly sorrow for sin, is a direct contradiction of terms as employed with reference to the grand and glorious scheme of Gospel salvation.

In F—— N—— I trust that both are savingly united. Though unable to speak when I entered his chamber, I found him in full possession of his other faculties, and he listened eagerly and attentively to what from time to time I whispered to him. A smile of the most perfect resignation played on his countenance, so that even an unconcerned spectator might have conceived, without any stretch of the imagination, that the almost lifeless form extended on the couch before him was gazing with delight on the sweet fields which bloomed and blossomed beyond the dark portals of the grave.

His hand, which he had extended to me on my first entrance, cold and clammy as it was with the dews of death, remained firmly clasping mine, and at every motion, which he seemed to fancy might be meant for its removal, its grasp was tightened as though he was unwilling to part from it except in death.

I tried long and patiently to catch the meaning of what he endeavoured to say to me, but the attempt was vain; at times he seemed most anxious to be understood, but at last, finding, no doubt, that I could not comprehend his meaning, he ceased from his efforts, at the same time giving utterance to a sound most deeply expressive of his sorrow at being deprived of the power of communicating his thoughts.

After some questions, to which he replied by a responsive clasp of the hand, I proceeded to commend his spirit to God in prayer; but the few first sounds had scarcely fallen from my lips ere prayer was of no avail. Without a struggle —with hardly one convulsive movement—without any of those signals which mark the final separation of matter and spirit, F—— passed from a world of sin and sorrow into the presence of his Maker, with the sweet composure of one falling calmly asleep on a pillow of down. . . .

* * * * *

April 17th.

Four months have passed away; gentle spring has taken the place of winter; nature smiles in her gayest dress, and amidst the multitude of others whom I have been called upon to attend in their last hours, and point to the path of penitence and consolation, the circumstances attending the scenes of F—— N——'s dying hours have almost passed from my recollection, and the pages of my Diary might alone have brought everything fresh to my memory but for an event which occurred to me this morning.

Among the certificates which the parish clerk brought me to sign and compare with the registers, from which they were extracted, I saw, "F——

N ———, Union Workhouse, December 21."
Repeating the name as I read it over, I inquired, " Who wants this certificate ?"

" O, sir, a respectable-looking man in a sailor's dress came and asked for it yesterday, and he is to call again this morning about twelve o'clock."

" Very well—when he comes tell him to call here for this paper; perhaps he may be able to give me some tidings about that poor old man who, I remember, interested me so much. Did he say for what purpose he wanted the certificate ?"

" Why, sir, all he told me was, that there was some little property coming to him, which he could not get till he had proved the old man's death."

About the time appointed my servant announced to me that a person had been sent by the clerk, and, at my orders, ushered in a man dressed in the manner previously described, about forty years of age, and respectful in his deportment, whilst at the same time he displayed that blunt honesty of manner so thoroughly characteristic of an English seaman. Whether it be that the perils they are obliged to undergo when at sea makes them more restless and ofttimes turbulent when ashore, certain it is that the discipline under which they are kept on board ship makes them uniformly civil and well-conducted when in the presence of their superiors.

I soon learnt that the man before me was the warrant carpenter on board the C—— frigate, and that his object in procuring the certificate was to be able to substantiate his claim to some property to which F—— N——, had he lived but a fortnight longer, would have come into possession.

"Are you, then, any near relation to N——?"

"I am the son of his only sister, your honour, and a better-hearted man than he was never trod a deck. He had only two children—one was a sailor like myself, who broke the old man's heart. Poor George! he came to a bad end, and had no one to thank but himself;—his other child, Ellen, was my wife, and she has now met her father in heaven!" . . . .

It would be wholly out of my power to preserve in the following narrative the same descriptive language adopted in the relation of it. There was a feeling displayed in the recital of many portions of it which would have moved the sternest heart. Its very simplicity gave it an additional charm, and I was thankful for the accidental event which put me in possession of the facts attending the former career of F—— N——.

* * * *

" I have told you, sir, that I am the nephew of the man by whose death I inherit the property to which he, had he lived, would have been entitled; and however much I may get by it, would that he were alive and well to share it, for he had troubles enough to contend against; . . . . . but he is at rest now, and I am not afraid that one who gave such good lessons as he did, and practised them himself, should die unhappily at last."

" He did not die unhappily, my friend, far, very far, from it; nevertheless, there was something on his mind which seemed to give him great uneasiness, and which he would not speak about."

" I don't wonder at it, sir; he had more than enough to drive many men mad; my only wonder is how he ever bore up against his troubles so long as he did, but the back is suited to the burden."

The last time I saw him alive he was grieving about his son, and no one could persuade him that he was not the cause of his untimely death; though, for my own part, I am sure that no boy ever had a better father, and no child ever less deserved one; but this is part of my story, and therefore I had better begin from the beginning; you must please to excuse a sailor's roundabout way, sir.

"It is more than five-and-thirty years ago that I can first remember my uncle, and although so many years have passed, and I have had to rough it in all parts of the world, I can remember him as almost an old man then! Poor uncle F———, as I used to call him; he was always kind to me! . . . . He did not marry till somewhat late in life, and until he had made a comfortable property with which to maintain a wife; and when he did make a match, it was a very unhappy one, so that he had little cause to regret the day which set him at liberty by making him a widower.

"Within a few months after her death, I was fated to lose my father, and it was then that my mother and myself took up our abode under the same roof as my uncle.

"Many a long year has passed away, sir; I have been in strange countries and seen strange things, but notwithstanding all, I can never forget the many happy hours I spent as a boy in my poor old uncle's cottage at L———.

"I was four years old when I went to live there; George was about one year older, and Ellen just two years younger than I. But for one circumstance it would have been impossible to find a happier family; my mother was a mother to Ellen and George, and their father was more than a father to me. Day by day we used to attend the school, and perhaps the partiality which Ellen displayed towards me, and the greater success I obtained, might have been the cause, but somehow or other George and myself were never friends long together, and there was scarcely an evening that we returned from school but my father had to settle some dispute between us. We saw little of him during the day, for his employ in the ship-building yard engaged him from morning till night; but when night came, and he did return to his home, the quiet of that home was constantly disturbed by our boyish quarrels. I cannot say that I never was in fault, although I know I always tried to keep friends with him; but the same unruly spirit which George showed as a boy displayed itself during the whole of his short life; and though I ought to be the last to say so, yet truth will out—it required a far tighter hand to keep him in than my poor uncle had either leisure or power to employ.

"He was about fourteen years of age when the first breaking up of the little family took place. Living as we did in a sea-port town, where all sorts of characters meet together, George very soon associated himself with companions who taught him everything but what was for his good. We were both apprentices to the same master, at the same trade which my uncle followed, for he very rightly thought that we should do better with any other person than with him, and therefore took the two boys of another boat-builder in exchange for George and myself, so that we might properly learn our business. George followed it up for about two years, and being very quick and sharp, bid fair to be one day a first-rate workman; but bad company was the ruin of him, and getting every day more and more idle, he at last finished by binding himself to an American captain, and without saying a single good-bye to any one, left us all.

"Ah, sir! 'twas a sad scene when the full truth was made known to his father, for he was not long in hearing the news. 'Twas the first real sorrow he had ever had, and the blow fell heavily upon him. From that time, sir, he was quite an altered man, and never did he appear to feel so strongly as when, according to his regular custom, we used to read aloud a chapter in the Bible each night before we separated.

"He loved his Bible, sir, and he made us love it too, always telling us it was the best of books, and that as long as we kept the word of God, we should never want a friend. And his words have come true. Many's the time I have had to rough it, and thought that my lot in life was very hard, but this blessed book has made me more than contented; it has made me praise God that I was far better off than I deserved to be, instead of giving way to murmuring!"

[My visitor at this part of his story produced a small Bible, bearing the well-known stamp of the Society for Promoting Christian Knowledge, and on my observing that I was glad to see it bore evident tokens of being well worn and used, he replied,]

"That Bible, Sir, was the gift of a dying mother!—she told me to use it." . . .

[He stopped for a moment, and tears moistened the weather-beaten cheek of the honest sailor.]

"I have obeyed her, and the more I use it

the more her dying words are impressed on my heart. When a child she taught me to repeat the simple hymn

> "'Holy Bible, book divine,
> Precious treasure, thou art mine!'

And her last words, as she blessed me and gave me this little treasure, were, 'Keep it, Charles; it is the book of comfort.'

* * * * *

"But I must get back, sir, to what I was talking about, or I shall never have done. I was saying that it was when we assembled at our evening duties we much so missed poor George, and that my uncle seemed to feel so deeply his loss. A letter however, which was received shortly after he left, told us that he was doing well, and we lived on in hopes that the prodigal, as the old man used to call him, would some day come back to his father's home! He did so, sir, but not as the prodigal. . . . Oh! it was a bad business altogether, sir, and I hardly know how to tell it!

"Many years passed away; my poor mother was laid in the grave, and trouble had worn my uncle down to a shadow of what he once was. Fond as he was of me, he could not forget his own son; and although it was only now and then we got any tidings of him, those tidings were not of the sort to make us happy.

"I had worked out my apprenticeship term, and was earning good wages at my trade, when one night I was unfortunate enough to fall into the hands of a press-gang, who soon transferred me to the decks of a king's ship lying off the coast. Resistance could do no good, so I made the best of a bad job, and having got leave for my things to be sent on board, I determined to do my duty in the situation in which God had placed me; and I have never had cause, sir, to repent doing so. After three years' service the ship was paid off, and in consideration of my good character I was allowed to go free.

"The first use I made of my liberty was, with my uncle's consent, to join my fortunes with those of my cousin Ellen. 'Twas a blessed day when it took place, and whilst, as we then thought, the only drawback to our happiness was that the prodigal had not yet come home, we had afterwards reason to curse the hour when he made his appearance.

"Eight years passed away, and except by an occasional line or two, which was never very satisfactory, we really knew nothing as to how George was going on. . . . . .

"I was the father of four healthy children, and it would have been a hard matter to find a more happy and contented home than ours;—the old man wanted but one thing to set his mind perfectly at rest, the presence of his son! Could he but have foreseen the . . . . but I'll tell it all in good time, sir . . . . 'twas a bad business. . . . .

"The first real trouble we knew was the death of three of our children by a fever which raged in the town, and which had well-nigh carried off the mother with them; but she had greater sorrows to suffer, such as the strongest could not have borne up under. She was always fond of her brother, and whenever, as a boy, he was found fault with, I can well remember even now how firmly she took his part . . . . little did she think, poor soul, that when grown up to manhood he would be, though unwillingly, the means of her death.

"You know, I dare say, sir, as well as I can tell you, that the little town of L—— has always been noted for the smuggling carried on; scarcely a week passed without something taking place connected with this business, and as most of the townspeople had a hand in it, 'twas no very easy birth for the revenue officers. Nothing was more common than to hear every now and then, in the middle of the night, firing of guns, and many a poor fellow has been lodged before morning in the gaol, who had been unluckily taken in the act of handing ashore some forbidden goods.

" I don't wish for a moment to defend smuggling,—it must be wrong to break any law,—but still I wish that law was changed, or something done so that there shouldn't be such a temptation to break it. . .

" The house in which we lived was close to the shore, and we had removed there but a few months before the dreadful event which broke up a happy family, and brought ruin, if not disgrace, on every member of it.

" It had been a wet and foggy day, and the same sort of dirty night followed it—such a night that we were glad to have a house to shelter us and a fire to warm us. We were sitting up, by almost a fatal chance, very much later than usual, and it was nearly midnight before we thought of leaving the cheerful fireside.

" My poor uncle had lately lost what to him was a large sum, which he had advanced to save a brother-workman from prison; and I well remember that our conversation was upon that subject, as to how the loss was to be made up. Many a plan was proposed one after another, but at last, having decided on one which appeared the most suitable, we were about to say 'Good night,' when the well-known, and to us almost familiar sound of fire-arms, told that mischief was abroad. The reports followed each other in such quick succession, that I at length opened the door for the purpose of learning, if possible, the reason of such a close attack.

Scarcely had I stood for a few minutes, and watched the lights which were moving to and fro on the shore, not more than a quarter of a mile from where I was, when a man hastily turned the corner of the street, and rushing past me into our cottage, tried to make fast the door, which he would have succeeded in doing but for my interference. A sudden scream, as you may well suppose, escaped from my wife at this unlooked for intrusion . . . and the scene which followed can never be forgotten! . . . 'tis more like a dream, sir, now that all is past . . . but such a dream . . . sleeping or waking . . . 'tis as fresh in my recollection as when it happened.

"No doubt with a view of frightening her into silence, though without any intention of carrying his threat into execution, the man levelled a pistol at my poor Ellen, and with a brutal oath exclaimed '——— be quiet! or by ——— this shall soon make you!' . . .

"My uncle, who had been almost stupified by the suddenness of the whole business, no sooner saw the act, and the raised pistol pointed at his child, than even before I could reach the spot, he sprang forward, and dashing it from the man's hand, thundered out, 'God's curse rest on you, villain! would you commit murder?'

* * * * *

"You should have seen, sir, what followed, ... I cannot tell it . . . . *the old man's voice did it all!* . . . .

"I must leave you to guess what happened, when I tell you that he from whose lips I had never before, on any occasion, heard a single oath,—who always reproved the sin in another, had in that moment of fearful excitement forgotten his duty to God, and *his first and last curse was pronounced on his long-lost son!*

* * * * *

"We had little time for explanation when once the recognition had taken place, so suddenly had everything come upon us, that we seemed deprived of the power of taking the most common and necessary precaution to save the poor fugitive who, by a strange providence (and His ways, sir, are often mysterious) had been led to seek shelter in his own home. His pursuers, though baffled for a time, were in close search after him; our's chanced to be the only house where a light was to be seen and voices heard, and scarcely had the lost one been recognised— and a hurried explanation given of his danger— when, '*in the king's name,*' the door was opened.

"The poor fellow had been too well noted in the affray to escape instant detection; all attempts to screen him were useless, and he whose return had been so long looked for, and so constantly prayed for, was taken from his father's house to pass the first night of his landing on his native shore within the walls of a prison! I won't attempt, sir, to speak of that wretched night;— 'twas enough to drive us all wild with despair. Much as my poor wife suffered—and her affliction was indeed great—what the aged father had to endure is known only to God. The curse seemed to ring in his ears, and the thought that he had uttered one on his first-born was more than he could bear.

"Morning brought no change with it. We tried to obtain the release of the unhappy prisoner, but, as you may suppose, without effect. .... The full tide of trouble was flowing, and it was of no use to try and make headway against it.

"In vain did the old man plead hard for his son on the trial which soon followed—in vain was every nerve strained to get him off—all his friends who came forward to help him could do nothing—the evidence was too strong to be shaken; two revenue officers had been killed in the fray, and though the murder could not be brought home to any one in particular, poor George had been most conspicuous—his previous wild life told against him, and at last, with two of his companions, he was found guilty, and sentenced to death, which was, however, afterwards changed to transportation for life!

* * * * *

"Poor fellow—he was spared the suffering of undergoing the full weight of the sentence: from whatever cause—he died before the convict ship sailed on her sad voyage; but I have every reason to hope that he lived long enough to repent of his sins, and ask pardon from God!

* * * * *

" His death was not the only consequence of George's crime ; those so nearly connected with him were doomed to feel more bitterly, and to suffer yet more severely. .... For months after I lived on in the hope that I at least should escape the blow which threatened to fall .... the hope was never realised .... and with a broken heart I soon laid in the last resting-place one whose loss can never be supplied. The shock she received from the sad changes had so shattered her, that reason soon failed, and never, but for one short hour before her death, did she recognise those around her—not even her husband or her child. .....

" I can't go on, sir ;—you know how the old man died .... thank God his troubles are over." . . , .

* * * * *

I saw that my guest was as unable as he might be unwilling to continue any longer; I therefore only made such simple inquiries as satisfied me how it happened that F—— N—— had become an inmate of the union with which I was connected. With these minor details I need not trouble the reader. The secret sorrow which disturbed the dying hour of the unhappy pauper was now explained—nor can we marvel that he shuddered at every expression from those around which in any measure recalled to his memory the sad recollection of his FIRST AND LAST OATH!

*

THE END.

LONDON:
G. J. PALMER, PRINTER, SAVOY STREET, STRAND.

SUBSCRIBERS.

Copies.

., Hon. Mrs , Upper Berkeley St., London   2

., Charles S. H., Esq., Upper Berkeley St., ιdon   1

orth, E., Esq., M.D., Cheltenham . . 1

ns, John, Esq., Cheltenham . . . 1

ns, Mrs. Robert, Holford . . . 1

, P. F., Esq., Clifton 1

son, S., Esq., Cheltenham . . . 2

age, J. L., Esq., Prestbury . . . 1

v, Rev. J., Ashchurch Rectory . . . 1

, Major, Worcester 1

ır, Rev. James, B.D , Twickenham . . 1

rd, Fulke T., Esq., Bristol . . . 3

rd, George T., Esq., Clifton . . . 1

rd, Thomas T., Esq., Bristol . . . 1

r, Rev. William, Cheltenham . . . 1

SUBSCRIBERS.

	Copies.
Bean, Lieutenant Colonel, Cheltenham	1
Beale, Thomas, Esq., Upton on Servon	3
Bernard, Lady Harriet, Cheltenham	2
Bernard, Lady Anne, Cheltenham	2
Benzie, Miss Charlotte., Cheltenham	1
Best, James, Esq. Worcester	1
Blayney, R., Esq., Evesham	1
Bowly, J. H., Esq., Cheltenham	1
Boyd, Rev. Archibald, Cheltenham	1
Briggs, Henry, Esq., Cheltenham	1
Broughton, Rev. Henry, Wellinborough Vicarage	1
Browne, Rev. John, Cheltenham	1
Bubb, John, Esq., Cheltenham	1
Buckle, William, Esq., Cheltenham	1
Cocks, Hon. and Rev. Somers, Worcester	1
Clifton, Rev. G. H., Ripple Rectory	1
Clarke, Miss C., Cheltenham	1
Cromie, Lady, Whitcombe	1
Capper, Robert, Esq., Cheltenham	2
Cheltenham, a Lady of	1
Clark, Rev. Joseph, London	1
Cole, Christopher, Esq., Cheltenham	1
Comyn, Stephen, Esq., M.D., Cheltenham	
Cooke, C. T., Esq., Cheltenham	1
Cooke, Charles James, Esq., Bristol	1
Corey, Rev. Charles, Alderton Rectory	2

SUBSCRIBERS.

Copies.

Corbett, C. Holland, Esq., Adminton House, Cambden	1
Cottle, Thomas, Esq., Cheltenham	1
Cosnaghan, Lieutenant, R.N., Cheltenham	1
Cousins, Mrs. Louis, Bristol	1
Coxwell, Rev. W. R., Dowdeswell Rectory	
Coxwell, Charles, R., Esq., Dowdeswell	1
Darell, Lady, Craycombe	1
Davies, Rev. C. G., Tewkesbury	1
Davies, Francis, Esq., Pershore	1
Dowdeswell, William, Esq., M.P., Pull Court	1
Eldon, Earl of, London	1
Exeter, Lord Bishop of, Bishopstowe	1
Egginton, Rev. J. C., Cheltenham	1
Elton, Rev. George, Worcester	1
Elwes, H. C., Esq., Spennells Court	1
Erskine, Rev. H. M., Forthampton	1
Evans, Charles, Esq., Worcester	1
Evans, W., Esq., Haverfordwest	1
Ford, Dowager Lady, Charlton Kings	1
Faussett, Rev. Bryan, Cropthorne	1
Feild, Rev. S. H., Gawcott Vicarage	1
Foley, Rev. E. W., Tewkesbury	1
Foley, Rev. John, Wadhurst Rectory	1

SUBSCRIBERS.

    Copies.

Fortescue, T., Esq., Cheltenham	1
Foxton, Rev. G. L., Worcester	1
Fowler, Charles, Esq., Cheltenham	1
Frampton, Edward, Esq., Cheltenham	1
Francis, H. Esq., Pershore	1
Gloucester and Bristol, Lord Bishop of,	1
Gardner, James Agg, Esq., Cheltenham	1
Garrow, Rev. E. W., Serenhampton	1
Grice, Rev. J. H., Upton on Severn	1
Griffiths, James, Esq., Haverfordwest	1
Gwinnett, W. H., Esq., Cheltenham	1
Haberfield, John Kerle, Esq., Bristol	1
Havergall, Rev. J., Worcester	1
Harris, W., Esq., Redruth, Cornwall	1
Hartland, N., Esq., Charlton Kings	1
Harvey, John, Esq., Haverfordwest	1
Hastings, Charles, Esq., M.D, Worcester	1
Hastings, Miss, Worcester	1
Hawkins, Rev. W., Cheltenham	2
Hemming, Rev. Benjamin, Pershore	1
Hicks, Rev. W., Cubberley Rectory	2
Hill, Rev. Francis, Kempsey	1
Hyde, John, Esq., Syndale House	1
Hyde, Colville, Esq., Trinity College, Cambridge	1
Hunt, Miss, Gateacre, Liverpool	1

SUBSCRIBERS.

                                              Copies.

	Copies
Jerrard, Rev. F. H., Long Stratton Rectory	1
Kendall, E. L., Esq., Cheltenham	1
Kent, Rev. A., Longdon	1
Keysall, Mrs., Cheltenham	1
Kingdom, J., Esq., Cheltenham	1
Kingdom, Mrs., Cheltenham	1
Kinsey, Rev. W. M., Greys Rectory, Oxon	2
Kington, Thomas, Esq., Clifton	2
Kirby, John, Esq., Bristol	1
Lyttleton, Lord, Hagley Park	1
Lace, Miss, Beaconfield, Liverpool	1
Lechmere, Rev. A. B., Hanley Vicarage	1
Lechmere, E. Hungerford, Esq., Great Malvern	1
Lingwood, R. S., Esq., Cheltenham	2
Madox, T., Esq., Haverfordwest	1
Malpas, Rev. Henry, Pershore	1
Matthews, Rev. H. C., Pershore	1
Maxwell, Mrs. Berkely, London	1
Milford, W. E., Esq., Truro, Cornwall	1
Monro, Frederick, Esq., Cheltenham	1
Morgan, William, Esq., Magdalen College, Oxon	1
Nightingal, Lady, London	1
Neumann, Rev. J. S., Hockliffe Rectory	1

SUBSCRIBERS.

Copies.

Newell, Rev. T. B., Cheltenham . . . 1
Newman, W. H., Esq., Gray's Inn, London . 1
Nuttall, Robert, Esq., Kempsey . . . 2

Oliver, Mrs., Hereford 1
Owen, Titus, Esq., Cheltenham . . . 1

Parker, Rev. William, Little Comberton . . 1
Parry, George, Esq., Haverfordwest . . . 1
Phillips, Rev. Dr., Worcester 1
Philllips, John, Esq., Haverfordwest . . 1
Phillips, George, Esq., Haverfordwest . . 1
Powell, J. Rogers, Esq., Haverfordwest . . 1
Pugh, Miss M. E., Haverfordwest . . . 1

Rees, Miss, 5, York Place, Clifton . . . 1
Robinson, Rev. C. W., Leominster . . . 1
Roughton, Mrs., Cheltenham 1
Russell, Miss Eliza, Litley Court, Herefordshire 1

Savage, Rev. J. A., Cheltenham . . . 1
Sculthorpe, Mrs., Senior, Beoley Vicarage . . 1
Shirley, Henry, Esq., Cracombe . . . 1
Shirley, Mrs., Cracombe 1
Stevenson, Rev. H. J., Hallow Vicarage . . 1
Strachan, J. G., Esq., Cheltenham . . . 1
Strode, Lieut. Col., The Heath, Upton on Severn 1

SUBSCRIBERS.

	Copies.
Strode, Miss, The Heath, Upton on Severn	1
Strickland, Jacob, Esq., Bristol	3
St. John, Rev. George, Worcester	1
Tenisson, Mrs., Cheltenham	1
Tennant, William, Esq., Ham Court, Upton on Severn	1
Tennant, Miss, Ham Court, Upton on Severn	1
Thomas, Mrs., White Ladies, Worcester	1
Thornhill, Mrs., Cheltenham	1
Thorpe, Venerable Archdeacon, Kemerton Rectory	1
Tombs, Rev. J., Huddersfield	1
Tombs, Joseph, Esq., Haverfordwest	1
Trye, Rev. C. B., Leckhampton, Cheltenham	1
Trye, Rev. J. R., Whitcombe Rectory	1
Turnbull, Rev. J. C., Cheltenham	1
Turner, J. H., Esq., Gray's Inn, London	1
Vivian, Quintus, Esq., Knaston Hall, Wellingboro'	1
Worcester, Lord Bishop of	1
Worcester, Very Rev. Dean of	3
Ward, Arthur, Esq., Tunbridge Wells	1
Ward, Neville, Esq., Tunbridge Wells	2
Wathen, James, Esq., Stanley Park, Stroud	1
Wathen, Miss, Stanley Park	1

SUBSCRIBERS.

	Copies.
Watkins, Mrs., Worcester	1
Webster, James, Esq., Hatherley Court	1
Welch, G. H., Esq., Arle Court	1
Whinyates, Misses	1
Whitehead, Rev. H. C., Ramsgate	1
Wilkinson, Joseph, Esq., Cheltenham	1
Williamson, Arthur, Esq., London	1
Wolseley, Rev. Sir R., Baronet	1
Woodhouse, J. G., Esq., Leominster	1
Woods, S., Esq., Liverpool	1
Woodyatt, Rev. Edward, Cheltenham	3
Woodyatt, Mrs. E., Cheltenham	1
Woodyatt, Lieutenant George, Cheltenham	1
Woodyatt, E., Esq., Portishead	1

WORKS

PUBLISHED BY

J. HATCHARD AND SON.

ADAM, REV. T.—AN EXPOSITION of the FOUR GOSPELS, of which the Notes on those by St. MARK, St. LUKE, and St. JOHN, have never before been published. By the late Rev. THOMAS ADAM, B.A. Rector of Wintringham; Author of "Private Thoughts on Religion," &c. With a MEMOIR of the AUTHOR. 2 vols. 8vo. cloth, 12s. published originally at 1l. 1s.

"Perhaps few were better fitted to write a practical and experimental commentary on any part of the Scriptures than this author, whose pregnant briefness of remark, and deep acquaintance with experimental religion, would preserve him from prolixity, and enable him to present the most useful view of the subject to the mind. The present posthumous work will be found characterised by all the best peculiarities of the author."—*Record*.

ALLEN, REV. I. N.—A DIARY of a MARCH through SCINDE, and AFFGHANISTAN, with the troops under the Command of General Sir W. Nott, &c., during the Campaign of 1842. By the Rev. I. N. ALLEN, Assistant Chaplain to the Hon. E. I. Company's Bombay Establishment. Post 8vo. cloth, with several Illustrations, 12s.

"That portion of the war of which the author treats has been hitherto almost untouched."—*Asiatic Journal*.

"Everything interesting the author examined with attention; and the account he has given of the proceedings of the army, the manners, customs, and mode of warfare of the Affghans, will be read with pleasure and with profit; and we recommend Mr. Allen's book to all who feel an interest in the country."—*Times*.

ANDERSON, REV. R.—A PRACTICAL EXPOSITION of the GOSPEL of ST. JOHN. By the late Rev. ROBERT ANDERSON, Perpetual Curate of Trinity Chapel, Brighton; and Chaplain to the Right Hon. Lord Teignmouth. 2 vols. 12mo. cloth. 14s.

" Written in that humble and reverential spirit, which can hardly fail to please and to improve the reader."—*British Critic.*
" A work admirably adapted for Family Reading."—*Christian Remembrancer.*

— A PASTORAL ADDRESS on REGENERATION; and POSTSCRIPT. Fcap. cloth, 1s. 6d.

— TEN DISCOURSES on the COMMUNION OFFICE of the CHURCH of ENGLAND. With an APPENDIX. Second Edition. 12mo. cloth, 7s.

— THE BOOK of COMMON PRAYER, a Manual of Christian Fellowship. Second Edition, with a Pastoral Letter written in 1842. Fcap. cloth, 1s. 6d.

ANLEY, MISS C.—INFLUENCE. A Moral Tale for Young People. By CHARLOTTE ANLEY. Fourth Edition, fcap. cloth, 6s.

— MIRIAM; or, the Power of Truth. A Jewish Tale. Eighth Edition, fcap. cloth, 6s.

— THE PRISONERS of AUSTRALIA. A Narrative. Fcap. cloth, 3s. 6d.

— ESSAY on the DISTINCTION between BODY, SOUL, and SPIRIT. 32mo. cloth, 8d.

ATKINS, REV. H.—A SERIES of THEOLOGICAL LECTURES, delivered in the Cathedral Church of Chichester, during Lent. In the years 1835, 36, 37, 38, 39, 40, 41. By the late Rev. HENRY ATKINS, M.A., Prebendary of Wightering. 12mo. cloth, 7s.

" Very pleasing, scriptural, and profitable."—*Churchman's Monthly Review.*

" The knowledge displayed in these Lectures, the justness of reasoning, the excellence of the style, and its suitableness to the subjects, are alike worthy of the high fame which Mr. Atkins enjoyed as a scholar and a divine."—*Gentleman's Magazine.*

BABINGTON, T.—A PRACTICAL VIEW of CHRISTIAN EDUCATION in its EARLY STAGES. By THOMAS BABINGTON, Esq. Ninth Edition. fcap. cloth, 5s.

BATEMAN, REV. J.—WHY do you BELIEVE the BIBLE to be the WORD of GOD? By JOSIAH BATEMAN, M.A., Vicar of Huddersfield. Second Edition. 12mo. cloth, 4s.

— SERMONS PREACHED in INDIA. 12mo. cloth, 5s.

BATHER, ARCHDEACON.—SERMONS, CHIEFLY PRACTICAL. By EDWARD BATHER, M.A., Archdeacon of Salop. 3 vols. 8vo., boards, each 12s.

BAXTER, REV. J. A.—THE CHURCH HISTORY of ENGLAND. By the Rev. JOHN A. BAXTER, M.A., Perpetual Curate of Christ Church, Coseley, Staffordshire. Dedicated by permission to the Right Rev. the Lord Bishop of Lichfield. 2 vols. post 8vo. cloth, 16s.

BEST, HON. & REV. S.—PAROCHIAL SERMONS. By the Hon. and Rev. SAMUEL BEST, A.M., Rector of Abbots Ann, Hants. 12mo. boards, 3s. 6d.

— PAROCHIAL MINISTRATIONS. 12mo. cloth, 3s. 6d.

BEVAN, REV. D. B.—FOOD for BABES; or, the First Sermons that very Little Children are able to Understand. By the Rev. D. BARCLAY BEVAN, M.A., Rector of Burton Latimer. Second Edition, revised and corrected. 18mo. cloth, 3s.

BIBLE STORIES, selected from the Old and New Testament, familiarised for the Use of Children; in Portions. By the Author of "Questions on the Epistles," &c. Third Edition. 2 vols. 18mo. half-bound. each 2s. 6d.

BIDDULPH, REV. T.—THE YOUNG CHURCHMAN ARMED. A Catechism for Junior Members of the Church of England. By the late Rev. THEOPHILUS BIDDULPH, A.M. Minister of St. Matthew's, Bristol. 18mo. cloth, 1s.

BIDDULPH, REV. T. T.—PRACTICAL ESSAYS on the MORNING and EVENING SERVICES, and on the Collects in the Liturgy of the Church of England. By the late Rev. THOMAS T. BIDDULPH, M.A. Minister of St. James's, Bristol. Third Edition. 3 vols. 8vo. boards, 1l. 7s.

BIRD, REV. C. S.—THE PARABLE of the SOWER. Four Sermons preached before the University of Cambridge. in the Month of May, 1845. By the Rev. CHARLES SMITH BIRD, M.A., F.L.S., Prebendary of Lincoln, and late Fellow of Trinity College, Cambridge. Fcap. cloth, 3s. 6d.

"This is a valuable exposition of one of our richest parables, and takes so wide a range in its discussions of great principles, viewed in their practical and experimental bearings, that we can most cordially recommend it for general circulation."—*Churchman's Monthly Review.*

BISSLAND, REV. T.—SERMONS. Preached in St. Paul's Chapel, Winchmore Hill. By the late Rev. THOMAS BISSLAND, A.M., of Balliol College, Oxon, Rector of Hartley Maudytt, Hants, and Chaplain to the Right Hon. Lord Bexley. 8vo. boards, 10s. 6d.

— THE PREACHING of the CROSS the effectual Means for the Conversion of the Sinner, and the Stability of the Church. 12mo. cloth, 3s. 6d.

BLACKLEY, REV. W.—EXPOSITORY LECTURES on the FIRST FOUR CHAPTERS of ST. MATTHEW'S GOSPEL. With One on Chapter v. 21—26. By the Rev. W. BLACKLEY, B.A., formerly of St. John's College, Cambridge, Author of "Brief Review of Baptismal Obligation." 12mo. cloth, 5s. 6d.

BLOMFIELD, REV. G. B.—SERMONS ADAPTED to COUNTRY CONGREGATIONS. By the Rev. GEORGE BECHER BLOMFIELD, A.M., Rector of Stevenage, Herts, and Canon of Chester. 2 vols. 12mo. cloth, each 5s.

BLUNT, REV. H.—POSTHUMOUS SERMONS. By the late Rev. HENRY BLUNT, M.A., Rector of Streatham, Surrey. Second Edition, 3 vols 12mo. cloth, each 6s.

— A FAMILY EXPOSITION of the PENTATEUCH. Second Edition, 3 vols. 12mo. cloth, each 6s.

— NINE LECTURES upon the HISTORY of SAINT PETER. Sixteenth Edition. 12mo. cloth. 4s. 6d.

— EIGHT LECTURES on the HISTORY of JACOB. Sixteenth Edition. 12mo. cloth, 4s. 6d.

— TWELVE LECTURES on the HISTORY of ABRAHAM. Eleventh Edition. 12mo. cloth, 5s 6d.

— LECTURES on the HISTORY of SAINT PAUL. Tenth Edition. 2 Parts. 12mo. cloth, each 5s. 6d.

— LECTURES on the HISTORY of our LORD and SAVIOUR JESUS CHRIST. Tenth Edition. 3 Parts. 12mo. cloth, each 5s. 6d.

— DISCOURSES upon some of the DOCTRINAL ARTICLES of the CHURCH of ENGLAND. Eighth Edition. 12mo. cloth, 5s. 6d.

— SERMONS preached in TRINITY CHURCH, CHELSEA. Fifth Edition. 12mo. cloth, 6s.

— A PRACTICAL EXPOSITION of the EPISTLES to the SEVEN CHURCHES of ASIA. Third Edition. 12mo. cloth, 5s. 6d.

— LECTURES on the HISTORY of ELISHA. Fourth Edition. 12mo. cloth, 5s. 6d.

— TWO DISCOURSES upon the TRIAL of the SPIRITS. Seventh Edition. 12mo. sewed, 1s. 6d.

— TWO DISCOURSES upon the SACRAMENT of the LORD'S SUPPER. Eighth Edition. 12mo. sewed, 1s.

— A SERMON on the LORD'S DAY. Sixth Edition. 12mo. sewed, 6d.

BOSANQUET, S. R.—VESTIGES of the NATURAL HISTORY of Creation. Its Argument examined and Exposed. By S. R. BOSANQUET, Esq. Second Edition. Post 8vo. cloth, 2s. 6d.

BRADLEY, REV. C.—SERMONS, preached chiefly at the Celebration of the Lord's Supper. By the Rev. CHARLES BRADLEY, Vicar of Glasbury, Brecknockshire, and Minister of St. James's Chapel, Clapham, Surrey. Second Edition. 8vo. cloth, 10s. 6d.

— PRACTICAL SERMONS for every Sunday and Principal Holy-Day in the Year. Complete in Two Volumes. Second Edition. 8vo. cloth, 1l 1s.

N.B. The Third Volume can be had in post 8vo. price 8s. to complete the early edition.

— SERMONS preached in the Parish Church of Glasbury, Brecknockshire. Eighth Edition. 8vo. cloth, 10s. 6d.

— SERMONS preached at St. James's Chapel, Clapham, Surrey, Sixth Edition. 8vo. cloth, 10s. 6d.

— SERMONS, preached in the Parish Church of High Wycombe, Bucks. Eleventh Edition. 2 vols. 8vo. cloth, 21s.

BRENTON, SIR J.—A MEMOIR OF VICE-ADMIRAL SIR J. BRENTON, Bart. & K.C B. chiefly drawn from Original Notes, arranged and published by the Rev. H. RAIKES, Chancellor of Chester. 8vo. cloth.

BROWNE, REV. J.—SERMONS, preached in the Church of the Holy Trinity, Cheltenham. By the Rev. JOHN BROWNE, LL.B., Curate. 8vo. boards, 12s.

BUDDICOM, REV. R. P.—THE CHRISTIAN EXODUS; or, the Deliverance of the Israelites from Egypt Practically Considered, in a series of Discourses. By the late Rev. R. P. BUDDICOM, M.A., F.A.S., Incumbent of St. George's Church, Everton, and formerly Fellow of Queen's College, Cambridge. Second Edition. 2 vols. 12mo cloth, 14s.

BUNYAN, J.—THE PILGRIM'S PROGRESS. In Two Parts. By JOHN BUNYAN. With Original Notes by the Rev. THOMAS SCOTT. Sixth Edition. 12mo. cloth, 5s.

BURTT, C.—EXEMPLA NECESSARIA; or, Elementary Latin Exercises on all the Parts of Speech; and the Substance of Syntax; containing English Words and Sentences to be turned into Latin, Latin into English, and numerous Examination Questions to be entered on with the Accidence. With an Introduction. Short Rules are also given to assist in reading Latin correctly, for the position of words in a sentence, and for construing. Intended for young persons just beginning, for those not well grounded in grammar, and those who begin late in life. By C. BURTT, Teacher of Latin, &c. Third Edition, much enlarged. 18mo. cloth, 2s. 6d.

BUTTERTON, REV. DR.—PAROCHIAL SERMONS on VARIOUS SUBJECTS. By the Rev. GEORGE ASH BUTTERTON, D.D., Head Master of the Royal Free Grammar School of Giggleswick, Yorkshire, late Head Master of Uppingham School, and formerly Head Master of St. John's College, Cambridge. 8vo. cloth, 7s. 6d.

CALCUTTA, BISHOP OF—EXPOSITORY LECTURES on ST. PAUL'S EPISTLE to the COLOSSIANS. In which the Apostle's argument respecting the Errors on the subject of the Mediation of Christ prevailing at Colosse, is applied to the present circumstances of our Protestant Church. By The Right Reverend DANIEL WILSON, D.D., Bishop of Calcutta, and Metropolitan of India. Second Edition, Revised and Corrected. Foolscap, cloth, 6s.

"It would not be easy to say how highly we value this short and effective commentary upon an epistle, which was evidently intended to bear on those corruptions now rapidly spreading amongst us. We receive it with thankfulness."—*Churchman's Monthly Review.*

— THE SUFFICIENCY of HOLY SCRIPTURE as the RULE of FAITH; being a Sermon delivered at the Cathedral Church of St. John, Calcutta, at an Ordination holden on Sunday, May 2, 1841. Second Edition. 12mo. sewed, 9d.

— SERMONS delivered in India. 8vo. cloth, 12s.

— THE EVIDENCES of CHRISTIANITY, in a Course of Lectures delivered in the Parish Church of St. Mary, Islington, containing the Lectures on the Authenticity, Credibility, Divine Authority, and Inspiration of the Holy Scriptures. Fourth Edition. 2 vols. 12mo. cloth, 9s.

— THE DIVINE AUTHORITY and PERPETUAL OBLIGATION of the LORD'S DAY asserted in Seven Sermons. Third Edition. 12mo. cloth, 3s. 6d.

— SERMONS on VARIOUS SUBJECTS of CHRISTIAN DOCTRINE and PRACTICE. Sixth Edition. 8vo bds. 12s., or 12mo. 5s.

— A PLAIN and AFFECTIONATE ADDRESS to Young Persons about to be CONFIRMED. Nineteenth Edition. 12mo. sewed, 4d.

— A PLAIN and AFFECTIONATE ADDRESS to Young Persons previously to Receiving the LORD'S SUPPER. Twelfth Edition. 12mo. sewed, 4d.

CARDALL, REV. W.—SERMONS, Preached in the Parish Church of Lancaster. By the Rev. WILLIAM CARDALL, B.A. 8vo. cloth, 8s.

CHESTER, BISHOP OF—A PRACTICAL EXPOSITION of the GOSPELS of ST. MATTHEW and ST. MARK, in the form of Lectures, intended to assist the practice of domestic instruction and devotion. By JOHN BIRD SUMNER, D.D., Lord Bishop of Chester. Sixth Edition. 1 vol. 8vo., or 2 vols. 12mo., cloth, 9s.

— A PRACTICAL EXPOSITION of the GOSPEL of ST. LUKE, in the form of Lectures. Third Edition. 1 vol. 8vo., or 2 vols. 12mo. cloth, 9s.

— A PRACTICAL EXPOSITION of the GOSPEL of ST. JOHN, in the form of Lectures. Third Edition. 1 vol. 8vo., or 2 vols. 12mo., cloth, 9s.

— A PRACTICAL EXPOSITION of the ACTS of the APOSTLES, in the form of Lectures. 1 vol. 8vo., or 2 vols. 12mo. cloth, 9s.

— A PRACTICAL EXPOSITION of the EPISTLE of ST. PAUL to the ROMANS, and the FIRST EPISTLE to the CORINTHIANS, in the form of Lectures. 1 vol. 8vo., or 2 vols. 12mo., cloth, 9s.

— A PRACTICAL EXPOSITION of ST. PAUL'S SECOND EPISTLE to the CORINTHIANS, and the EPISTLES to the GALATIANS, EPHESIANS, PHILIPPIANS, and COLOSSIANS; in the form of Lectures. 1 vol. 8vo., or 2 vols. 12mo., cloth, 9s.

— A PRACTICAL EXPOSITION of the GENERAL EPISTLES of JAMES, PETER, JOHN, and JUDE, in the form of Lectures. 1 vol. 8vo., or 2 vols. 12mo., cloth, 9s.

— CHRISTIAN CHARITY; its Obligations and Objects, with reference to the present state of Society. IN A SERIES OF SERMONS. Second Edition. 8vo. cloth, 9s., or 12mo., 6s.

— APOSTOLICAL PREACHING CONSIDERED, in an Examination of St. Paul's Epistles. Also, Four Sermons on Subjects relating to the Christian Ministry, and preached on different occasions. Eighth Edition, enlarged, 8vo. cloth, 10s. 6d.

— SERMONS on the PRINCIPAL FESTIVALS of the CHRISTIAN CHURCH: to which are added, Three Sermons on Good Friday. Fifth Edition, 8vo. cloth, 10s. 6d.

CHESTER, BISHOP OF.

— THE EVIDENCES of CHRISTIANITY, derived from its NATURE and RECEPTION. Sixth Edition, 8vo., cloth, 10s. 6d.; or 12mo. 6s.

— A SERIES of SERMONS on the CHRISTIAN FAITH and CHARACTER. Eighth Edition, 8vo. cloth, 10s. 6d.; or 12mo. cloth, 6s.

— A TREATISE on the RECORDS of the CREATION, and on the MORAL ATTRIBUTES of the CREATOR. Fifth Edition. 2 vols. 8vo. cloth, 1l. 1s.

— SIX CHARGES delivered to the CLERGY of the Diocese of CHESTER, at the Triennial Visitations in 1829, 1832, 1835, 1838, 1841, and 1844. 8vo. cloth, 7s.

THE CHILD'S VISION; or, the ANGEL and the OAK. By the Author of the "Priestess." Square 12mo. cloth extra 3s. 6d.

CHRISTIAN SYMPATHY; a Collection of Letters addressed to Mourners. 32mo. cloth, gilt edges, 2s. 6d.

CHRISTMAS IMPROVEMENT; or, Hunting Mrs. P. A Tale, founded on Facts. Intended as a Christmas Box for those who wish to begin the New Year without Her. Third Edition, 18mo. cloth, 2s. 6d.

CHRIST OUR EXAMPLE. By the author of "The Listener." Seventh Edition. Foolscap, cloth, 6s.

CONTENTS.

1. In the Object of Life.
2. In the Rule of Life.
3. In his Intercourse with the World.
4. In the Condition of Life.
5. In his Sorrows.
6. In his Joys.
7. In his Death.

CHRISTIAN OBSERVER, conducted by Members of the Established Church, from 1802 to 1846; and continued monthly, 1s. 6d.

CLARK, REV. F. F.—PLAIN SERMONS to COUNTRY CONGREGATIONS. By Francis Foreman Clark, A.B., Head Master of the Grammar School, Newcastle-under-Lyne, and late Minister of Christ Church, Chorley. 12mo. cloth, 6s.

CLARK, MRS. T.—THE COUNTRY PARSON'S WIFE. Being intended as a Continuation of, and Companion to, "Herbert's Country Parson." By Mrs. Thomas Clark, of East Bergholt, (late Louisa Lane.) Fcap. cloth, 2s. 6d.

CLOSE, REV. F.—CHURCH ARCHITECTURE SCRIPTURALLY CONSIDERED, from the Earliest Ages to the Present Time. By the Rev. F. CLOSE, A M., Perpetual Curate of Cheltenham. 12mo. cloth, 3s. 6d.

— FIFTY-TWO SKETCHES of SERMONS on MISCELLANEOUS SUBJECTS. 8vo. cloth, 6s.

— MISCELLANEOUS SERMONS. Preached at Cheltenham. Second Edition. 2 vols. 8vo. bds. each 12s.

— A COURSE of NINE SERMONS, intended to Illustrate some of the Leading Truths contained in the Liturgy of the Church of England. Preached in the Church of the Holy Trinity, Cheltenham, in the year 1825. Seventh Edition, 12mo. cloth, 5s.

— THE CATHOLIC DOCTRINE OF THE SECOND ADVENT of our Lord and Saviour Jesus Chris., considered in a course of Four Sermons, preached in the Parish Church, Cheltenham, in the season of Advent, 1845. 12mo cloth, 2s. 6d.

COMPANION to the BOOK of COMMON PRAYER, of the United Church of England and Ireland.

CONTAINING,
1. Subjects of Meditation for every Sunday throughout the year.
2. Texts of Scripture to be committed to memory.
3. Reading Lessons for every Sunday morning and evening.
4. A Catechism on a new plan.

24mo. cloth, 2s.

CONFIDENCE in GOD the ONLY TRUE REST for the SOUL, and REFUGE in these ALARMING TIMES. Fcap. bds. 5s.

CONSISTENCY. By CHARLOTTE ELIZABETH. Fifth Edition. 18mo. boards, 2s. 6d.

CONVERSATION on the ADVANCE WE HAVE MADE in CHRISTIAN CHARITY; or, Why is it not Enough for a Man to be Sincere? 18mo. cloth, 1s.

COOKESLEY, REV. W. G.—SERMONS. By the Rev. WILLIAM GIFFORD COOKESLEY, M.A., Assistant Master of Eton College. 2 vols. 12mo. cloth, each 5s.

"Sound and moderate in doctrine, earnest in their exhortations, and well suited for the purposes of family and domestic worship."—*Church and State Gazette.*

"These Sermons are eminently suited to the sober temper and practical objects of family worship, as they never, in developing the Gospel dispensation, forget the important place assigned in it to the faithful discharge of temporal duties."—*Britannia.*

CRAIG, REV. E.—BRIEF HINTS to CANDIDATES for HOLY ORDERS. By the Rev. EDWARD CRAIG, Curate of Burton Latimer. Fcap. cloth, 3s.

Contents:— Choosing the Profession—Preparatory Study—Reading for Holy Orders—The Formularies—Composition — Sermon-Making—Preaching—Reading—Schools—Visiting—Dissent—Popery—Consistency, &c.

CRUDEN, A.—A COMPLETE CONCORDANCE to the HOLY SCRIPTURES of the OLD and NEW TESTAMENT; or, A DICTIONARY AND ALPHABETICAL INDEX TO THE BIBLE. In Two Parts. To which is added, A CONCORDANCE TO THE APOCRYPHA. By ALEXANDER CRUDEN, M.A. The Ninth Edition. To which is added, a Life of the Author, by ALEXANDER CHALMERS, F.S.A. 4to. boards, 1l. 1s.

CUNNINGHAM, REV. J. W.—SERMONS. By the Rev. J. W. CUNNINGHAM, A.M., Vicar of Harrow, and late Fellow of St. John's College, Cambridge. Fifth Edition. 2 vols. 8vo. bds. 1l. 1s.

— A WORLD WITHOUT SOULS. Fourth Edition. 12mo. cloth, 5s.

— SIX LECTURES on the BOOK of JONAH. Fcap. bds. 3s.

— MORNING THOUGHTS, in PROSE and VERSE, on Portions of the Successive Chapters in the Gospel of St. Mark. Third Edition. Fcap. bds 2s. 6d.

— THE VELVET CUSHION. Eleventh Edition. Fcap. bds. 5s.

DAILY READINGS. Passages of Scripture selected for Social Reading, with Applications. By the Author of "The Listener," "Christ our Example," &c. Second Edition. 12mo. cloth, 6s.

DAUTREY.—THE BIBLE in PALESTINE; or, Hints from Scripture by which to determine the localities of the Crucifixion, the Transfiguration, and other great events of our Saviour's Life. Together with Notes of a Tour through the Holy Land, during the Summer of 1843. By Mr. and Mrs. DAUTREY. 12mo. cloth, 8s.

DEALTRY, REV. DR.—SERMONS, CHIEFLY PRACTICAL, Preached in the Parish Church of Clapham, Surrey. By WILLIAM DEALTRY, D.D., F.R.S., Rector of Clapham, and Chancellor of Winchester. Second Edition, 8vo. boards, 10s. 6d.

DEBRETT—COMPLETE PEERAGE of the UNITED KINGDOM of GREAT BRITAIN and IRELAND. A New Edition, arranged alphabetically. Edited by WILLIAM COURTHOPE, Esq. 8vo. half-bound, 1l. 10s.

— BARONETAGE of ENGLAND. Seventh Edition, with Additions. Edited by WILLIAM COURTHOPE, Esq. With a New Set of Arms. 8vo. half-bound, 1l. 8s.

DIMOCK, REV. J. F.—THE THIRTY-NINE ARTICLES of the CHURCH of ENGLAND, Explained, Proved, and Compared with her other Authorized Formularies, the Homilies and Liturgy, in a Plain and Popular Manner. By JAMES F. DIMOCK, M.A., Curate of Stilton, Huntingdonshire. 2 vols. 8vo. boards, 15s.

DRUMMOND, H.—SOCIAL DUTIES on CHRISTIAN PRINCIPLES. By HENRY DRUMMOND. Fifth Edition. Fcap. cloth, 4s.

DRUMMOND, REV. S. R.—ELEMENTS of the CHRISTIAN RELIGION; being Sketches of Sermons preached at St. John's, Brighton. By the Rev. SPENCER RODNEY DRUMMOND, M.A., Perpetual Curate of St. John's, Chaplain to Lord Viscount Melville. Fcap. cloth, 2s. 6d.

EIGHTEEN MAXIMS of NEATNESS and ORDER. To which is prefixed an Introduction by THERESA TIDY.

"For want of a nail, the shoe was lost;
For want of a shoe, the horse was lost;
For want of a horse, the rider was lost,
(Being overtaken and slain by the enemy,)
And all for want of care about a horse-shoe nail."
Poor Richard.

Twenty-fourth Edition. 18mo. sewed, 6d.

EDELMAN, REV. W.—SERMONS on the HISTORY of JOSEPH. Preached in the Parish Church of St. Mary, Wimbledon. By the Rev. W. EDELMAN, late Curate of Wimbledon. 12mo. cloth, 5s.

EDWARDS, REV. E.—TWENTY-ONE PLAIN SERMONS, DOCTRINAL and PRACTICAL. Originally preached before a Country Congregation. By the Rev. E. EDWARDS, Perpetual Curate of Marsden, in the Diocese of Ripon. 12mo. cloth, 6s.

"To Mr. Edwards's Sermons we invite the public attention: they realise our notion of practical Sermons."—*Church of England Quarterly Review.*

ELWIN, REV. F.—A VOLUME of SERMONS. Preached at the Octagon Chapel, Bath, and printed at the request of the Congregation. By the Rev. FOUNTAIN ELWIN, Vicar of Temple, Bristol, and one of the Ministers of the Octagon. 12mo. cloth, 5s.

— SEVEN SERMONS on the CHARACTER of GIDEON. Preached at the Temple Church, Bristol, and at the Octagon Chapel, Bath. Second Edition, 12mo. cloth, 4s.

THE FAMILY PASTOR; or, Short Sermons for Family Reading. By a Clergyman of the Church of England. 12mo. cloth, 3s. 6d.

FINCHER, J.—THE ACHIEVEMENTS of PRAYER, Selected exclusively from the Holy Scriptures. By JOSEPH FINCHER, Esq. With a Testimony to the Work by James Montgomery, Esq. of Sheffield. Third Edition. 12mo. cloth, 6s.

— THE INTERPOSITION of DIVINE PROVIDENCE. Selected exclusively from the Holy Scriptures. 12mo. cloth, 6s.

FLETCHER, W. E.—THE CHILD'S GUIDE THROUGH the BIBLE; or, a Help to understand the Bible, as the Record of God's Plans for Teaching Men Religion. By W. EVANS FLETCHER, B.A. Fcap. cloth, 4s.

FORTY FAMILY SERMONS. By the Editor of the "Christian Observer." Dedicated, by permission, to the Bishops of Winchester and Chester 8vo. cloth, 12s.

FUTURE DAYS. A Series of Letters to my Pupils. Intended as a Present for Young Ladies leaving School. 12mo. cloth, 5s.

Among the contents will be found:—Content and Occupation—Mental Cultivation—Conversation—Marriage—Wives of Celebrated Men—Training the Young—Servants—A Sketch—Liberality—The Christian's Hope—Biographical Notices.

"The tone is unexceptionable, and the morality inculcated not of too impracticable a character."—*Spectator*.

GARBETT, REV. J.—PAROCHIAL SERMONS. By the Rev. J. GARBETT, Rector of Clayton, Sussex, and Professor of Poetry in the University of Oxford. 2 vols. 8vo. cloth, each, 12s.

"These volumes form an excellent addition to our stock of standard works on Christian faith and practice. For private study or household reading, they are the best that have fallen under our view."—*Britannia*.

— CHRIST as PROPHET, PRIEST, and KING; being a Vindication of the Church of England from Theological Novelties, in Eight Lectures, preached before the University of Oxford, at Canon Bampton's Lecture, 1842. 2 vols. 8vo. cloth, 1*l*. 4s.

"An able, learned, and valuable publication, the fruits of many years' study and reflection."—*Christian Observer*.

"We have read these volumes with interest, and we hope with edification. We regard them as very valuable, on the grounds of their intrinsic merit."—*Churchman's Monthly Review*.

— A REVIEW of Dr. PUSEY'S SERMON; and the Doctrine of the Eucharist, according to the Church of England. 8vo. sewed, 6s.

GARDNER, J.—THE GREAT PHYSICIAN; or, an Attempt to trace the Connection of Diseases and Remedies with the Truths of Revelation. By JOHN GARDNER, M.D., Editor of "Liebig's Letters on Chemistry." 8vo. cloth, 10s. 6d.

"The work before us displays learning and ability."—*Morning Chronicle*.

"This work, 'The Great Physician,' is evidently the production of a clear-thinking head and a sound heart; the subject, a new and most interesting one. * * I am no critic; I only know when I myself am pleased, and I can only say, that, without giving an unqualified assent to some of the positions, the work, as a whole, has interested me much."—*Author of the Christian Gentleman's Daily Walk*.

GIBBON, E.—THE HISTORY of the DECLINE and FALL of the ROMAN EMPIRE. By EDWARD GIBBON, Esq. New Edition. 8 vols. 8vo. cloth, 3*l*.

THE GIPSIES. Dedicated, by permission, to James Crabb, the Gipsies' Friend. Fcap. cloth, 4s. 6d.

GOODE, REV. F.—A NEW VOLUME of SERMONS. By the late Rev. FRANCIS GOODE, Lecturer at Clapham. 8vo. cloth, 10s. 6d.

— THE BETTER COVENANT PRACTICALLY CONSIDERED, from Hebrews viii. 6, 10—12; with a SUPPLEMENT on Philippians ii. 12, 13. Fourth Edition. 8vo. boards, 10s. 6d.

GOODE, REV. W.—TWO TREATISES on the CHURCH. By DR. T. JACKSON and BISHOP SANDERSON; with a Letter of Bishop Cosin, on the Orders of the Foreign Reformed Churches. Edited, with Introductory Remarks, by WILLIAM GOODE, M.A., Rector of St. Antholin. Fcap. cloth, 5s.

— MODERN CLAIMS to the GIFTS of the SPIRIT, Stated and Examined. With Appendix. Second Edition. 8vo. bds. 10s. 6d.

— TRACTS on CHURCH RATES. 8vo. bds. 7s. 6d.

— THE CASE AS IT IS; or, a Reply to Dr. Pusey's Letter to the Archbishop of Canterbury; including a Compendious Statement of the Doctrines and Views of the Tractators as expressed by themselves. Third Edition. 8vo. sewed, 1s.

— ALTARS PROHIBITED by the CHURCH of ENGLAND. 2 Parts in 1. 8vo. sewed, 2s. 6d.

— A LETTER to a LAY FRIEND, in Answer to Inquiries respecting the State of Things in the Church, and the Course which the Present Crisis demands from those who tender its Welfare. Second Edition, enlarged. 8vo. sewed, 1s.

— TRACT 90 HISTORICALLY REFUTED; or, a Reply to a Work by the Rev. F. Oakeley, entitled, "The Subject of Tract 90 Historically Examined." 8vo. sewed, 5s.

THE GOSPELS COLLATED. Presenting in one view the Concurrent Testimony of the Evangelists. By a BARRISTER of Lincoln's Inn. Royal 8vo. cloth, 1*l*. 1s.

"We feel it our duty to give this volume our warmest recommendation."—*Oxford Herald.*

GOULD, MISS H.—THE GRAHAME FAMILY; or, Historical Portfolio Opened. By Miss HUSSEY GOULD. With Woodcuts. Fcap. cloth, 6s.

GRAY, MRS. H.—THE HISTORY of ETRURIA. Part I. TARCHUN AND HIS TIMES. From the Foundation of Tarquinia to the Foundation of Rome. Part II. FROM THE FOUNDATION OF ROME TO THE GENERAL PEACE OF ANNO TARQUINIENSIS, 839, B. C. 348. By Mrs. HAMILTON GRAY. 2 vols. post 8vo. cloth, each 12s.

" A work which we strongly recommend as certain to afford pleasure and profit to every reader."—*Athenæum*.

" Mrs Gray's works are entitled to a most prominent place in the literature of this country."—*Herald*.

— TOUR to the SEPULCHRES of ETRURIA in 1839.

Contents:—Introduction—Veii—Monte Nerone—Tarquinia—Vulci—Tuscania—Cære or Agylla—Castel d'Asso—Clusium—Conclusion.

Third Edition. With numerous Illustrations, post 8vo. cloth, 1l. 1s.

" Mrs. Gray has won an honourable place in the large assembly of modern female writers."—*Quarterly Review*.

" We warmly recommend Mrs. Gray's most useful and interesting volume."—*Edinburgh Review*.

GRAY, REV. J. H.—SERMONS in ROME. During Lent 1838. By the Rev. JOHN HAMILTON GRAY, M.A., of Magdalen College, Oxford; Vicar of Bolsover and Scarcliff. 12mo. cloth, 7s. 6d.

— EXPLANATION of the CHURCH CATECHISM. With Scripture Proofs, for the use of Sunday Schools. Second Edition. 12mo. cloth, 1s.

— On the ORDAINING INFLUENCE of the HOLY GHOST. 12mo. cloth, 2s. 6d.

GRIFFITH, REV. T.—THE APOSTLES' CREED, considered in relation to the wants of the Religious Sense, and certain errors of the Present Day. By the Rev. THOMAS GRIFFITH, A.M., Minister of Ram's Episcopal Chapel, Homerton, Author of " The Spiritual Life," &c. &c. 12mo. cloth, 10s.

" We have perused this work with pleasure, for there is in it sound scholarship, a correct, and often elegant, exposition of doctrinal points, and a truly pious and devout spirit."—*Gentleman's Magazine*.

GRIMSTON, HON. MISS.—ARRANGEMENT of the COMMON PRAYER BOOK and LESSONS, Dedicated, by Permission, to Her Majesty.

The peculiar advantage of this arrangement consists in having the entire Morning and Evening Service printed in a large clear type, in two portable volumes, one for the Morning and the other for the Evening.
The following are the prices:—

	£	s.	d.
The largest size demy 12mo. Morocco elegant	2	0	0
Ditto plain	1	15	0
Ditto calf gilt leaves	1	10	0
The second size, royal 18mo. Morocco elegan	1	15	0
Ditto plain	1	10	0
Ditto calf gilt leaves	1	5	0
The smallest size, royal 32mo. Morocco elegant	1	4	0
Ditto plain	1	1	0
Ditto calf gilt leaves	0	16	0

GRYLLS, REV. T.—SERMONS preached in the Cathedral Church of St. Peter's, Exeter, by the late Rev. THOMAS GRYLLS, A.M., of Trinity College, Cambridge, Prebendary of Exeter, and Rector of Cardynham, Cornwall. With a Biographical Sketch of the Author, by the Rev. J. PUNNETT, M.A., Vicar of St. Erth, and formerly of Clare Hall, Cambridge. 8vo. cloth, 10s. 6d.

" We have looked into this Volume with great satisfaction. The interesting biographical sketch which precedes the Sermons (twenty in number) prepared us to expect what we found, an earnest and sincere piety, and sound scriptural views, enforced and adorned by the graces of a highly cultivated mind."—*John Bull.*

HANKINSON, REV. T. E.—SERMONS. By the Rev. THOMAS EDWARDS HANKINSON, M.A., late of Corpus Christi College, Cambridge, and Minister of St. Matthew's Chapel, Denmark Hill. 8vo. cloth, 10s. 6d.

HARE, REV. A. W.—SERMONS to a COUNTRY CONGREGATION. By AUGUSTUS WILLIAM HARE, A.M., late Fellow of New College, and Rector of Alton Barnes. Sixth Edition. 2 vols. 12mo. cloth, 16s.

" They are, in truth, as appears to us, compositions of very rare merit, and realise a notion we have always entertained, that a sermon for our rural congregations there somewhere was, if it could be hit off, which in language should be familiar without being plain, and in matter solid without being abstruse."—*Quarterly Review.*

HASTINGS, REV. H. J.—PAROCHIAL SERMONS, from Advent to Trinity Sunday. By the Rev. HENRY JAMES HASTINGS, M.A., Rector of Areley Kings. 8vo. cloth, 12s.

—PAROCHIAL SERMONS, from Trinity to Advent Sunday. 8vo. cloth, 12s.

" These Sermons appear to us to be written in the spirit of a true Churchman; and we may safely assure our readers that they will find them replete with edifying matter, and well calculated to serve the purpose of a companion and guide to the services of the ecclesiastical year."—*Churchman's Monthly Review.*

HATHERELL, REV. J. W.—NINE SERMONS Preached at the Palace Chapel la Valetta, at Malta, in October, November, and December, 1841. To which are added TWO THEOLOGICAL ESSAYS, read on public occasions. By the Rev. J. W. HATHERELL, D.D., Brasenose College, Oxford, and Rector of Charmouth, Dorset. 12mo. cloth, 3s. 6d.

HENDRY, MISS E. A.—CRESSINGHAM RECTORY. Family Conversations on various Subjects. By ELIZABETH ANNE HENDRY. 12mo. cloth, 3s.

HIFFERNAN, REV. J. M.—CHARACTERS and EVENTS in SCRIPTURE HISTORY PRACTICALLY CONSIDERED. A Series of Lectures. By the Rev. JOHN M. HIFFERNAN, A.M., Curate of Fethard, in the Diocese of Cashel. 12mo. cloth, 5s.

HINTS to PROMOTE a LIFE of FAITH; or, the Ratification of the Baptismal Covenant. By a Member of the Church of England. Fcap. cloth, 4s. 6d.

" This work is intended to aid inexperienced inquirers to attain a life of faith. It is written in a truly pious, practical, and devotional spirit."—*English Review*.

HINTS on EARLY EDUCATION and NURSERY DISCIPLINE. Fifteenth Edition. 12mo. cloth, 3s. 6d.

" I think I may say that of all men we meet with, nine parts out of ten are what they are, good or evil, useful or not, by their education."—*Locke*.

HINTS for REFLECTION. Compiled from various Authors. Third Edition. 32mo. cloth, 2s.

HISTORY of JOB, in Language adapted to Children. By the Author of the " Peep of Day," " Line upon Line," &c. 18mo. cloth, 1s.

HITCHEN, REV. I.—TWELVE SERMONS. Preached in St. Mary's Episcopal Chapel, Glasgow, 1842. By the Rev. ISAAC HITCHEN, M.D., Assistant Minister. 8vo., cloth, 7s. 6d.

HOLLOWAY, REV. DR.—THE ANALOGY of FAITH; or, an Attempt to Show God's Methods of Grace with the Church of Christ, as set forth in the experience of David. By the Rev. THOMAS HOLLOWAY, D.D., Some time Fellow of Exeter College, Oxford, and Minister of Fitzroy Chapel, Fitzroy Square. 8vo. cloth, 10s. 6d.

— EUCHARISTIA; or, a Vindication of the Lord's Supper from the Superstition and Idolatry of Modern Innovations. Being the Substance of a Course of Sermons preached before the Congregation assembling to Worship at Fitzroy Chapel. Fcap. cloth, 3s. 6d.

HOPE, MRS.—SELF-EDUCATION and the FORMATION of CHARACTER: Addressed to the Young. By MRS. HOPE. Second Edition, Revised. 18mo. cloth, 2s. 6d.

" Parents and teachers will gain many useful hints from the perusal of this volume."—*Record*.

HOPE, DR.—MEMOIRS of the LATE JAMES HOPE, M.D., Physician to St. George's Hospital, &c. &c. By MRS. HOPE. To which are added, REMARKS on CLASSICAL EDUCATION. By Dr. HOPE. And LETTERS from a SENIOR to a JUNIOR PHYSICIAN. By Dr. BURDER. The whole edited by KLEIN GRANT, M.D., &c. &c. Third Edition. Post 8vo. cloth, 7s.

" The general, as well as the medical reader, will find this a most interesting and instructive volume."—*Gentleman's Mag.*
" A most interesting and valuable volume."—*Britannia.*
" A volume of universal interest."—*Morning Post.*
" A very interesting memoir to every class of readers."—*Christian Observer.*

HOPWOOD, REV. H.—ELISHA'S STAFF in the HAND of GEHAZI, and other Sermons. By the Rev. HENRY HOPWOOD, M.A., Queen's College, Cambridge. Late Inspector of Schools for the National Society. 12mo., cloth, 2s. 6d.

Any profits accruing from these Sermons will be devoted towards defraying the expenses of erecting an Altar-Screen and an Organ, in Christ Church, Worthing.

HOWARD, J.—MEMOIRS of JOHN HOWARD, the Christian Philanthropist: with a Detail of his extraordinary Labours; and an Account of the Prisons, Schools, Lazarettos, and Public Institutions he visited. By THOMAS TAYLOR, Esq., Author of " The Life of Cowper," &c. &c. With a Portrait. 12mo. cloth, 7s.

HOWELS, REV. W.—SERMONS. By the late Rev. W. Howels. With a Memoir of the Author, &c., By Charles Bowdler. Second Edition, 2 vols. 8vo. With a Portrait, 24s.

— A COURSE of SERMONS on the LORD'S PRAYER, printed in a separate volume. 8vo. boards, 5s.

HURNALL, REV. J.—EPOCHS of the CHURCH of LYONS. A Fragment in the History of the Church of Jesus Christ. Translated from the French. Edited by the Rev. J. Hurnall, M.A. Second Edition, fcap. cloth, 3s. 6d.

JEWSBURY, MISS M. J.—LETTERS to the YOUNG. By Maria Jane Jewsbury. Fifth Edition. Fcap. cloth, 5s.

JOHNSTONE, REV. J.—THE WAY of LIFE. Set forth in several Sermons preached before, and dedicated by permission to, Her Majesty the Queen Dowager. By John Johnstone, M.A., late Minister of All Saints, Rotherhithe. 8vo. cloth, 10s. 6d.

JONES, REV. J.—LECTURES on the PRINCIPAL TYPES of the OLD TESTAMENT. By the Rev J. Jones, M.A., Incumbent of St. Andrew's Church, Liverpool. Vol. 1, 12mo. cloth, 5s. 6d.

— EXPOSITORY LECTURES on SELECT PORTIONS of the ACTS of the APOSTLES. 2 vols. 12mo. cloth, 10s.

THE JOYS of HEAVEN. By a Layman. 12mo. cloth, 4s. 6d.

" You seem to have compared with much diligence, and connected with skill, the intimations which are scattered throughout Scripture on this most interesting and important subject; and, as a whole, I think the book displays a power of thought which will recommend it to the few who reason, and a felicity of illustration, which will make it attractive to the many who feel."
—*Extract from a Letter from Mr. Dale.*

KAY, J.—THE EDUCATION of the POOR in ENGLAND and EUROPE. By Joseph Kay, B.A., of Trinity College, Cambridge, Travelling Bachelor of the University. With numerous Statistical Tables. 8vo. cloth, 14s.

" The matter treated of in this volume 'is one of engrossing interest to every christian and philosophic mind, and the writer has brought to his task real earnestness, industry, and intelligence. We take leave of it in the sincere hope that it may be, as it deserves, extensively read. It shows not merely the evils of our deficient education, but the remedies; and these not theoretically but by examples."—*Times.*

KENNION, REV. T.—SERMONS. By the late Rev. THOMAS KENNION, M.A., of Christ Church, Cambridge, and Incumbent Minister of Christchurch, High Harrogate. 8vo. cloth, 10s.

KEY-STONE of GRAMMAR LAID; or, the Governess's Assistant in simplifying that Science. By T. C. 18mo. cloth, 2s.

LADIES' SUNDAY-SCHOOL ASSISTANT; or, Mother's Guide to the Four Gospels. Being an explanation of each chapter according to the verses, with occasional Practical Hints. 12mo. cloth, 5s.

LANDMANN.—A UNIVERSAL GAZETTEER; or, Geographical Dictionary of the World. Founded on the Works of Brookes and Walker; with the addition of several thousand names not to be found in any other work, the Latitude and Longitude throughout, and the relative Distances most carefully examined. By GEORGE LANDMANN, Esq., C.E., late a Lieutenant-Colonel in the Corps of Royal Engineers. 8vo. bound, 15s.

LECTURES on the DESTINY of the JEWS, and their Connexion with the Gentile Nations. By Ten Clergymen of the Church of England. 12mo. cloth, 9s.

LE MESURIER, REV. J. T. H.—GARRISON SERMONS. Being Twenty Discourses preached to her Majesty's Troops in the Island of Malta. By the Rev. J. T. H. LE MESURIER, M.A., Chaplain to the Forces, &c. 12mo. cloth, 6s.

LE PAGE, M.—PETIT MUSEE de LITTERATURE FRANCAISE; or, the French Speaker: a Chronological and Critical Table of the eminent writers of France, from the Fourteenth to the Nineteenth Centuries. Illustrated with selections in Prose and Verse, from the best Authors in the three last periods. By M. LE PAGE, Professor of the French Language, author of " L'Echo de Paris." 12mo. bound, 8s. 6d.

" The selections have been carefully made, and show at once the style and the power of the writer. We strongly recommend the ' Petit Musée' to all those desirous of becoming acquainted with the literature of France."—*Argus.*

WORKS PUBLISHED BY

LE VERT, C.—A GENERAL and PRACTICAL SYSTEM of TEACHING and LEARNING LANGUAGES. Applicable to all Languages, and particularly the French. By C. LE VERT, Teacher of French. 12mo. cloth, 5s.

⁎ A book composed for the benefit of Young Persons engaged in teaching, either as assistants in schools, Governesses in private families, or daily Teachers; also of Mothers who educate their children themselves, or wish to superintend their education; lastly, of persons who are not able to procure a master.

" This work is no less distinguished by its great sound sense and general intelligence, than by its thorough mastery of every practical detail of teaching."—*Foreign Quarterly Review.*

LIGHT in the DWELLING; or, a Harmony of the Four Gospels, with very Short and Simple Remarks adapted to Reading at Family Prayers, and arranged in 365 sections, for every day of the year. By the Author of "The Peep of Day," "Line upon Line," &c. Revised and corrected by a Clergyman of the Church of England. 8vo. cloth, 14s.

" The Author of the 'Peep of Day' and its sequel 'Line upon Line,' two most valuable series of early religious instruction for the infant mind—could not have done better than apply her powers to the production of such a work; and we are happy to report that she appears to have done so with great success. The author is well equal to her task, and we hope this will not be her last contribution to the Church."—*Churchman's Monthly Review.*

" Brief remarks, always to the point, full of spiritual meaning, and what is far better, of spiritual feeling, meet us in every page of this work."—*Christian Ladies' Magazine.*

" Those who use this interesting and beautifully written manual, will have 'Light in the Dwelling.' We can, with a good conscience, and an enlightened conviction, recommend the work, both for family and private reading.—*Evangelical Magazine.*

LINE UPON LINE; or, a Second Series of the Earliest Religious Instruction the Infant Mind is capable of receiving; with Verses illustrative of the Subjects. By the Author of "The Peep of Day," &c. Part I. twenty-fifth thousand. Part II. twenty-second thousand. 18mo. cloth, each 2s. 6d.

LINDSAY, LORD.—A LETTER to a FRIEND on the EVIDENCES and THEORY of CHRISTIANITY. By LORD LINDSAY. 12mo. cloth, 3s.

M'FARQUHAR, REV. W. P.—SERMONS. Preached in St. Mary's Episcopal Chapel, Dumfries; and designed more especially to illustrate Christian Truth and Obligation, in connexion with some of the leading Anniversaries of the Church of England, with the Ordinance of the Ministry, and with the mode of salvation by faith in Christ Jesus. By the Rev. W. PITT M'FARQUHAR, B. A., Incumbent of St. Mary's Episcopal Chapel. 12mo. cloth, 6s.

M'NEILE, REV. H.—THE CHURCH and the CHURCHES; or, the Church of God in Christ, and the Churches of Christ Militant here on Earth. By the Rev. HUGH M'NEILE, M.A., Hon. Canon of Chester, and Incumbent of St. Jude's Liverpool. 8vo. cloth, 12s.

" Mr. M'Neile's fame as a writer has been long established, but it will be greatly increased by the volume now before us, and which is in every respect worthy of its highly gifted author. We hail with much satisfaction the appearance of this very seasonable publication."—*Morning Herald.*

" Mr. M'Neile has, in our opinion, accomplished the task he has undertaken with admirable judgment, great ability, and striking effect. We recommend this work in the strongest terms to the attention of our readers."—*Record.*

" We desire earnestly that this work may be read and studied by all our clergy, and by thousands of their congregations, as well as by the leaders of thought among our Dissenting brethren. For scriptural soundness, original thought, and a vigorous and bold expression of gospel truth, with a powerful and effective exposure of the anti-christian delusions that now assail us, there is no work of the day which deserves a higher place."—*Churchman's Monthly Review.*

— LECTURES on the CHURCH of ENGLAND, delivered in London, March, 1840. Eighth Edition. 12mo. cloth, 5s.

— LECTURES on the SYMPATHIES, SUFFERINGS, and RESURRECTION of the LORD JESUS CHRIST, delivered in Liverpool during Passion Week and Easter Day. Third Edition. 12mo. cloth, 4s. 6d.

— SERMONS on the SECOND ADVENT of our LORD JESUS CHRIST, with Notes. Fifth Edition. 12mo. cloth, 4s. 6d.

— SEVENTEEN SERMONS. Third Edition. 12mo. cloth 7s.

MANASSEH, a TALE of the JEWS. With several Illustrations. Fcap. cloth, 5s.

MARRIOTT, REV. H.—A PLAIN and PRACTICAL VIEW of the LITURGY of the CHURCH of ENGLAND. Taken from a course of Sermons formerly preached in Margaret Chapel in the city of Bath. Newly arranged and corrected. By the Rev. HARVEY MARRIOTT, Rector of Claverton, and Chaplain to the Right Honourable Lord Kenyon. 12mo. cloth, 4s. 6d.

— SERMONS on the CHARACTER and DUTIES of WOMEN. 12mo. boards, 3s. 6d.

MARRIOTT, REV. H.

— FOUR COURSES of PRACTICAL SERMONS. 8vo. boards, each 10s. 6d.

— EIGHT SERMONS on "The SIGNS of the TIMES." 8vo. boards, 6s.

MARRIOTT, REV. J.—SERMONS. By the late Rev. JOHN MARRIOTT, A.M., Rector of Church Lawford, Warwickshire. Edited by his Sons, the Rev. John Marriott, A.M., and the Rev. Charles Marriott, A.M. 8vo. cloth, 10s. 6d.

MARSHALL, MISS. — EXTRACTS from the RELIGIOUS WORKS of FENELON, Archbishop of Cambray. Translated from the Original French. By MISS MARSHALL. Tenth Edition, with a Portrait. Fcap. cloth, 4s. 6d.

MEEK, MRS.—THOUGHTS on the RESPONSIBILITY of MAN; With a view to the Amelioration of Society; addressed to the Higher and Middle Classes. By EMMA MEEK. Foolscap, cloth, 3s. 6d.

MEEK, REV. R.—THE MUTUAL RECOGNITION and EXALTED FELICITY of GLORIFIED SAINTS. By the Rev. ROBERT MEEK, M.A., Rector of St. Michael, Sutton Bonnington, Notts, (Late of Richmond, Yorkshire) Fourth Edition, fcap. cloth, 3s. 6d.

— REASONS for ATTACHMENT and CONFORMITY to the CHURCH of ENGLAND. Third Edition, revised, corrected, and enlarged. 18mo. cloth, 2s. 6d.

— THE CHURCH of ENGLAND, a Faithful Witness against the Errors and Corruptions of the Church of Rome. 8vo. boards, 12s.

— PASSION WEEK; a Practical and Devotional Exposition of the Gospels and Epistles appointed for that Season, composed for the Closet and the Family. 12mo. boards, 4s.

MONTGOMERY, REV. R.—THE GREAT SALVATION and our SIN in NEGLECTING IT. A Religious Essay, in Three Parts. By the Rev. ROBERT MONTGOMERY, M.A., Oxon, Author of "The Omnipresence of the Deity," "Luther," "The Gospel in Advance of the Age," &c. &c. Fcap. cloth, 5s.

— CHRIST OUR ALL in ALL. Third Edition. Fcap. cloth, 4s. 6d.

MOUSLEY, REV. W.—MORAL STRENGTH; or, the Nature and Conquest of Evil Habits Considered. By WILLIAM MOUSLEY, M.A., Vicar of Cold Ashby, late of Queen's College, Cambridge; Author of "Plain Sermons on some of the leading Truths of the Gospel." 12mo. cloth, 4s.

"An excellent subject well treated; very well arranged, and containing much good and practical information."—*British Magazine.*

MORNING and EVENING SERVICES EXPLAINED to CHILDREN, and enforced by Scripture. 18mo. cloth, 1s. 6d.

MUSTON, REV. C. K.—RECOGNITION in the WORLD to COME; or, Christian Friendship on Earth Perpetuated in Heaven. By the Rev. C. K. MUSTON, A.M., Chelmsford. Fourth Edition, 12mo. cloth, 7s.

— SERMONS at ROTTERDAM. 8vo. cloth, 12s.

NEWNHAM, W.—A TRIBUTE of SYMPATHY ADDRESSED to MOURNERS. By W. NEWNHAM, Esq., M.R.S.L.

Contents:—1. Indulgence of Grief. 2. Moderation of Grief. 3. Excessive Sorrow. 4. Advantages of Sorrow. 5. Self-examination. 6. Resignation. 7. Sources of Consolation. Fcap. cloth, 5s.

— THE RECIPROCAL INFLUENCE of BODY and MIND CONSIDERED: As it affects the Great Questions of Education—Phrenology—Materialism—Moral Advancement and Responsibility—Man's Free Agency—The Theory of Life—The Peculiarities of Mental Property—Mental Diseases—The Agency of Mind upon the Body—Of Physical Temperament upon the Manifestations of Mind—and upon the Expression of Religious Feeling. 8vo. cloth, 14s.

" It is impossible to read this work without the conviction that the author has bestowed very much thought on a very large number of most important subjects, and has accomplished the very difficult task, viz. of writing a book on an abstruse subject, which general readers may understand, and scientific men profit by. Few will rise from its perusal without being sensible that on some points their views have become more clear, and that new trains of thought have been suggested to them ; and no one can close it without feeling much respect both for the principles and abilities of the author."—*British and Foreign Medical Review.*

NEWTON, REV. J.—SIXTY-SIX LETTERS from the REV. JOHN NEWTON, late Rector of St. Mary, Woolnoth, London, to a Clergyman and his Family, between the Years 1791 and 1801. Never before Published. 12mo. cloth, 5s.

NIGHT of TOIL; or, a Familiar Account of the Labours of the First Missionaries in the South Sea Islands. By the Author of "The Peep of Day," &c. Second Edition. Fcap. cloth, 5s.

NIND, REV. W.—LECTURE-SERMONS. Preached in a Country Parish Church. By WILLIAM NIND, M.A., Fellow of St. Peter's College, Cambridge, and Vicar of Cherry Hinton. 12mo. cloth, 6s.

"Discourses which could not be read or listened to without profit."—*Gentleman's Magazine.*

NORTH, REV. J. W.—SERMONS on the LITURGY. By the Rev. J. W. NORTH, M.A., Chaplain of the Isles of Scilly. Late Curate of Fulham. Post 8vo. cloth, 10s.

OXENDEN, REV. A.—THE COTTAGE LIBRARY. Vol. I. The Sacrament of Baptism. By the Rev. ASHTON OXENDEN, late Curate of Barham, Kent. 18mo. sewed, 9d.

"A little book of probably large usefulness. It avoids disputed points, but conveys a clear and simple view of the holy rite of baptism. It is admirably suited to the cottage, as well as to all places in which ignorance reigns upon the subject."—*Church and State Gazette.*

— THE COTTAGE LIBRARY, Vol. 2. THE SACRAMENT OF THE LORD'S SUPPER. 18mo. sewed, 9d.

PARKER, MISS F. S.—TRUTH WITHOUT NOVELTY; or, a Course of Scriptural Instruction for every Sunday in the Year, principally designed for Private Family Instruction, and Sunday Schools. By FRANCES S. PARKER, Author of "The Guiding Star, and other Tales," "The First Communion," &c. Second Edition. Fcap. cloth, 4s. 6d.

PARRY, SIR W. E.—THOUGHTS on the PARENTAL CHARACTER of GOD. By Captain Sir WILLIAM EDWARD PARRY, R.N. Third Edition. 18mo. cloth, 1s. 6d.

PARRY, REV. J.—DISCOURSES on VARIOUS SUBJECTS. Delivered to Congregations in the Eastern District of London. To which are added, Two SERMONS preached before the University of Oxford. By the Rev. JOHN PARRY, M.A., Late Fellow of Brasenose College, Oxford, and now Rector of St. John of Wapping. 12mo. cloth, 5s.

PEARSON, REV. DR.—MEMOIRS of the LIFE and CORRESPONDENCE of the REV. CHRISTIAN FREDERIC SWARTZ. To which is prefixed, A Sketch of the History of Christianity in India. By HUGH PEARSON, D.D., M.R.A.S., Author of "The Life of Buchanan." Third Edition. 2 vols. post 8vo. cloth. With a Portrait and Map. 16s.

PEARSON, REV. J. N.—SUNDAY READINGS for the FAMILY and the CLOSET. By the Rev. J. NORMAN PEARSON, M.A. Incumbent of the District Church, Tunbridge Wells. 12mo., cloth, 7s.

"Sound and practical."—*British Magazine.*
"A most valuable work."—*Church of England Magazine.*

PEEP of DAY; or, a Series of the Earliest Religious Instruction the Infant Mind is capable of receiving. With Verses illustrative of the Subjects. Fortieth thousand, revised and corrected. 18mo. cloth, 3s.

POYNDER, J.—LITERARY EXTRACTS from ENGLISH and OTHER WORKS; collected during Half a Century; Together with some Original Matter. By JOHN POYNDER, Esq. 2 vols. 8vo. cloth, 1l. 10s.

PRACTICAL SUGGESTIONS TOWARDS ALLEVIATING the SUFFERINGS of the SICK.
Part I. Third Edition. 12mo. cloth, 3s.
Part II. Fourth Edition. 12mo. cloth. 6s. 6d.

PRACTICAL TRUTHS from HOMELY SAYINGS. Second Edition. 18mo. cloth, 2s. 6d.

PRAYERS, FAMILY AND PRIVATE.

A FORM of PRAYERS, Selected and Composed for the Use of a Family principally consisting of Young Persons. Thirteenth Edition. 12mo. cloth, 2s. 6d.

FAMILY PRAYERS. By the late HENRY THORNTON, Esq., M.P. Nineteenth Edition. 12mo. cloth, 3s.

FAMILY PRAYERS. By the late W. WILBERFORCE, Esq., Edited by his Son, the Rev. R. I. Wilberforce, Archdeacon of the East Riding of Yorkshire; Vicar of Burton-Agnes, late Fellow of Oriel College. Ninth Edition. Fcap. 8vo. sewed, 1s. 6d.

FAMILY PRAYERS for a FORTNIGHT. 18mo. cloth, 2s.

FAMILY PRAYERS for Every Day of the Week. selected from various portions of the Holy Bible, with References. Third Edition. 12mo. boards, 2s. 6d.

FAMILY PRAYERS, chiefly from ARCHBISHOP LEIGHTON. 18mo. cloth, 2s.

FAMILY PRAYERS for Every Day in the Week. By CLERICUS. 18mo. cloth, 1s. 6d.

PRAYERS, FAMILY AND PRIVATE.

PRAYERS and OFFICES of DEVOTION for Families, and for Particular Persons, upon most occasions. By BENJAMIN JENKS. Altered and Improved by the Rev. Charles Simeon. 12mo. roan, 4s. 6d. or 18mo. 3s.

HELPS to DEVOTION; Morning and Evening Prayers for every day in the week, adapted for the use of Families. By the late Rev. H. TATTAM, M.A. 12mo. boards 2s. 6d.

SHORT FAMILY PRAYERS for Every Morning and Evening of the Month. Selected and Arranged from the Liturgy, Psalms, and various eminent Writers. By WILLIAM SOLTAU, Esq. Member of the Church of England. 12mo. cloth, 3s.

A COURSE of MORNING and EVENING PRAYERS, for the use of the Families of the Poor. 12mo. sewed, 6d., or 5s. per dozen.

SHORT PRAYERS for Every Day in the Week, to be used either in the Family or Private. By the late RICHARD SHEPHERD, M.A., Incumbent of St. Margaret's, Stanstead, Herts, and late Curate of St. Mary's, Whitechapel. 12mo. sewed, 2d., or 1s. 6d. per dozen.

FORMS of PRAYERS, adapted for the use of Schools and Young Persons. By J. SNOW. 18mo. cloth, 2s. 6d.

PRIVATE PRAYERS for YOUNG PERSONS. By M. A. Fcap. cloth, 2s.

A FEW PLAIN SHORT PRAYERS, intended to be sent with each set of Baby Linen lent to Poor Women. 24mo. sewed, 3d., or 2s. 6d. per dozen.

PRAYERS for CHILDREN and YOUNG PERSONS. 24mo. sewed, 3d. or 2s. 6d. per dozen.

A COMPANION to the ALTAR, with Occasional Prayers. By GEORGE A. E. MARSH, A.M., Rector of Bangor, Flintshire, and late Minister of St. Mary's Chapel, Park Street, Grosvenor Square. Third Edition. Boards 1s. 6d., sheep 2s., calf, 3s.

NEWLY ARRANGED MANUAL for COMMUNICANTS at the LORD'S SUPPER, including the Service for the Holy Communion. 24mo. bound, 3s.

THE PRIESTESS. An Anglo-Saxon Tale of the Early Days of Christianity in Britain. By the Translator of "Margaret; or, the Gold Mine." Post 8vo. cloth, 7s. 6d.

"A stirring story of Pagan temples, rites, Priests and Priestesses, Christian converts and religious vows. We can justly recommend this volume to every class of readers."—*Literary Gazette.*

QUESTIONS and PRACTICAL REMARKS on the PORTIONS of SCRIPTURE selected as the Epistle for each Sunday in the Year. By the Author of "Bible Stories," &c. 18mo. cloth, 2s. 6d.

QUESTIONS and PRACTICAL REMARKS on the PORTIONS of SCRIPTURE selected as the Gospels for each Sunday in the Year. By the Author of "Bible Stories," "Questions on the Epistles," &c. 18mo. cloth, 2s. 6d.

QUESTIONS on the COLLECTS of the CHURCH of ENGLAND, for every Sunday in the Year, Designed to Promote a Better Understanding of those comprehensive Forms of Prayer; with a Key, containing suitable Answers and Scriptural proofs, for the use of Young Persons. 18mo. cloth, 1s. 6d.

RADCLYFFE, REV. W.—THE PULPIT HELP to PRAYER. By the Rev. W. RADCLYFFE, M.A., of Queen's College, Oxford, and Curate of Moor Critchill, Devon. 18mo., cloth, 3s.

RICHMOND, REV. L.—THE ANNALS of the POOR. By the late Rev. LEGH RICHMOND. With Engravings by EDWARD FINDEN. Fcap. cloth, 5s.

ROBERTS, W.—THE PORTRAITURE of a CHRISTIAN GENTLEMAN. By W. ROBERTS, Esq., of Lincoln's Inn, Editor of the "Life of Mrs. H. More." Second Edition. Boards, 6s.

ROOSE, E. M.—ECCLESIASTICA; or, the Church, her Schools, and the Clergy. By EDWARD MAHON ROOSE, Esq., of Lincoln's Inn. Second Edition. 8vo. cloth, 10s. 6d.

ROSE UNIQUE; or, Errors Expiated. Fcap. cloth, 4s.

ROWE, REV. S.—AN APPEAL to the RUBRIC; in a Review of the several Clauses of the Ritual Code; with Suggestions for General Uniformity in the Public Services of the United Church of England and Ireland. By SAMUEL ROWE, M.A., of Devon. Fcap. cloth, 3s. 6d.

RUSSELL, DR.—THE HISTORY of MODERN EUROPE. With an Account of the Decline and Fall of the Roman Empire; and a view of the Progress of Society, from the Rise of the Modern Kingdoms to the Peace of Paris in 1763. In a series of Letters from a Nobleman to his Son. New Edition, continued to the death of William the Fourth of England. In 4 vols. 8vo. £2. 12s.

THE SACRED PRECEPTOR; or, a Series of Questions and Answers, elucidating the Doctrine, Practice, and Natural History of Scripture; for the use of Schools and Young Persons. 12mo. half-bound, 3s.

SALTER, REV. H. G.—THE BOOK of ILLUSTRATIONS; or, Scripture Truths exhibited by the aid of Similes, Original and Selected. By the Rev. H. G. SALTER, A.M., Curate and Lecturer of Glastonbury. 8vo. cloth, 10s. 6d.

These illustrations are drawn from Nature, History, the Arts and Sciences, and the Kingdoms of Grace and Providence. It is believed that no similar work has been published since Mr. Spencer's in 1658, of which the most valuable portions are here incorporated.

SAMUEL, REV. J.—THE REMNANT FOUND; or, the Place of Israel's Hiding Discovered. Being a summary of proofs, showing that the Jews at Daghistan, on the Caspian Sea, are the Remnant of the Ten Tribes. The result of personal residence and investigation. By the Rev. JACOB SAMUEL, Senior Missionary to the Jews for India, Persia, and Arabia. 8vo., cloth, 5s.

SCENES in OUR PARISH. By a Country Parson's Daughter. 2 vols. 12mo. bds. each 5s.

SCOTT, REV. T.—THE HOLY BIBLE; containing the Old and New Testament according to the Authorised Version; with Explanatory Notes, Practical Observations, and copious Marginal References. By the Rev. THOMAS SCOTT, late Rector of Ashton Sandford, Bucks. A New Edition, with the Author's last Corrections and Improvements, and with numerous Illustrations and Maps. 6 vols. 4to. cloth, 6l. 6s. or 3 vols. imperial 8vo. cloth, 3l. 3s.

— THE HOLY BIBLE; with the Practical Observations. 2 vols. imperial 8vo. cloth, 1l. 5s.

— ESSAYS on the MOST IMPORTANT SUBJECTS in RELIGION. With a MEMOIR of the AUTHOR. Fifteenth Edition. 12mo. 5s.; 18mo. 3s. 6d.

SCRIPTURE CATECHISM; extracted chiefly from the Rev. Edward Bickersteth's "Scripture Help." Designed to assist the Young in acquiring a Knowledge of the Holy Bible, and to commend it to their love. By E. W. 18mo. cloth, 2s.

SELECTION of FABLES from FLORIAN and OTHER AUTHORS, Translated and Versified. To which are added, A Few Scraps from a Portfolio. By THERESA TIDY. 18mo. cloth, 1s.

SELKIRK, REV. J.—RECOLLECTIONS of CEYLON, after a Residence of nearly Thirteen Years, with an Account of the Church Missionary Society's Operations in that island, and Extracts from a Journal. By the Rev. JAMES SELKIRK, Curate of Myddleton Tyas, Yorkshire. 8vo. cloth, with a Map and various Illustrations, 14s.

"Containing a very clear and succinct account of Ceylon; and may be safely recommended to those who wish a coup d'œil of the island."—*Spectator*.

"The author has afforded, we think, the most complete information we have ever had, respecting this magnificent island, and developes a number of original traits which have escaped the notice of other travellers."—*Literary Gazette*.

SERMONS and EXTRACTS CONSOLATORY on the LOSS of FRIENDS. Selected from the Works of the most eminent Divines. Third Edition. 8vo. cloth, 12s.

SHERWOOD, MRS.—THE HISTORY of JOHN MARTEN. A Sequel to "The Life of Henry Milner." By Mrs. SHERWOOD. 12mo. cloth, 7s. 6d.

— THE HISTORY of HENRY MILNER. 3 vols. 12mo. cloth, each 6s.

— THE HISTORY of the FAIRCHILD FAMILY; or, The Child's Manual. Fifteenth Edition, 12mo., cloth. 5s.

— THE HISTORY of the FAIRCHILD FAMILY. Volume 2. Third Edition. 12mo. cloth, 5s.

— JULIETTA DI LAVENZA. A Tale 18mo. cloth, 2s.

— THE HEDGE of THORNS. Fifth Edition. 18mo. cloth, 1s.

— VICTORIA. 12mo. bds. 4s.

— THE ORPHANS of NORMANDY. Third Edition. 12mo. bds. 2s. 6d.

— THE LITTLE MOMIERE. 12mo. cloth, 3s.

SINCLAIR, REV. W.—THE DYING SOLDIER. A Tale founded on Facts. By the Rev. W. SINCLAIR, M.A., Minister of St. George's, Leeds. 18mo. cloth, 1s. 6d.

SLEEMAN, LIEUT.-COLONEL.—RAMBLES and RECOL-
LECTIONS of an INDIAN OFFICIAL. By Lieutenant-Colonel W.
H. SLEEMAN, of the Indian army. With numerous Coloured Illustrations.
2 vols. royal 8vo. handsomely bound in cloth, 2l. 12s. 6d.

"This work is not only replete with valuable information, but richly en-
livened with anecdote, story, and legend, splendidly bound up, and illumi-
nated with beautiful engravings. The contents are various and interesting."
Literary Gazette.

"The coloured lithographs that illustrate these volumes, in a rich profusion
which proves that cost has not been considered, are effective and splendid
presentments of the magnificent architecture of the East, and would alone
make the work valuable. Paper, type, and binding, are all so many
luxuries.—*Athenæum.*

"This is one of the best works that have been published on the subject
of Hindostan."—*Spectator.*

"We earnestly recommend this work to the attention of the reading
public, as the most interesting and best written that has been issued on
India for a number of years. The plates are perfect architectural drawings,
with rich illuminations in colour, to convey more accurately a true idea of
the originals."—*Britannia.*

THE SOLACE of an INVALID. Fourth Edition. Fcap. cloth,
5s. 6d.

SOLACE of a MOURNER. Fcap. cloth. 4s. 6d.

SORELLI, G.—THE STUDENT'S HELP for the ATTAIN-
MENT of the ENGLISH, FRENCH, and ITALIAN LANGUAGES.
By GUIDO SORELLI, Author of "My Confessions to Silvio Pellico," &c.
&c., Professor of Languages. 12mo. cloth, 5s.

A SPONSOR'S GIFT. Being Familiar Essays on those things
"which a Christian ought to know and believe," in a Series of Letters
to an absent Godchild. Second Edition, 12mo. boards, 3s.

STEWART, REV. J. H.—Lectures upon the FIFTY-FIFTH
CHAPTER of the PROPHET ISAIAH. By the Rev. JAMES HALDANE
STEWART, M.A., Incumbent of St. Bride's, Liverpool, and Chaplain to the
Most Noble the Marquis of Bute, and the Marquis of Breadalbane.

— THE FAMILY which JESUS LOVED; or, Lectures upon
the HISTORY of MARTHA, and MARY, and LAZARUS. Second
Edition. 12mo. cloth, 6s.

— THE PARENTAL PROMISE FULFILLED; a Brief
Memoir of his Eldest Son, W. C. Stewart, who departed this life in perfect peace, Dec. 3, 1834, aged seventeen. Third Edition. 12mo. cloth,
3s. 6d.

STOPFORD, REV. J.—PAGANO-PAPISMUS; or, an Exact Parallel between Rome-Pagan and Rome-Christian in their Doctrines and Ceremonies. By JOSHUA STOPFORD, B.D., Rector of All Saints, in the City of York. (Being a reprint of a work published in 1675.) 1 vol. 12mo. cloth, 7s.

STOWELL, REV. H.—TRACTARIANISM TESTED by HOLY SCRIPTURE and the CHURCH of ENGLAND, in a Series of Sermons. By the Rev. HUGH STOWELL, M.A., Incumbent of Christ Church, Manchester, and Hon. Prebendary of Chester. 2 vols. 12mo. cloth, each 6s.

Contents of Vol. 1:—Private Judgment—The standard of faith—Apostolical Succession, and the Powers of the Clergy—The Church of England and the Reformation—How Separatists are to be regarded—The Importance of Preaching—On Reserve in the communication of Christian Doctrine.

Contents of Vol. 2:—Justification by faith—On Baptism—Sin after Baptism—The Sacrament of the Lord's Supper—Fasting and Voluntary Humility—Forms—Church Architecture and Church Furniture—Recapitulation and Improvement.

N.B. The object of this work is not merely nor mainly to confute Tractarianism, but rather to inform and establish the minds of Churchmen on certain perplexing questions, respecting which definite views are much needed.

"We have read these discourses with unmixed pleasure, not only because of the importance of the subject of which they treat, but for the admirable spirit which they breathe. They are, in truth, models of controversial writing. It is impossible for us to imagine such questions to be handled with greater candour or ability."—*Glasgow Courier.*

STRANGE PLANET, an Allegory, and other Tales, for Sunday Reading. By the Author of "Aids to Developement." Illustrated with Woodcuts. 18mo. cloth, 3s.

TALES for MY GRANDCHILDREN. 18mo. cloth, 2s.

"A work adapted to the capacities of very young children, to afford instructive amusement for Sunday evening."

TEIGNMOUTH, LORD.—MEMOIRS of the LIFE and CORRESPONDENCE of JOHN LORD TEIGNMOUTH. By his Son, LORD TEIGNMOUTH. 2 vols. demy 8vo. cloth, 24s.

"Re..'e e \ i h inte esting matter."—*Christian Observer.*

"It is impossible to read these two volumes without being impressed with a since e respect for the cha acter and virtue of Lord Teignmouth, which r ed him deservedly to th e eminence he attained, for the spotless integrity he preserved in the midst of corruption, and for his sincere and unassuming piety."—*Asiatic Journal.*

— **LETTERS ADDRESSED by LORD TEIGNMOUTH** to his SON on his DEPARTURE for INDIA. 18mo. cloth, 1s.

THOMPSON, REV. E.—A VOLUME of SERMONS upon the FUTURE STATE of HAPPINESS. By the Rev. EDWARD THOMPSON, M.A., Minister of Charlotte Chapel, Pimlico. Dedicated, by permission, to Her Majesty the Queen Dowager. Second Edition. Post 8vo. cloth, 6s. 6d.

— POPULAR LECTURES upon the DIFFERENCES EXISTING BETWEEN the CHURCH of ENGLAND and the CHURCH of ROME. Enriched with copious Notes. Post 8vo. cloth, 6s. 6d.

THOMPSON, REV. F. E.—TWELVE LECTURES preached in St. George's Chapel, Old Brentford, in the Season of Lent 1844 and 1845. By the Rev. F. E. THOMPSON, B.A., of Trinity College, Cambridge, and Incumbent of Old Brentford. 12mo. cloth, 5s.

" These are sketches it is true, but they are sketches by the hand of a master. Mr. Thompson's style is original, and we may venture strongly to recommend this little work."—*Church and State Gazette.*

" In a theological point of view his object is very successfully accomplished by Mr. Thompson. In a literary sense the plan of the writer gives purpose, variety, and interest to his discourses. Biography and applied morality are superadded to the general matter of a Sermon. The style is agreeable—the manner rapid and impressive."—*Spectator.*

THISTLETHWAITE, REV. W.—TWENTY-ONE SERMONS for CHARITY SCHOOLS. By the late Rev. W. THISTLETHWAITE, A.M., Incumbent of St. George's, Bolton. To which is prefixed a MEMOIR of the AUTHOR, with a Portrait. 12mo. cloth, 10s.

THORNTON, H.—FEMALE CHARACTERS. By the late HENRY THORNTON, Esq., M.P. With Prayers adapted to the Lectures. Second Edition. Fcap. cloth, 3s.

— ON the TEN COMMANDMENTS, with PRAYERS. Second Edition. 12mo. cloth., 2s. 6d.

— LECTURES upon the SERMONS on the MOUNT. Second Edition. 12mo. cloth, 5s.

— FAMILY PRAYERS, in a Series for a Month. Sixteenth Edition. 12mo. cloth, 3s.

TRACTS FOR DISTRIBUTION.

FEED MY LAMBS, a Lecture for Children in Words of One Syllable. By the Rev. T. G. HATCHARD. 3d. each, or 2s. 6d. per dozen.

TRACTS FOR DISTRIBUTION.

MOLLY GAY; or, the Aged Christian Widow. By the Author of "Charity in Religion." 18mo. sewed, 9d.

THE CREATION and FALL of MAN. Arranged as nearly as possible in the Words of Scripture. For the Lower Classes in the National Schools. Part I. 18mo. sewed, 4d.

THE GOOD MOTHER and HER TWO SONS. Intended for Sailors and Emigrants. Second Edition. 2d., or 1s. 6d. per dozen, or 10s. per 100.

THE FOURTH COMMANDMENT EXPLAINED. By a Sunday School Teacher. 3d., or 2s. 6d. a dozen.

HOW OLD ART THOU? 2d. each.

A FEW HINTS on INFANT BAPTISM. By the Rev. Lord Arthur Hervey, M.A. 6d. each, or 5s. per dozen.

THE TEACHER'S ASSISTANT IN NEEDLE-WORK. Seventh Edition. 6d. each, or 5s. per dozen.

THE KNITTING TEACHER'S ASSISTANT. Ninth Edition. 6d., or 5s. per dozen.

A MISFORTUNE CHANGED into a BLESSING. 12mo. 6d., or 1s. in cloth boards.

ELIEZER; or, The Faithful Servant. 12mo. 3d., or 2s. 6d. per dozen.

PORTIONS OF SCRIPTURE, arranged with a view to promote the RELIGIOUS OBSERVANCE OF THE LORD'S DAY. By a LADY. 3d. each, or 2s. 6d. per dozen.

HOW CAN I GO TO CHURCH? Or, A Dialogue between a Lady and a Poor Woman. 3d each.

WHY SHOULD I NOT GO TO THE MEETING-HOUSE? 3d. each.

HAPPINESS AND MISERY; or, The Life of Faith and the Natural Life. Seventh Edition. 1½d. each.

A FRIEND to the SICK and AFFLICTED. Sixth Edition. 3d. each, or 2s. 6d. per dozen.

TRACTS FOR DISTRIBUTION.

THE SERVANT'S POCKET COMPANION: containing Prayers for Morning and Evening, and on Particular Occasions; with Short Addresses on the Duties of Servants. 18mo. 1s. boards.

NARRATIVE OF POLL PEG, of Leicestershire. 3d., or 2s. 6d. per dozen.

REPAIRING THE CHURCH. 3d. each, or 2s. 6d. per dozen.

A SHORT ADDRESS TO POOR WOMEN, on the Duty of bringing their Children early to be Baptized. 6d. each, or 5s. per dozen.

NO FRIEND LIKE AN OLD FRIEND. 18mo. 6d.

VILLAGE CONVERSATIONS on the LITURGY of the CHURCH of ENGLAND. By the Rev. GEORGE DAVYS, Bishop of Peterborough. 18mo. 1s.

By the same Author,

VILLAGE CONVERSATIONS on the PRINCIPAL OFFICES of the CHURCH. Forming a Sequel to the above. 18mo. 1s.

THE CURATE CATECHISING; or, an Exposition of the Church Catechism. By the Rev. W. THISTLETHWAITE, A.M. 8d. Sixth Edition. 18mo. 1s.

By the same Author,

THE CHURCH COMMUNICATING; or, An Exposition of the Communion Service of the Church of England. 18mo. 6d.

TRENCH, REV. F.—THE PORTRAIT OF CHARITY. By the Rev. FRANCIS TRENCH, Author of "Travels in France and Spain," "Scotland, its Faith and its Features," &c. &c. Fcap. cloth, 3s. 6d.

TUPPER M. F.—PROVERBIAL PHILOSOPHY. A Book of Thoughts and Arguments, Originally treated. By MARTIN FARQUHAR TUPPER, Esq., of Christchurch, Oxford. Sixth Edition. Post 8vo. cloth, 7s.

" A work which may be read over and over again with pleasure and profit."—*Post.*

— THE SECOND SERIES of PROVERBIAL PHILOSOPHY. Post 8vo. cloth, 7s.

" Superior to its predecessor."—*Christian Remembrancer.*

TUPPER M. F.
— A MODERN PYRAMID. To commemorate a Septuagint of Worthies. Post 8vo. cloth, 7s. 6d.

— GERALDINE, and other Poems. A Sequel to Coleridge's Christabel. Post 8vo., cloth, 7s.

— AN AUTHOR'S MIND. Post 8vo. cloth, 10s. 6d.

— A THOUSAND LINES. Now first offered to the world we live in. Post 8vo. cloth, gilt leaves, 2s. 6d.

TYTLER, MISS A. F.—LEILA; or, the Island. By ANN FRASER TYTLER. Fourth Edition. Fcap. cloth, 5s.

— LEILA in ENGLAND. A Continuation of "Leila; or, the Island." Third Edition. Fcap. cloth, 6s.

— MARY and FLORENCE; or, Grave and Gay. Seventh Edition. Fcap. cloth, 5s.

— MARY and FLORENCE at SIXTEEN. Fourth Edition. Fcap. cloth, 6s.

"These works are excellent. Miss Tytler's writings are especially valuable for their religious spirit. She has taken a just position between the rationalism of the last generation and the puritanism of the present, while the perfect nature and true art with which she sketches from juvenile life, show powers which might be more ambitiously displayed, but cannot be better bestowed."—*Quarterly Review.*

VERSCHOYLE. A Roman Catholic Tale of the Nineteenth Century. 12mo. cloth, 6s.

WHITE, REV. G.—THE NATURAL HISTORY and ANTIQUITIES of SELBORNE. By the Rev. GILBERT WHITE, M.A. With the Naturalist's Calendar; and the Miscellaneous Observations extracted from his papers. A New Edition, with Notes, by Edward Turner Bennett, Esq., F.L.S., &c. 8vo. cloth, 18s.

WILKINSON, REV. W. F.—CHRIST OUR GOSPEL. Four Sermons preached before the University of Cambridge, in the Month of January, 1846. By the Rev. W. F. WILKINSON, M.A., of Queen's College, Theological Tutor of Cheltenham College. Fcap. cloth, 2s. 6d.

— THE PARISH RESCUED; or, Laymen's Duties, Rights and Dangers. Fcap. cloth, 3s. 6d.

"Almost every page is suggestive of some important truth, which is especially entitled to consideration at the present crisis."—*Sheffield Mercury.*
"This is an excellent work, and deserves a very extensive sale."—*Cheltenham Journal.*

WILKINSON, REV. W. F.
— THE RECTOR in SEARCH of a CURATE. Post 8vo. cloth, 9s.

Contents:—1. The Parish—2. The Curate—3. The Temporary Curate—4. 5. The Evangelicist—6. The Evangelicals—7. The Unfortunate Man—8. The Scholar—9. The Millennarian—10. The Anglo-Catholic—11. The Approved—12. The Ordination.

"A lively and entertaining book."—*Christian Observer.*
"A work calculated to obtain a general reception in all the reading circles."—*Herald.*
"Interesting and attractive."—*Spectator.*

WILKS, REV. S. C.—CHRISTIAN ESSAYS. By the Rev. SAMUEL CHARLES WILKS, M.A. Second Edition, 8vo. boards, 12s.

WILLYAMS, MISS J. L.—CHILLON; or, Protestants of the Sixteenth Century. An Historical Tale. By JANE LOUISA WILLYAMS. 2 vols 8vo. cloth, 18s.

"We think highly of this pathetic story. A true spirit of cheerful piety pervades its pages; the characters are nicely discriminated, and many of the scenes are very vividly portrayed. All who read it may derive benefit from its perusal."—*Britannia.*
"The book before us furnishes proof of considerable ability."—*British Quarterly Review.*

WINCHESTER, BISHOP OF.—THE MINISTERIAL CHARACTER of CHRIST PRACTICALLY CONSIDERED. By CHARLES RICHARD SUMNER, D.D., Lord Bishop of Winchester. Second Edition, enlarged. 8vo. cloth. 12s.

WOODROOFFE, MRS.—SHADES OF CHARACTER: Or, Mental and Moral Delineations; Designed to promote the formation of the Female Character on the basis of Christian principle. By ANNE WOODROOFFE. Fourth Edition. 2 vols. fcap. cloth, 12s.

— THE HISTORY OF MICHAEL KEMP, THE HAPPY FARMER'S LAD. A Tale of Rustic Life, illustrative of the Spiritual Blessings and Temporal Advantages of Early Piety. Sixth Edition, fcap. cloth, 4s.

— MICHAEL THE MARRIED MAN. A Sequel to the above. 12mo. cloth, 6s.

WORDS of WISDOM for MY CHILD, being a Text for Every Day in the Year, for the use of very Young Children. Second Edition. 32mo. cloth, 2s.

YORKE, MISS C. J.— REFLECTIONS for LEISURE HOURS on the Duties, Hopes, and Privileges of Life, &c. By CAROLINE JANE YORKE. Fcap. cloth extra, 5s.

LONDON: PRINTED BY G. J. PALMER, SAVOY STREET, STRAND.